Ben Jonson and Theatre

Ben Jonson and Theatre is an investigation and celebration of Jonson's plays from the point of view of the theatre practitioner as well as the teacher. Reflecting the increasing interest in the wider field of Renaissance drama, this book bridges the divide by debating how Jonson's drama operates in performance. *Ben Jonson and Theatre* includes:

- discussions with and between practitioners
- essays on he staging of the plays
- edited trai cripts of interviews with contemporary practitioners.

This radical re-evaluation of Jonson's theatre is original and innovative in both form and content. It explores the vibrant relationships between actors, directors and academics in their approaches to Jonson. In an effort to open the repertoire to the diversity of Jonson's work, attention is given to rehearsal methods, workshop practices, design, acting, directing, marketing and marginalised theatre history, and all these are considered in the light of recent critical theory.

The volume includes contributions from Joan Littlewood, Sam Mendes, John Nettles, Simon Russell-Beale, Genista McIntosh and Geoffrey Rush, Oscar-winning actor for his role in *Shine*.

Richard Cave is Professor of Drama and Theatre Arts at Royal Holloway College, University of London. **Elizabeth Schafer** is a Lecturer in Drama and Theatre Studies at Royal Holloway College. **Brian Woolland** is a Lecturer in Drama at the University of Reading.

Ben Jonson and Theatre

Performance, Practice and Theory

Richard Cave, Elizabeth Schafer and Brian Woolland

London and New York

First published 1999
by Routledge
11 New Fetter Lane, London EC4P 4EE

Simultaneously published in the USA and Canada
by Routledge
29 West 35th Street, New York, NY 10001

Typeset in Perpetua by
M Rules, London
Printed and bound in Great Britain by
Biddles Ltd, Guildford and King's Lynn

British Library Cataloging in Publication Data
A catalogue record for this book is available from the British Library

Library of Congress Cataloguing in Publication Data
Ben Jonson and theatre: performance, practice, and theory / [edited by]
Richard Cave, Elizabeth Schafer, Brian Woolland. p. cm.
   'This book has grown out of a conference held at Reading University
in January 1996'–P. 3.
   Includes bibliographical references and index.
   1. Jonson, Ben, 1573?–1637–Dramatic production–Congresses.
   2. Jonson, Ben, 1573?–1637–Dramatic works–Congresses.
   3. Jonson, Ben, 1573?–1637–Stage history–Congresses.
   4. Theater–Production and direction–Congresses. I. Cave, Richard
Allen, 1943–. II. Schafer, Elizabeth, 1959–. III. Woolland, Brian,
1949–.
   PR2642.D7B46   1999
   822'.3–dc21   98-29160
                                         CIP

ISBN 0 415 17980-7 (hbk)
ISBN 0 415 17981-5 (pbk)

Contents

List of illustrations

Notes on contributors

Richard Cave is Professor of Drama and Theatre Arts in the Department of Drama and Theatre at Royal Holloway College, University of London. He has authored numerous publications in a range of fields: Irish drama (particularly on Wilde, T.C. Murray and W.B. Yeats, whose plays he has both edited and staged); modern English theatre (*New British Drama in Performance on the London Stage: 1970–1985*); stage design (monographs on Charles Ricketts and Robert Gregory); theatre history; the relation of dance with drama; and Renaissance theatre (studies focused on Webster and Jonson).

Colin Ellwood is a freelance theatre director and Artistic Director of Strangers' Gallery Theatre Company. He was Assistant Director to Sam Mendes' production of *The Alchemist* and has worked regularly for the RSC and the Traverse Theatre.

Andrew Gurr is Professor of English at the University of Reading. He is a director of the Globe project in London, chairing the New Globe Research Department. He has edited several Renaissance plays, including *Richard II* and *Henry V* for the New Cambridge Shakespeare. Other publications include *The Shakespearean Stage 1574–1642*; *Playgoing in Shakespeare's London*; *Rebuilding Shakespeare's Globe* (with John Orrell) and *The Shakespearean Playing Companies*. He has written extensively about the archaeology and the sociology of the London theatres of Shakespeare's time.

Mick Jardine is Head of English at King Alfred's University College, Winchester. His research interests are in the early modern period, particularly drama, and modern critical theory. He is currently working on a book on Shakespeare's Histories and a shared project on 'The Shakespeare Phenomenon', a study of the cultural reception and reproduction of Shakespeare in the modern world.

Joan Littlewood's work with Theatre Workshop, Stratford East has become legendary. High-profile productions include *Oh, What a Lovely War!*, *A Taste of Honey*, *The Hostage*, *The Quare Fellow*; however, Littlewood also directed a large number of classical plays, generally offending the critics with her overtly politicised readings of the classics. Theatre Workshop was remarkable for its commitment to a collective working practice, its complete lack of financial support from government funding bodies and its trailblazing use of techniques (for example, in-depth research and free-ranging improvisations in support of productions of classical texts) which now are taken for granted in British theatre.

Genista McIntosh is Executive Director of the Royal National Theatre, where she has worked with both Sir Richard Eyre and Trevor Nunn. Prior to this appointment she worked for many years as Casting Director for the Royal Shakespeare Theatre.

Sam Mendes has been Artistic Director of the Donmar Warehouse since 1992. He has also directed regularly for the Royal National Theatre (including the recent production of *Othello* with Simon Russell-Beale as Iago), and for the Royal Shakespeare Company, for whom he directed *The Alchemist* in 1991 at the Swan, Stratford and the Barbican. His productions have won numerous accolades, including the *Evening Standard*, *Manchester Evening News*, Critics' Circle and Olivier Awards.

John Nettles is perhaps best known for his starring television role as Bergerac and, amongst younger audiences, for his line of villains in pantomime; but he has played extensively in radio and in the classical and modern repertory at Bristol, Edinburgh, Exeter and Manchester. In several notable seasons with the Royal Shakespeare Company his roles have included Thersites, Lucio, Bassanio and Albany (1976–7); Leontes, Page and Octavius (1992–3); Meercraft in *The Devil is an Ass*, Brutus and Buckingham (1995–6).

Geoffrey Rush is best known internationally for his Oscar-winning performance as David Helfgott in *Shine*. However, Rush is also a Lecoq-trained stage actor of great distinction. His work ranges widely over classical and modern drama and Rush has often achieved great success working with director Neil Armfield. Rush was particularly acclaimed for his Proposhkin in Armfield's production of *Diary of a Madman*, a production which toured Russia and Georgia in 1991. Rush also has extensive experience as a theatre director in Australia.

Simon Russell-Beale was educated at Gonville and Caius College, Cambridge and at the Guildhall School of Music and Drama. Though he has acted at the Traverse, the Edinburgh Lyceum and the Royal Court, much of his earlier career was based in the Royal Shakespeare Company with whom he is an Associate Artist. His many roles in Renaissance drama include Ariel, Edgar, Richard III, Edward II, Thersites and Edward Knowell in *Every Man in his Humour*. At Greenwich Theatre he has played Ferdinand in *The Duchess of Malfi* and for the Royal National Theatre Mosca in *Volpone* and Iago. He recently starred on television in *A Dance to the Music of Time*.

Julie Sanders is a Lecturer in the Department of English at Keele University. Educated at the universities of Cambridge and Warwick, she is the author of *Ben Jonson's Theatrical Republics* (Macmillan, 1998) and co-editor (with Kate Chedgzoy and Susan Wiseman) of *Refashioning Ben Jonson* (Macmillan, 1998). She has published several articles, including work on Jonson, Margaret Cavendish and Richard Brome.

Elizabeth Schafer is a Lecturer in the Department of Drama and Theatre at Royal Holloway College, University of London. She is the author of *MsDirecting Shakespeare: Women Direct Shakespeare*; she co-edited (with Peta Tait) *Australian Women's Drama: Texts and Feminisms*; she has also edited Thomas Middleton's *The Witch*.

Brian Woolland is a Lecturer in the Department of Film and Drama at the University of Reading. He has published extensively on theatre, film and educational drama. He has edited *The Alchemist* for Cambridge University Press. He also works as a director (productions include *The Devil is an Ass* and *The Magnetic Lady*) and is a playwright, whose plays have been produced and toured in several European countries.

Acknowledgements

We would like to express our gratitude to all the delegates at the Reading conference on Ben Jonson and the Theatre, whom we list in the Appendix to this book, and to Professor Jacky Bratton (Head of the Department of Drama, Theatre and Media Arts at Royal Holloway College, University of London) and to Douglas Pye (then Head of the Department of Film and Drama at the University of Reading), who gave generously from departmental funds to sponsor that initial project out of which this book has grown. Also we offer warm thanks to the academic contributors to the volume and to the theatre personnel who took time out from hard-pressed schedules to talk with us about their involvement with Jonson in performance: their infectious enthusiasm made these interviews delightful as well as highly informative occasions. Our particular thanks to Colin Ellwood, whose workshop on *The New Inn* illuminated the play and energised the conference participants; and to Peter Barnes, whose enormous enthusiasm for Jonson and great generosity were influential in setting up the Reading conference. Christopher Murray of University College, Dublin, gave us much valued information about the staging of Jonson's plays in Ireland and the problems of teaching the playtexts within the Irish educational system. Grateful mention must be made of valued friends, students and associates, who have helped solve various problems we encountered: Martine Pelletier, Peter Rankin, Howard Goorney, Katherine Newey, Penny Gay, Iris Luppa, Colette Conroy, Graham Barwell, Katie Lewis. Librarians who have given us valuable advice and assistance include David Ward, Academic Services Manager, and his staff in Founder's Library at Royal Holloway College; Marian Pringle and the staff of the Shakespeare Centre Library at Stratford-upon-Avon; and the archivist and staff of the Manuscripts and Rare Books Room in the Library of University College, London. Together their efficiency made the fundamental processes of research remarkably smooth and streamlined. The student casts of Brian Woolland's productions of *The Devil is an Ass* and *The Magnetic Lady* at Reading University earn his particular thanks and indeed the gratitude of all the contributors who saw those remarkable stagings which profoundly illuminated both plays. Finally we wish to thank Talia Rogers, Jason Arthur and Sophie Powell at Routledge for their time, patience, enthusiasm and invaluable advice at all stages of the publishing process.

Preface

This book has grown out of a conference held at Reading University in January 1996, which was organised by Brian Woolland and Richard Cave and sponsored by their respective departments. The conference was itself unusual in that it deliberately mixed academics with theatre practitioners (actors, a playwright, directors, an administrator); the papers, panel discussions and interview-sessions were sound recorded and the various workshops recorded on video too. *Ben Jonson and Theatre* is not, however, to be viewed as the proceedings of the conference. Time has elapsed since then and our thinking and research about Jonson, though undoubtedly fuelled by the conference, has moved on. More practitioners have been interviewed since the project got under way. Rather than assemble an anthology of papers in the conventional way, we decided to attempt a different structure and one that was inspired from the first by the complex strategies that Jonson himself evolved in his drama, which seem designed to present multiple perspectives on to his themes, provoking, cajoling, challenging and teasing spectators into defining their own individual relationships to the action unfolding before them onstage. Hence a 'venture tripartite' between three author-editors to create a multivocal approach to Jonson the dramatist. But our separate narratives are broken into, interspersed and connected by other voices from the academy (Julie Sanders, Andrew Gurr and Mick Jardine) and from theatre (John Nettles, Simon Russell-Beale, Sam Mendes, Genista McIntosh, Joan Littlewood and Geoffrey Rush) who contest, combat and occasionally endorse, from the perspectives of their personal experience, what we three have to offer. The whole project has been conceived in the spirit of a dramatised, Jonsonian *discovery*, destabilising conventions to come at more clear-sighted views shaped by performance, practice and theory.

Readers will observe that certain scenes in particular plays are examined by several of the contributors: this is not an oversight on our part and care has been taken to avoid repetitive overlapping; the intention rather is to demonstrate through varying analytical methods the richness of interpretation that a Jonsonian text yields to actor, spectator and reader.

All writers on Jonson are confronted with a major dilemma of scholarship when attempting to discuss the full range of his plays: the want of a readily accessible modern edition of the complete works. Three of the comedies (*Volpone, The Alchemist* and *Bartholomew Fair*) are available in a wealth of good editions but it is a conscious part of our agenda to avoid privileging these particular plays and to seek to open up all Jonson's dramatic output to the repertoire. While Herford and the Simpsons' massive, eleven-volume edition (Oxford: Clarendon Press, 1925–52) covers the full range of the plays, their texts observe period spelling, which is not a great help to writers seeking to recommend Jonson to present-day theatregoers and readers for his *modernity*! The two-volume edition of the plays published by Dent in their Everyman's Library (1910) covers the full range, is still accessible and is in modern spelling, but the texts fall short of scholarly accuracy. Compromise has inevitably been forced on us; and we have chosen to follow the example of several recent commentators on Jonson's drama in reproducing the text of the Oxford edition edited by Herford and the Simpsons, respecting their punctuation but modernising the spelling. The only exception to this procedure occurs when, for the sake of the argument, the texts of the 1616 and 1640 Folios are being quoted. All act, scene and line references are to the Oxford edition.

The three of us have been individually responsible for the chapters ascribed to us, though we have edited, discussed and contested each other's ideas and their expression. We have together edited the remaining contributions. Though Richard Cave drafted the Induction and Epilogue, these sections define a shared agenda and, most importantly, a mutual passion and respect for Jonson and for theatre.

Richard Cave
Elizabeth Schafer
Brian Woolland

Induction

Tyrone Guthrie once opined that there was a list of roles, starting inevitably with Hamlet, Romeo and Benedict, that any aspiring classical actor should essay; next in the list, surprisingly, comes Mosca in *Volpone* (Guthrie 1959: 178).[1] How many young actors today would see Mosca as a necessary role through which to further a career? After McKellen's fine interpretation of Face or, for that matter, Wolfit's or Scofield's Volpone, it might have been expected that future generations of actors, young or mature, would begin to see such roles as touchstones through which to prove themselves in the way that Hamlet or Macbeth are deemed in theatrical circles to be benchmarks indicative of a performer's technical development. There have been only one or two major impersonations of Volpone each decade since Wolfit ceased to play the role. Revivals of Jonson's major plays (*Volpone*, *The Alchemist* and *Bartholomew Fair*) are sound in number but limited in range; several of the lesser-known works (*Every Man in his Humour*, *The New Inn*, *Epicoene*, *The Devil is an Ass*) have recently had an airing; but the revivals over the last decade of Marlowe's *Doctor Faustus* have been legion compared with the one revival of *The Devil is an Ass*. Webster's two tragedies have undergone regular, first-rate stagings; in 1995 there were no fewer than three professional productions of Ford's *The Broken Heart*; Shakespeare's *The Merry Wives of Windsor*, once thought to be an unpopular and unperformable play, has had numerous restagings by the RSC but no company has seen fit to revive *A Tale of a Tub*, which is as fine an example of rural social comedy. Why is this culturally the current situation? Why is there no recording of a Jonson production contained within the archives of the British Film Institute? Why does the BBC have only a truncated version dating back to the early 1950s of Wolfit's *Volpone* in its archive of televised drama (though, to be fair, BBC radio has done Jonson proud over the years, largely because of the pioneering efforts of Peter Barnes as adaptor and director)? Is this a reflection of the view that Jonson's plays are so preoccupied with the nature of theatre and of acting that they do not appear to advantage in another medium? If that view seriously obtains, then why are the plays not *staged* with greater frequency?

Newspaper reviewers have noticeably tended to greet most Jonsonian revivals over the last decade with enthusiasm and write of the need for a wholesale restaging of the corpus of his works; and yet the next revival still finds them hailing that production as a rediscovery. How and why has this come about, especially within a cultural climate that would appear to be ideal for a re-evaluation of Jonson's subversive satire and inexorable exposure of the levels of *performance* within all ranks of social life and all manner of experience? How best might audiences be re-educated and a culturally apt taste created for a greater appreciation of his drama? It is often claimed that Jonson's texts are difficult, that actors and consequently audiences shy away from his apparent verbosity (and a verbosity which has dated). But is this actually so? Why should Jonson be deemed intrinsically more *difficult* than Webster or Ford, Marlowe or Shakespeare? Are there political and ideological issues that need tackling in this apparent privileging of his many contemporaries over Jonson? If so, where are these best tackled to effect a change in the prevailing situation: within the theatre or at a pedagogical level?

Reference has so far been made to actors, directors and reviewers; but there is also the issue of Jonson's plays in relation to the challenges they offer to actresses. Many actresses now clearly see the performing of such roles as the Duchess of Malfi, Vittoria in *The White Devil* or Beatrice-Joanna in *The Changeling* as touchstones in mid-career, where before they were content with a progression from Juliet and Ophelia through Rosalind to Lady Macbeth (they now probably add Cleopatra, where once they added Constance in *King John* and Katherine of Aragon in *Henry VIII*). There is no Jonsonian role in the contemporary list. Fiona Shaw played Frances Frampul in *The New Inn* in 1987 and volubly expressed her dislike of a role in which she clearly acted with a lack of sympathy; and Shaw is an influential figure. To what extent has her experience coloured other actresses' responses to the possibilities that late Jonsonian comedy might offer them, despite the more sensitive playing of Deborah Findlay as Pru in that same production? To what degree was Shaw's attitude to play and role influenced by the prevailing view that Jonson is the archetypal misogynist? Is that judgement accurate or partial? Jonson, more than any other English playwright in the Renaissance, had a chance to write for actual women, to have women's bodies onstage during his masques. Ought we not to take account of this, especially in the context of the plays he wrote after this experience later in his career, instead of focusing solely on comparatively early works when judging him as misogynist? How can one reconcile 'Jonson the misogynist' with the Jonson who wrote poetry to, and was patronised and befriended by, learned aristocratic women of his time? How might this be related back to our appreciation of women's roles within the plays?

It is often argued, for example, that Doll is an inferior role to that of Face or Subtle in *The Alchemist*, that the actress has less stage-time than the two men in their venture tripartite and less flashy possibilities to display as impressive a range of technical accomplishments. Yet it could equally well be argued that Doll's role marks a significant turning point in Jonson's representation of women. It is Doll who has the intelligence to see the dangerous consequences of the uproar that her quarrelling colleagues are causing at the start of the play and the authority of voice and presence to quell their violence; she shows herself as adept at acting as Face or Subtle in her fit of talking (a virtuosic turn modelled on one of the major lazzi for female players in commedia dell'arte) and as the Queen of Faery; and she is the one, not Subtle, who immediately suspects a trick when, as she and Subtle are leaving Lovewit's house, Face insists they leave baggage and keys behind them. Doll's role demonstrates psychological insight, social acumen, force of personality and a brilliant line in acting skills. Only if these qualities are present in a performance of the role will Face's parting words to her carry the shockingly cynical bite that registers the profound cruelty of his dismissal, when he offers to write references for her to 'Mistress Amo . . . or madam Caesarean'. Doll may have come from a life in the Jacobean sex trade but to be so ruthlessly consigned back to it (as whore and backstreet abortionist) is disturbing, given her expertise as a *performer*. Yet the role would at first have been played by a young male, demonstrating in the very act of impersonating Doll how Jacobean society closed off from a woman like her one potential outlet as actress for her remarkable talents. Jonson would appear through Doll's role to be interrogating the conventions of cross-dressed playing, inviting debate and reappraisal of its assumptions and inherent, repressive sexism. When will a modern actress and director interrogate text and role in this way? Would doing so begin to challenge and destabilise the view of Jonson as misogynist? Women are increasingly editing Jonson's texts. Maybe this will produce less simplistically defined concepts of Jonson's misogyny. If so, then what are the likely consequences of this for professional performers, especially actresses? How can professional productions of the plays become informed by feminist readings of Jonson? It is generally agreed that in their investigation of the perils of acquisitiveness and of spiritual and moral apathy Jonson's plays hold up a startlingly precise mirror to our times. When will his explorations of gender and sexual stereotyping and his concern for the status of women in society also be appreciated for their precision of insight? What is required to effect these changes in perspective?

Questions, questions and yet more questions. Questions are designed to provoke, disturb, interrogate, appraise, destabilise, probe, challenge; they refuse categorical assertion yet invite considered response; they change the perspective the better to instigate debate or reassessment. These are also the functions and effects of the inductions to Jonson's plays, which also establish a particular relationship with the audience for the ensuing performance. Jonson desired alert not passive spectators and his inductions teased them into an appropriate frame of mind. Often he deliberately factionalised his audience as if to highlight both the importance of individual reaction and enjoyment of the freedom within the communal event that is theatre in performance to reach for personal insight. This volume begins with questions by way of induction, inviting readers to share in the shaping of the argument by engaging in debate. The intended agenda is to destabilise currently conventional approaches to Jonson's plays; use aspects of contemporary critical theory to change the perspectives on which traditional judgements have been based; and to determine the grounds (theatrical, pedagogical, theoretical) which would justify a more constant presence for the full range of his drama within the contemporary repertory. Always our concern has been with Jonson and the theatre: the perspective may shift at times to Jonson in the schoolroom or the academy, but the aim is to interrogate ongoing assumptions about his work which have a bearing on why certain plays are or are not regularly staged. Postmodernism refuses to acknowledge a canon or traditions in playing or in shaping a repertoire; and it is within the context of a spirited postmodernism that this induction and this volume have been conceived. Since drama thrives on opposition, we follow this induction with a prologue that promptly offers a counter-view.

Note

1　His remaining choices are Young Hardcastle in *She Stoops to Conquer* and Valentine in *Love for Love*.

Prologue

Who is Lovewit? What is he?

Andrew Gurr

Staging Jonson now is a particular challenge because his own texts were so securely of his age, and not for all time. He lacks the midwifery of the education syllabus that has made Shakespeare so much for *our* time. Adapting *Volpone* for the modern stage is manageable, if only because cupidity is still so much with us, but the more localised games that Jonson played in plays like *Poetaster*, *Bartholomew Fair* and *The Staple of News* with his characters and his time are more of a problem. My question about Lovewit offers a small challenge about how we might cope with just one element in the problem of modernising Jonson's plays for the stage. As an exemplar of the general difficulty of staging Jonson today, it may help to clarify a few of the particular challenges they face us with, even if it offers no easy answer.

My essential question is, who from his own time did Jonson have in mind when he composed the winner-takes-all character Lovewit for *The Alchemist* in 1610? Lovewit is a problem in terms of plot even today, since he is the exception to the generally moralistic rule of the endings in Jonson's comedies, that all the gulls are held up to ridicule for their foolishness while all the knaves are punished in a fitting way for their crimes. In the long series of Jonson plays which normally allow neither the wits nor the virtuous to win very much at the end, Lovewit gets away with material gains strikingly better than any other character. There is no justice, poetic or otherwise, in *The Alchemist*'s conclusion. What, we should therefore ask, is so special about Lovewit? The short answer to that lies in the immediate local conditions of London in 1610, and Jonson's personal and business relations at the time he wrote the play. It is essentially a part of his writing for his own time, and one that cannot easily be accommodated in ours. So the longer answer depends on how we think we should stage Jonson today.

The playtext itself makes it clear that *The Alchemist* was written to be intimately involved with the Blackfriars playhouse, its audience in 1610, and its immediate neighbourhood, which Jonson knew intimately. Jonson was born in Westminster in 1572 or so, and spent almost all his life in London. In 1610 Westminster was one of the two cities of London. As today, the richer neighbourhoods were to the west, on the Westminster side, while the poorer were to the north and east, although unlike today the inner city was wealthier than were the suburbs. Jonson was born a citizen of Westminster, but he was also a paid-up member of one of the companies of the city of London, and therefore a freeman of London.

One of the minor mysteries about his inner life is what having that freedom of London meant to him. Jonson's stepfather made him a member of the Tilers and Bricklayers, which made him technically a freeman of the city, capable of lawfully buying property and trading inside the walls. The fact that he continued to pay his dues as a member until 1612, even when he was finding favour with noble patrons, meant that he was derided for his consequent status as a brick-layer for the rest of his life. Much of his aggression must have come from his deprived childhood. He was proud of the people he killed; he became a Catholic when it was most dangerous and potentially disloyal to be one; he separated from his wife. From 1603 he climbed socially by living with his noble patrons. He cultivated a circle of learned friends among the nobles and gentry, including his former teacher at Westminster School, Camden, and the Cotton of the British Library's famous manuscript collection. He was far more deeply and inti-mately entangled in the immediacies of the social and cultural life of his time in London than, for all we know, was his friend Shakespeare.

Two of his plays celebrate highly specific local features of London's life in his time. Unless we count *Epicoene*, written for a boy company a year or so before, as a London play (it has a non-specific setting), *The Alchemist* was the first of his plays actually and precisely set in London. That innovatory feature of the play tends to be obscured by the fact that *Every Man in his Humour*, originally set like *Volpone* in Italy, was transferred to London for the Folio version, and the fact that *Bartholomew Fair*, set in Smithfield on the feast-day and festival of Saint Bartholomew, together with some of the later plays (notably *The Staple of News*) were also explicitly set there. Jonson was actually quite late in joining the fash-ion for plays set in London, a fashion Shakespeare never wore, but which many of their contemporaries were trying on by the turn of the century. The choice of a location in the Blackfriars for *The Alchemist* was an innovation in Jonson's *œuvre* that we should not take lightly.

In the early years of the seventeenth century Jonson himself was living in the Blackfriars where he set *The Alchemist*. He wrote a dedication to 'the two famous universities' for the publication of *Volpone*, which he dated 11 February 1607 and addressed as 'from my house in the Blackfriars'. The placing of *The Alchemist* was emphatic, and is clearly signalled in the text. Its seventeenth line locates its place 'here in the Friars'. The whole play is redolent not just of the London of 1609–10, but of the playhouse's immediate neighbourhood. Such a setting, for a play actually staged in the same neighbourhood, had an obvious metatheatri-cal value. Its metatheatricality, however, as we shall see, went much further than the 'liberty' that it shared with its playhouse.

It is a cliché of *Alchemist* criticism that the play held a mirror up to nature, the stage, according to sound classical theory, reflecting its audience as in a mirror, presenting the life that Jonson's audiences in 1610 knew at first hand. That hand is a bit remote from us now, so it is worth indicating just a few of the things that Jonson must have expected his first audiences to recognise of themselves in the play. By 1610 it was no longer a new thing to make London the setting for a play, but in this most innovatory of his London plays Jonson did it more wholeheartedly than any of his peers. His scheme for what he was mirroring embodied a great deal more than just a touristic evocation of its contemporary London setting.

It was written for Shakespeare's company, the King's Men, to perform in their opening season, late 1609–10, after a long closure for plague, at their newly acquired hall playhouse in the Blackfriars. Its location 'here in the Friars' is at the same time a house in the residential district of Blackfriars and the play-house known as the Blackfriars. The Blackfriars district was a 'liberty' up to 1608, a precinct of the Benedictine Order up to the Reformation, and then a private precinct free from the city's control, even though it was inside the city walls. In 1608 James, being very short of cash (the court's wine bills alone were running at hundreds of thousands of pounds a year), finally allowed it to come under the city's government in return for a huge loan. Not that the city gained much from it, except rectifying a jurisdictional anomaly. As a residential district it was far too affluent to cause many riots, and its residents could use their influence on the Privy Council. It housed the Office of the Revels. Despite that so-potent presence, and the control it exercised over the professional play-ers, the district's main troubles came from the playhouse. Even then trouble did not come from the riotous behaviour of the crowds but from their numbers, and especially from the nobility's coaches forcing their way through the narrow lanes to deliver their wealthy passengers at the playhouse door. The first notice of trouble from traffic jams ever to appear in the London records apart from the chronic squeezes on London Bridge itself was a result of the crowds flocking to the Blackfriars playhouse.

It was a wealthy neighbourhood, occupied by a distinct mix, both of social classes and of social attitudes. The Lord Chamberlain and the Revels Office both occupied rooms adjacent to the playhouse. At the same time the preacher at the parish church, Stephen Egerton, was famous for, amongst many other things, his sternly voiced disapproval of playgoing. There were some rigorous puritans living there, including some of the Anabaptists and dissenters who were begin-ning to prepare themselves in Amsterdam to sail to the Americas and found a new society there. It had many of the richest noblemen in town, besides num-bers of the richer citizens. As part of that general affluence, it had vendors of high-class things like feathers – all of London's gallants and ladies who wanted feathers to decorate themselves went to Blackfriars for them – and the superior products sold there were drugs rather than drapery, wine rather than beer.

Abel Drugger with his beginnings of a tobacco shop would have been typical of the traders who catered to the richer residents of Blackfriars. Artisan traders and the handicraft shops, shoemakers, cobblers and makers of industrial goods, worked in other parts of the city, to the north in Cheapside if they were grocers and food merchants, near St Paul's if they were booksellers, and further to the east if they were mercers.

The Blackfriars theatre was located in the cultural rather than the commercial heart of London, the beginnings of the West End. But although London was growing very fast, approaching a quarter of a million people by the turn of the century, and at four hundred thousand by 1650 ready to become the biggest city in Europe, it was still a tightly knit community, small enough to have its stock of gossip and scandals held in common. *The Alchemist* is packed with references to places in the city that everyone knew, and to recent events that everyone knew about. They include Simon Read, convicted in Southwark in 1608 for raising spirits. He conjured up devils to locate some stolen money for a young clerk rather like Dapper in the play. It names Gamaliel Ratsey, a famous highwayman executed in 1605, and the notorious Mediterranean pirate Ward, an Englishman. Ward's adventures were the subject of a play, *The Christian Turned Turk*, which was staged in 1609 while Jonson was writing *The Alchemist*. John Dee, one of the real alchemists, who worked for Queen Elizabeth and became famous for his learning, particularly his collection of esoteric books which was the subject of a notorious fracas, had died in 1608. Broughton, whose manic prophecies Doll spouts to trigger the explosion at the heart of the play, was another element in the common currency of London gossip at the time.

The Alchemist is packed with the everyday currency of common London chat. There is a mention of the New Exchange in the Strand, opened in 1609, and a reference to the New River scheme, a water-works project for London started by the then Lord Mayor, Edward Myddleton, work on which began in 1609. Other then-familiar places mentioned include St Paul's, which was the central locality of town and the meeting-place for all gossips; pie-corner, a place selling pork products near Smithfield market; the artillery yard, a field just outside the walls near Bishopsgate where the gunners from the Tower of London practised; Lothbury, a street of copper-founders and brass-makers; Sea-coal Lane, near Fleet Street; the Wool-sack Inn in Farringdon, the Dragon Inn, and the Pigeon Inn up-river at Brentford; and of course the rogues' escape to Brentford, a famous rendezvous for lovers and fugitives outside London, seven miles up the Thames on the western side of the city. We also get Ratcliff, Pimlico, the madhouse at Bedlam, and Pickt-hatch, a well-known loitering-place for prostitutes near the Charterhouse (the play is full of current London euphemisms for prostitutes – bona robas, cockatrices, guinea birds, punk device).

The gullible characters in the play designedly mirrored the Blackfriars locals, though they were neatly designed to include a wider range of locals in its mirror than the actual audience for the first performances. The two puritans, Ananias and Tribulation Wholesome, would not have been playgoers, though such dark-suited figures were familiar enough in the streets outside. They represent the Amsterdam Brethren, members of the company of anti-episcopal preachers excluded from the established church for the Calvinist rigour of their views – in the play they use the name 'Christ-tide', for instance, instead of Christmas, because in the view of the Brethren the suffix 'mass' sounded too Catholic. They refer to their exiled colleagues as the 'silenced saints', and the 'exiled saints', because the Church of England refused to allow them to preach – hence their base in Amsterdam, the chronic need to raise funds, and the longer-term plan to sail for the Americas. We might argue that their depiction had a spread of allusiveness beyond the silenced saints, since in the early years of the play at the Blackfriars even a Church of England dignitary might be compared to the biblical Ananias.[1]

Abel Drugger and his ambition to be a tobacconist, along with the slightly more upmarket Dapper, were both traders who catered for the rich residents like Sir Epicure Mammon. The play is full of references to citizens and citizen ambitions, such as the Company of the Grocers, one of the twelve livery companies from whom the Lord Mayor was elected, and the naughty suggestion that Drugger might one day be called to the scarlet, meaning that he would become a Sheriff, in scarlet gown, on the Dick Whittington model. The Whittington story, where the bells call him back to become thrice Lord Mayor of London, had become hugely popular in the 1590s, especially among the apprentices who made up the largest proportion of audiences at the amphitheatre playhouses in these years, though not at the exclusive Blackfriars, where the price of the cheapest admission was six times what it was at the Globe.

At the Blackfriars, the largest of the communities contributing to the early audiences for Shakespeare's company were the Inns of Court. Located within easy walking distance of the Blackfriars, the two Temples, Lincoln's Inn, and the three lesser inns had more than eight hundred students or ostensible students of law who flocked to the plays, and especially to what in 1610 was London's sole indoor playhouse, the Blackfriars. In *The Alchemist*'s mirror they are not represented on the stage side, but the play has an ample number of references to the terms and vacations which determined their comings and goings. I suspect that Jonson was relying on the student component in the Blackfriars audience to pick up his exotic uses of strange language like Subtle's alchemical jargon, and to enjoy his explosions of comic verbal excess in Doll's outpouring of Broughton.

Two other things in the play were characteristic of London precisely in 1610. One was the bubonic plague, which has made Lovewit, the owner of the house, flee into the country, where everyone who could afford to went when the number of deaths reached epidemic proportions, as in many summers it did. There had been a particularly intense run of plague from early in 1608 right through 1609. No performing at any of the London playhouses was permitted from July 1608 or earlier, right until January 1610. In the 121 parishes of London the deaths of 2,262 people from the plague were recorded in 1608, and 4,240 for 1609. For many years the Privy Council had required each of the London parishes to keep a record of plague deaths separate from those that were due to other causes, and every Thursday it added up the 121 totals. When the number of deaths from plague in any week for all 121 parishes rose to thirty it ordered the closure of all public meetings, including the playhouses. As part of the attempt to limit the epidemic by inhibiting crowds it postponed the new law terms, which would normally have brought many outsiders with lawsuits into London; and it tried to restrict travel generally – except for those who had country homes and were heading out of the city, of course. In 1610, while Jonson was writing *The Alchemist*, the plague epidemic was an all-too recent event. Lovewit's absence, leaving his butler Jeremy to mind the house, was a familiar practice in the Blackfriars precinct.

The other of the characteristically London things the play makes use of is the easy access that the trickster characters in the play have to Spanish stage costumes. This was partly a reminder of the metatheatrical game, the pretence that the house in Blackfriars was not supposed to be a theatre. The play opens with the three rogues quarrelling, and several verbal parodies of the most famous of the old plays, Thomas Kyd's *The Spanish Tragedy*, first staged twenty-three years before, and revised by Jonson for Henslowe a decade or so before he wrote *The Alchemist*. In Act 4 Face, when he goes to get a second Spanish costume to match Surly's, actually says that he will go to the players and get 'Hieronimo's old cloak, ruff, and hat', the costume of the leading character in Kyd's play. Here the metatheatrical jokery began to extend its scope. While for the moment it would merely have seemed like a theatrical in-joke, this identification of the alchemists as close friends of the play-actors develops an important function in the play's conclusion. In effect it begins to highlight the play's underlying game. The full metatheatrical mirror makes the Blackfriars audience into a real audience of Blackfriars people, and the tricksters into the real actors of the Blackfriars playhouse, the 'counterfeiting' players who are playing their games of deceit and disguise in order to make outrageous profits from their audience.

But before looking more closely at this aspect of the play it is worth sketching in a little about Jonson's relations with Shakespeare, for reasons which relate to the question of just who in 1610 the original for the character Lovewit might have been: the subject of a deliberate if covert 'application' (the Elizabethan term), the practice of which as Jonson said in his epistle to *Volpone* had recently 'become a trade'. Setting aside the legend that Jonson got his first notice as a playwright for *Every Man In* through Shakespeare's backing, we know that Jonson recurrently wrote plays for the Shakespeare company. His first famous plays through

1597–99 were written for them, then he left them for the new Blackfriars Boys, returning intermittently with *Sejanus* in 1603, *Volpone* in 1605, *The Alchemist* in 1610, and subsequently *Catiline*. Both his and Shakespeare's playtexts show multiple instances of their interaction through these years.

Initially, when they were colleagues and rivals, this interaction appears as games of covert allusion which chiefly are concerned with asserting which should be the proper mode for comedy, Juvenalian (Jonson) versus romantic (Shakespeare), and this is particularly the case in *Every Man Out* and *Twelfth Night*.[2] Later more complex jibes were delivered on both sides. In *Poetaster*, 4.9., Ovid and Julia play out a perfect parody of Romeo and Juliet's balcony scene. Julia '*appeareth above, as at her chamber window*', and calls to Ovid, who promptly replies from below. 'I high, thou low? O, this our plight of place / Doubly presents the two lets of our love', complains Julia. When he leaves '*Shee calls him backe*', and when she goes '*He calls her backe*'. There is evidence of a more complex interaction between the two in the way *Volpone*'s imagery of deformed nature bears a distinct relation to that in *King Lear*, both plays written in 1605 for the Globe company. From Shakespeare's side at the time of *The Alchemist* came *The Winter's Tale* and *The Tempest*, one spanning sixteen years and stretching from Sicily to the seacoast of Bohemia, the other set on a single island taking only the three hours actual traffic of the stage, from two till five 'glasses'. The two plays together challenged Jonson's allegiance to the neo-classical unities.[3] In 1609–10, when Jonson once again began writing for Shakespeare's company at their new playhouse, the Blackfriars, for which Jonson had recently finished *Epicoene*, they both wrote magician plays, *The Tempest* and *The Alchemist*.[4] It is inconceivable that each of them did not know a fair amount about what the other was doing, and that their plays did not include specific if semi-private jibes at one another. I have elsewhere argued that Jonson's copy of the notorious book usually called *Aretino's Postures*, to which Mammon refers, was utilised by Shakespeare in *The Winter's Tale*.[5]

Later, when he wrote a new prologue to *Every Man In* for the Folio book of his plays, Jonson was to attack the old fustian of 'York and Lancaster's long jars', along with *Henry V*'s choruses wafting you, as Heywood's also did, 'o'er the seas' (though Shakespeare used no 'creaking throne' coming down the 'boys to please' until 1609 or later in *Cymbeline*). In the same prologue Jonson also mocked the 'roll'd bullet' and 'tempestuous drum' warning of storms like *King Lear*'s, for all his own recent use of them in *Catiline*. Through the years from 1607 to 1614 when Shakespeare was writing the last of his plays Jonson regularly criticised them, notably the popular *Pericles* as a 'mouldy tale'. In the *Bartholomew Fair* Induction he drew the line at 'a servant-monster' and 'a nest of anticks', in 'tales, tempests, and such-like drolleries'. Against that explicit criticism, we can set first Jonson's quite exceptional familiarity with Shakespeare's plays, from characters like Justice Silence, Doll Tearsheet, Falstaff and Pistol,

Osric and Polonius, to single lines from a wide range of the plays, not least *Julius Caesar*, where he is on record as mocking a couplet which only survives now in a modified form.

Jonson was not at all resistant to using some of the things he scorned, and not only when writing for Shakespeare's company, as he did with his nest of antics in *Volpone* and the storm noises in *Catiline*. His masques are full of materials that show his familiarity with Shakespeare's plays, not just in the 1611 *Masque of Oberon*, with its borrowings from *A Midsummer Night's Dream*, and *Love Restored* of the same Christmas, but the 1609 *Masque of Queens*. His last unfinished play, *The Sad Shepherd*, is set in a Shakespearean forest of Arden. Jonson's assertive independence prevented him from admitting any debts, but the links between the two playwrights are so intense and consistent that we cannot doubt a close human link too. The bond may have been especially potent in 1610, when Shakespeare was beginning to detach himself from daily work for the King's Men, and Jonson had returned to write for the company at its new Blackfriars playhouse after his five years away writing for the boy's company playing at the same venue.

All the plays of this period, culturally still something of a novelty in the London of 1610, were prone to what Jonson chose to call dismissively and disingenuously the 'trade' of application. Every fictional story put on the stage was thought liable to be fitted to the actual events of the day, at least so far as censorship allowed, whether it was the Essex rebellion or King James's foreign policy in *A Game at Chess*. The law was strict in declaring that no living person could be represented onstage. The players of course flouted that law – for *A Game at Chess* they actually got hold of a suit of the Spanish Ambassador's own clothing, and his notorious sedan chair, which was equipped with a special commode-seat to accommodate the painful fistula he suffered from. The art or trade of 'application' was a major pleasure of the playgoing game for Londoners. Jonson was cautious about making things too hot for himself with the censor, and chose to characterise familiar types rather than specific individuals. But the 'application' was usually pretty obvious. In a play like *The Alchemist*, to be performed at a playhouse crowded with Inns of Court students, he could rely on the audience recognising all the types while not actually identifying themselves personally in the reflections they saw on the stage's mirror.

In the prologue to the play Jonson announces what he is doing. 'Our scene is London', he proclaims, ' 'cause we would make known, / No country's mirth is better than our own.' More to the point, he defends what the play does:

> Though this pen
> Did never aim to grieve, but *better* men,
> Howe'er the age he lives in doth endure
> The vices that she breeds, above their cure.

Instead, his aim is better than that of the age:

> But when the wholesome remedies are sweet,
> And, in their working, gain and profit meet,

– everyone knows that all writers since Aristotle have claimed profit and delight as the reward of drama –

> He hopes to find no spirit so much diseased,
> But will with such fair correctives be pleased.
> For here he doth not fear who can *apply*.

– And just in case there are any devotees of the 'trade' of application present –

> If there be any that will sit so nigh
> Unto the stream, to look what it doth run,
> They shall find things, they'd think, or wish, were done;
> They are such natural follies, but so shown,
> As even the doers may see, and yet not own.

In other words, you might 'apply' these doings to yourself, but you can conceal your own folly by refusing to acknowledge that it is you in the mirror.

The Alchemist was designed to show the spectators a set of characters who were deliberate parodies of their neighbours and themselves, shown by their referential names to be types, not personally recognisable individuals. The cast is a mixture of gulls or fools, including Surly and Dame Pliant, set against the trio of rogues and tricksters who prey on them. There is only one exception to this division. The gulls, who range in social status from Sir Epicure Mammon and his gentleman friend Surly through young Kastril, the land-owning would-be hawk and his sister, the young widow Dame Pliant, to the Puritans, and to Dapper and Drugger, are with the exception of the Puritans a deliberate conspectus of the kind of society that might have been reflected in the audience at the Blackfriars in 1610. Their common factor is their greed and their gullibility, their willingness to let themselves be deceived by the play-acting tricksters. Face is the man who can play many parts, the many-costumed and multi-pseudonymed disguiser, Subtle is the fake alchemist and spouter of nonsensical alchemical jargon, loud of voice and actorly of manner, and Doll is a mixture of both.

In *Volpone*, the last play Jonson wrote for Shakespeare's company before *The Alchemist*, every character is punished in the end with 'poetic' justice that accords exactly with his or her deserts. Volpone, who tricked his gulls by pretending to be ill and on the point of death, is condemned to work in a hospital until he is sick indeed. Mosca, the servant and parasite who has worked so hard to serve himself, is condemned to new service chained to a galley's oar. The old man Corbaccio, whose greed made him try to disinherit his son, is required to relinquish his whole estate to him, and so on. Like the Mikado, Jonson makes the punishments fit the crimes. But *The Alchemist* ends differently. All the gulls are certainly exposed as fools, and their greed makes them suffer as they lose their investments in the alchemical project, some without ever knowing that they have been gulled. They all suffer consistent punishments for the way greed makes fools gullible. By contrast the rogues are not punished in any judicial way. They simply revert to the status they all occupied before the play began. Subtle, the fake alchemist, and his Doll escape penniless back to the streets they came from, with no profit from their elaborate con. They are restored to precisely the state of social outcasts they were in before the play started. So is Face, who returns to his former role as the house-owner's butler.

But once the owner, Lovewit, returns unexpectedly at the end of Act 4, and manages finally to make his way into the house, he becomes a complicating factor in the resolution. Face manages to outwit Subtle and Doll and send them away penniless. By securing Lovewit's backing he can fool all the gulls too, and send them away without their 'pelf'. But he himself can only return to his former role as Jeremy, Lovewit's butler. All three members of the 'venture tripartite' therefore end up where they began before the play started. They suffer far less than the gulls, who all lose their wealth. The one beneficiary, whom we should give careful attention to, the one character who is enabled to profit from all the loot that the gulls have brought to the house, without doing anything to deserve it, is Lovewit. He is the only real winner at the end of the play, and we should ask why.

In *Volpone* all the punishments fit the crimes with the macabre precision of 'poetic' justice. In *The Alchemist* the punishments are of three kinds, and none of them conform to any sense of regular justice. The gulls lose their wealth and are exposed as fools for their gullibility. The rogues are returned to where they were before the play started. In losing nothing, the knaves do better than the fools. Lovewit, the latecomer, is the only one who wins, both the wealth and the wife. This apparent inequity ought to make us ask why Jonson, the arch-maker of ingenious plots and devotee of neat closures, should have laid out such a manifestly discordant ending to his most London-centred play, and given all the profit with no obvious justice, poetic or otherwise, to this passive and suggestible latecomer Lovewit.[6]

The explanation I can offer to explain this is rather contorted, but it fits the evidence of the text surprisingly well, whatever it may suggest about how it may be possible to stage any contemporary production of the play that allows a director to take account of its inequity. The whole play works best as a mirror of playing, a metadrama. The gulls mirror the original audience as the experienced

Jonson expected to find them. The rogues are not merely trickster-outsiders but types of the stage-players who perform the play. The function of the players' profession is to con their audiences. Playing was commonly said to be a deception, a 'counterfeit'. Such a claim was a commonplace about the theatre that by 1610 was old enough to be made a joke in itself, as Jonson does in this play. The Blackfriars audience is gulled by the tricksters, play-actors whose 'application' is their identity as players, staging their deceptive show of alchemical magic and verbal mumbo-jumbo to a gullible audience in the Blackfriars. The 'Argument' which Jonson attached to the printed version of the play, a typical verse which spells out the play's title in an acrostic, uses the language of playing to describe what the rogues do in the play. Noting Face as the servant to the Blackfriars house, and Subtle and Doll as the tricksters, we are told

> only wanting some
> *House* to set up, with him they here contract,
> Each for a *share*, and all begin to *act*.
> Much company they draw, and much abuse.

As sharers in the playing company, they are the people who drew up the contract for the use of the playhouse they were to play in, they draw in their large audience, and they abuse them. Seeing the play's action as a model of the theatrical experience, a metaphor for the staging process, tells us directly what Jonson is up to.

It is a play about a play about stage-trickery, a counterfeit set in the Blackfriars precinct in 1610 as that neighbourhood mirrored itself inside the Blackfriars theatre. The Blackfriars audience has been gulled out of its cash by the players, just as the gulls onstage are conned of their money by the tricksters who deceive them. That creates a neat distinction between actors and audience, and registers itself as an all-too apt version of the game of 'application', since the players have taken the audience's money in the expectation that they would be performing exactly the sort of con-trick with verbiage and gulling that Face and Subtle and Doll perform on the Blackfriars stage to the Blackfriars gulls. But that leaves Lovewit out of the equation. He has left London because of the plague, and now returns in time to reap his profits. What, as the house-owner and only profiteer, is his role in relation to the company of players?

Can we 'apply' the character of Lovewit to anyone at the real Blackfriars? For all his superior status as house-owner, Lovewit is able to act a part when Face calls on him to do so; and his relationship with Face becomes an intriguing inversion of their former master–servant roles. Lovewit starts the concluding speech to the play, and then hands it over to Face, his now-restored Jeremy the butler. The butler is, as the audience have seen, the supreme actor of roles. He started the play as a profit-making thief calling himself Face, and he ended back playing his butler role once again, sharing his profits with his boss. He is the supreme representative of the player as a con-man, who teaches some of his play-acting to his master in the interests of their mutual profit.

In his final speech Lovewit complacently tells the audience, in the rhyming verses that signalled the play's end, and in his character as beneficiary of all the loot thanks to Face, of his gratitude to this colleague who is the master-player and con-man.

> That master
> That had received such happiness by a servant,
> In such a widow, and with so much wealth,
> Were very ungrateful, if he would not be
> A little indulgent to that servant's wit,
> And help *his* fortune, though with some small strain
> Of his own candour. Therefore, gentlemen,
> And kind spectators, if I have outstripped
> An old man's gravity, or strict canon, think
> What a young wife and a good brain may do:
> Stretch age's truth sometimes, and crack it too.   (5.5. 146–56)

Then he hands the epilogue over to Jeremy/Face, who says:

> Gentlemen,
> My part a little fell in this last scene,
> Yet 'twas decorum. And though I am clean
> Got off from Subtle, Surly, Mammon, Doll,
> Hot Ananias, Dapper, Drugger, all
> With whom I traded; yet I put myself
> On you, that are my country; and this pelf
> Which I have got, if you do quit me, rests,
> To feast you often, and invite new guests.   (5.5. 157–65)

Decorum? He claims that although his 'part' in the finale didn't involve as many disguises and play-acting as in the previous acts he has got money, thanks to his master's generosity, and he claims that he will use his profit, 'this pelf which I have got', to present more plays in the future, 'To feast you often, and invite new guests', namely another load of the Blackfriars gulls.

For me there is only the one possible 'application' for Lovewit the master and owner of the house in his collaborative and mutually beneficial relation to his servant, the player Jeremy/Face. He is not only the owner of the house in which the con-trick was played, but the chief and only real profiteer from the con-trick itself. The owner of the Blackfriars 'house' is a lover of wit, who has been absent from the house because of the plague. So who were the lovers of wit who owned the Blackfriars playhouse in 1610? The answer to that fits the metadramatic structure of the plot with remarkable neatness. In 1608, after ten years of use by a boy's company, the Blackfriars had reverted to the possession of its owners, Richard and Cuthbert Burbage, who inherited it from their father in April 1597. They, having run the Globe through those ten years, from 1599 to 1608, as members of a consortium of five of the sharers from the playing company who were performing at the Globe, designed a new contract in 1608. In effect, they extended the ownership of the Blackfriars to the same consortium. Consequently, when the Blackfriars playhouse reopened in early 1610, after the long closure for the plague, while Jonson was still writing his play, the owners of the Blackfriars had become those five Lovewits: Richard and Cuthbert Burbage, John Heminges, Henry Condell and, last but far from least, that most famous lover of wit, William Shakespeare.

It may be incidental that Shakespeare returned to Stratford in 1609, after the new contract for the ownership of the Blackfriars theatre had been signed, while the players continued to wait for permission to reopen the London playhouses. Shakespeare went home then after his mother died, perhaps chiefly to sort out his properties in and around Stratford. He kept contact with the players through 1609 and 1610 while writing *The Tempest* (I have argued elsewhere that the time allocated in that play to Ariel for his changes of costume indicate close contact with the playhouse[7]), but from then on his visits to London were intermittent, and conceivably unexpected. He was certainly free even under his sharer contract with the company to remain in Stratford so long as the plague kept the theatres shut. There is evidence that by 1610 the leading players used to send their juniors on tour, while they themselves remained in the vicinity of London.[8] Lovewit's absence and return does consort with Shakespeare's division of his times and places between London and Stratford in these years. In 1610, when *The Alchemist* was staged at the Blackfriars, he was no longer a regular member of the company, though no doubt he could still play a part onstage when called on. But from his new retirement any visit to London would have been chiefly as a playhouse owner. The few hints of his activities in these years suggest that his time in London was as much to invest his profits as to meet the players. He did business for his Stratford friends there, and he bought an apartment in the Blackfriars gatehouse. He was no longer to be regarded as the common player, member of the playing company, that Richard Burbage, player of Face, still was.

Like so many of Jonson's plays, *The Alchemist* is a testimony to the capitalistic practices of its time. Even in the unique world of the London theatre the chief profits went to the landlords. You might say that Lovewit bought Jonson's play, and made money from it at the expense of the Blackfriars residents of London. The Lovewits of the new Blackfriars playhouse enjoyed their plays, and they enjoyed the profit they made from the players who enacted the con-tricks which the plays enacted on their gullible audiences. Jonson depicted Shakespeare/ Lovewit, for all his love of games, as a new London capitalist.

Shakespeare as Lovewit evidently did not take offence at this identification of him as the chief profiteer. He had made fun of Jonson in *The Winter's Tale*, probably written a bit earlier than *The Alchemist*, in his reference to the statue by Giulio Romano and Hermione's 'natural posture', which I suspect is a reference to Jonson's ownership of a copy, mentioned first in *Volpone*, of *Aretino's Postures*. Shakespeare also chose to give Bohemia a sea-coast for Perdita to be left on. Bohemia's shore, a display of ostensible ignorance that the literal-minded Jonson could still deride when talking to Drummond of Hawthornden some years later, was made from a deliberate reversal of the locations in the source, *Pandosto*. Instead of sailing from Greene's Bohemia to Sicily, Antigonus was made to take the reverse journey, landing on a coast that Jonsonian literalists would know could not exist. More to the point, in Shakespeare's own alchemical play, *The Tempest*, written while Jonson was finishing his magician play, he mocked Jonson's well-advertised devotion to the neo-classical unities by locating his play on a single island, and timing its action to fit precisely the three hours traffic of stage-time, from two o'clock till five o'clock, a feat easily outdoing Jonson's own devotion to the hours of daylight for a play that he took care to signal so strongly in *The Alchemist*.

It is scarcely conceivable that such heavy trading in semi-private allusions and mutual mockery could have been indulged in by only one of the pair. Inevitably, *The Alchemist* contained its author's counter-attack. Jonson, enthusiastic for money like his fellow but much less possessive about it, set up an image of his fellow lover of wit that made him in strictly financial terms into the sole beneficiary of all the con-tricks that the King's Men were now practising when they staged their plays at the Blackfriars.

Sadly, such in-jokes were coins in the local (counterfeit) currency of their time which lost its value as soon as the time was past. At least semi-private in their own time, such allusions have proved elusive or invisible even to current commentators on the plays. That is one of the major problems for any producer of Jonson on the modern stage. Theatre is always for its own time, and has to be read differently in other times. We might now stage a Lovewit dressed in the familiar image of pointy-bearded and ruffed Shakespeare, but almost all the niceties of the 1610 game of 'application' that made Lovewit into Shakespeare would still be lost. For students of the real Jonson, I would argue, an awareness of his metatheatrical games can enhance everything that is there in Jonson's games of mirroring and application, but the losses in a modern performance are considerable.

Notes

1 A spiritual biography about Joan Drake, a citizen Londoner in the 1630s, reports that when she started making derisive comments on religious matters Dr John Dod lodged in her house in an attempt to reform her, but she 'would laugh and jest at all he said in derision: In her thoughts likening him unto *Ananias*, one whom at a play in the Black-Friers shee saw scoft at, for a holy brother of *Amsterdam*.' See Pritchard 1994: 92–5 (here p. 94).

2 See, for instance, Gras 1989: 545–64.

3 See Gurr 1982: 52–62.

4 See Levin 1971: 47–58.

5 See note 3.

6 Critics have grappled with Lovewit in a variety of ways. See, for example, Arnold 1969: 151–66, and revised 1972; Rebhorn 1980: 355–75; Watson 1986: 332–65; and the overviews in books such as Barton 1984: 150–2, and Haynes 1992: 117–18. All offer incisive comments on Lovewit's anomalous function in the play. None of them take the question quite far enough to sufficiently explain why Jonson should have chosen to give him his anomalous triumph, however.

7 Gurr 1988: 91–102.

8 Gurr 1996: ch. 3.

Part I

Ben Jonson and the theatre (as it is and as it might be)

Richard Cave

1 Script and performance

Richard Cave

To begin where most rehearsals for a production of one of Jonson's plays will begin: the script. Read-throughs of a Jonsonian text according to Simon Russell-Beale are notorious in today's theatre for their length, for the exhaustion (and at times the despair) they induce in the casts set upon giving that text dramatic life. Yet as rehearsals evolve and start to inhabit what is to be the playing space, actors find that text generating a remarkable dynamism and stimulating them with an exhilarating vitality. Are the texts, then, as *playtexts* somehow at fault? Do they give off the wrong signals and, if so, why? Why do they not on an initial encounter appear to give actors the right kind of purchase on the play by revealing to them the potential their respective roles offer? Or, to hit the bottom line, why are modern actors *afraid* of encounters with Jonson? If we set aside the myths and stories about Jonson's relations with actors in his own day and his attack on audiences for not appreciating the excellences of those of his plays which failed to gain enthusiastic applause at their first viewing (issues which editors tend to rehearse in the introductions to the twentieth-century editions of the plays with a relish that must prove daunting to an actor who reads them), will we find any explanation for this state of affairs in the actual *texts*? The subtext of Andrew Gurr's Prologue to this volume implies an answer which is strongly affirmative. This needs investigation.

Focusing on issues of language and Jonson's precision of reference, Gurr argues that Jonsonian drama is not for all time but locked in a particular past. Yet he concludes with the observation that 'theatre is always for its own time, and has to be *read differently* in other times';[1] offers by way of demonstration a reading of *The Alchemist* as metatheatrical game-playing; but then warns that with such a reading 'the losses are considerable'. Certainly there are losses (only a dedicated scholar of Jacobean life and theatrical practice could offer the particular reading that he has attempted); but are there no corresponding *gains* in insight for a contemporary audience? This is to imply that only initial audiences contemporary with a play's composition and staging can experience that play in depth. Are subsequent generations of audiences to be condemned to receiving that play superficially? Surely not. Gurr's is in large measure the purist's argument and, as such, open to the same kind of criticism that Granville Barker levelled against William Poel's attempts at recreating *authentic* Renaissance staging practice: namely that, however sensitive or imaginative an Edwardian audience may be who are watching *The Two Gentlemen of Verona* on a stage designed to imitate the Fortune Theatre peopled by actors in Renaissance costumes, they can in no way be described as having a genuine Elizabethan experience.[2] Granville Barker preferred to try and discover the basic principles underlying Elizabethan staging practice and then find modern *equivalences* for these. Could this method not be applied equally well to the playtext in performance? Surface dialogue is generally the means (for actors and audience) to access the inner (subtextual) life of a drama, its thematic coherence. Through engaging with that inner life, equivalences might be found which would bring depth to an audience's reception of a playtext in performance. Questing for such a pattern of analogies frankly admits our difference from the past but simultaneously reveals the potential for kinship. This implies an alert and self-aware audience; but that in the staging of Jonson's plays is precisely the kind of response that his dramatic strategies seem to demand (he devises ever subtler means to bring an audience back to an awareness of its place within the constructed performance, both in terms of its relation to the world of the play onstage and of a necessary detachment from that world). How are actors to gain access to that inner dynamic of a play by Jonson and perceive or sense the stimulus it offers to their creativity at a *reading* of the text? This raises an issue about the texts available for reading.

Comparing the 1616 Folio of Jonson's *Works* with the 1623 Folio of Shakespeare's, Andrew Gurr detects a marked and pointed difference between them. Shakespeare's plays are printed from copy that in various ways was designed primarily for actors' use; Jonson's he sees as the product of careful editing, even rewriting and expansion, and designed for a readership. In other words: Shakespeare's works are offered to posterity as playtexts, Jonson's as literature.[3] He substantiates this claim by comparing the kinds of stage directions that are to be found in both Folio and Quarto printings of Shakespeare's and Jonson's plays. Shakespeare's directions are relatively few in number because as actor and shareholder he would be present at rehearsal to control the initial staging. Jonson's are fewer still and record merely visual effects not wholly deducible from the dialogue (such as his fondness for the 'discovery' of a leading figure in the drama at an early stage in the performance).[4] From the playtexts Gurr deduces in Shakespeare's case a complex usage of the levels within the playing space and the power-structuring possible through such usage, especially in episodes involving those levels for purposes of spectacle. Visual spectacle, other than what is required by a conscious theatricality, occurs rarely in Jonson in Gurr's view: the emphasis, by implication, is wholly on what is spoken (and Gurr makes much of Jonson's stated preference for auditors rather than spectators). In theoretical terms this means that the performance text of a Jonsonian drama is all but synonymous with the playtext. But why then, one might question, is our attention drawn to the plays' evident and self-conscious *theatricality*, if Jonson is in fact offering them to us for appreciation as literature? Peter Barnes, a dramatist and practised director of

Jonsonian comedy, would take a decidedly contrary view: 'To criticise him [Jonson] from the text alone is like criticising an opera for the libretto.'[5] Two points need addressing before Barnes's judgement can be supported and Gurr's argument contested: firstly, what exactly is meant by 'stage directions' in relation to the Folio of 1616; and secondly, what is to be understood by the term 'visual spectacle' in relation to Jonson's plays? Both issues impact on how one sets about *reading* Jonson, especially as a practitioner.

When Jonson came to supervise the printing of the playtexts he chose to include in the 1616 Folio, he had no precedents in the way of contemporary publishing to follow: that was the daring of the enterprise. The plays of classical authors, Greek and Roman, were objects of close study from schooldays upwards and, though acted frequently enough, were perceived primarily as literature. Jonson's Folio copies the principles of such texts in terms of scene divisions.[6] What was highly innovatory was his layout of the dramatic text upon the page (one can note the differences most markedly in respect of certain plays which had previously been published as quartos). Gurr is right in one sense: there are very few stage directions in the Folio of the conventional kind, which are set as bracketed insertions between lines of text and printed in an italic typeface to distinguish them from the surrounding dialogue. But there are others (again relatively few but of great significance) which are printed as marginal annotations in some of the plays included in the 1616 Folio (and again within the texts of the additional plays contained in volume two of the Second Folio of 1640) which, without distracting attention from the main columns of text, add necessary glosses about characters' movements, stage business and, occasionally, appearance. There is for example the note accompanying the characters' entrance in *The Alchemist* at 3.5.1. '*Subtle disguised like a Priest of Faery*'; or later in the scene at l.25 the comment '*He* [Dapper] *throwes away as they bid him*' beside Face's instruction: 'If you have a ring about you, cast it off'. Asterisks within the dialogue in *The Sad Shepherd* at 1.6.33–6 indicate precisely where Robin is to kiss Marian, just as in smoking sequences in *Every Man in his Humour* and the Induction to *Cynthia's Revels* dashes in the text of the dialogue show where the actors are to puff on their pipes. A more complex example still of such a marginal annotation is again to be found in *The Sad Shepherd* at 3.4.43–9 where the direction 'Enter *Maudl*[in]: like *Marian*. *Maudl*: espying *Robin-Hood* would run out, but he staies her by the Girdle, and runs in with her. He returns with the Girdle broken, and shee in her own shape' indicates a series of intricate visual effects, which are not clearly apparent from the dialogue. These glosses clearly indicate the nature of *performed* actions, and in some instances the timing of speech with action to create a particular rhythm in performance. While undeniably they act as a guide to readers to help envisage the nature of such moments in performance, they also reflect Jonson's intentions about staging. It oversimplifies the issue to claim like Gurr that these directions take the form they do solely for the benefit of readers.

In fact the layout deserves closer attention still. Herford and the Simpsons observe that Jonson 'liked the look of a clean page in which the text stood out clear'.[7] This is true: the dialogue immediately captures and sustains attention in consequence. But at the periphery of one's vision as one reads, there are these guides which illuminate what is being focused on by the eye but in a manner that need not necessarily disturb one's concentration on the flow of dialogue. The glosses in other words help to realise a sense of the play in performance and as such, I would argue, can be interpreted as assisting the reader *or* as instructing the performer over a range of usually crucial matters concerning pace and clarity of action. Claire Cochrane has questioned whether perhaps the modern practitioner needs a specially edited text of a Jonsonian play which would indicate a director's way through the action.[8] There would be a potential danger in this in that such an edition would privilege a particular reading of the play which might circumscribe actors' creativity with the text: it would be memorialising one particular reading at the expense of others. Jonson's own mode of laying out the dramatic text in the 1616 Folio (the principles of which are imitated in the enlarged 1640 Second Folio) in my view subtly achieves Claire Cochrane's ambition by intimating the potential for performance without inhibiting a practitioner's creative input. Brilliantly through his chosen format Jonson has found a way of circumventing the limitations of the hand-held book such that one rests in a kind of half-illusion that one is in the theatre experiencing a performance. Jonson has created a plurality of texts within the one held text: performance text and literary text cohabit the page and one can, therefore, *choose* a mode of reading. The problem for today's practitioner is that, with the exception of Herford and the Simpsons, modern editors since Gifford in 1816 have tended to ignore the implications of the layout of the 1616 Folio, have observed more traditional conventions in setting plays, and so have lost touch with Jonson's innovative 'plurality' and consequently lost access to Jonson's evocation of the play as performance.

There are other indications within the Folio text to support this interpretation of its layout. Consider the appearance of the dialogue at the opening of *The Alchemist*, for example (or any other sequence of rapid, cross-fire talking in the play). Modern editors break up the verse lines in order to isolate speeches and speakers for ease of reading, whereas the Quarto and Folio by contrast preserve the verse lines intact and distinguish the speakers' names within any given line by use of a different type face (Roman capitals).[9] The modern editor finds a visual way of showing the pattern of verse lines but misses the sheer vitality of Quarto or Folio where you have a real sense of people trying to shout each other down. Quarto and Folio reproduce the effect of performance; the modern text is by contrast too clean, too decorous: literary not theatrical. Seeing the text as literature inclines one to bring a set of presuppositions to a reading which fasten on the need for significances and meanings, which arrest the evocation of what in the theatre must be a fast-flowing action. Actors with experience in Jonsonian comedy repeatedly recall that the moment the play took off in rehearsal was when they finally discovered the pace of particular scenes.[10] Why should they spend time with modern editorial formats searching for that pace, when Jonson's own texts devise ways of giving them immediate access to the required tempo?

The device has other connotations for performance worth commenting on, which are exemplified by the closing lines of that opening scene of *The Alchemist*. The quarrel has scarcely been resolved when a knock comes 'w*ithin*', Doll is sent to spy on who has arrived and reports back that it is a young man with the appearance of a clerk; Face identifies the man as a new intended gull, Dapper; the name means nothing at first to his accomplices, till Face reminds them of information about the man's longing for a *familiar* which he had previously imparted; the trio have now to decide how best to handle the situation. Within six tight lines the scam is all set up. Set out in the Folio as described above in six uninterrupted lines of verse with the names of the varying speakers being distinguished by a different typeface the sheer verve and rapidity of the episode is deftly caught and recreated in one's imagination as one reads. Set out by modern conventions with each new speaker having a new line in the text (even when only a single word is to be spoken) those six lines sprawl down the page with quite a different impact on the reader's sensibility. There is clearly at this moment in the action a need for quick thinking and the Folio's preserving of the verse lines conveys a real sense of the trio's brilliant if demonic intelligences. They have to improvise on the spur of the moment: a new gull requires a new technique of trickery appropriate to his social standing and his particular longing; Face and Subtle must create the outline of an agreed scenario within which they can immediately begin to operate. The layout of the modern edition slows down the pace of it all, as it becomes visually a series of questions and answers and in consequence there is little sense that the trio are (in modern parlance) winging it or that they have recovered a unity of intent after their divisive quarrel. The Folio text shows us why Doll was so anxious about the future of their 'venture tripartite' throughout the men's aggression: everything depends on their ability to respond to any given situation as a *team*. The Folio text here implies much about pace, characterisation and a necessary ensemble work for the actors involved. The exhilarating audacity of the moment, the breathtaking expertise with which cues and roles are decided on, and the relish with which Face and Subtle plunge straight into *performance* are all exactly contained within the chosen layout. This is not just dramatic verse; it is *theatrical* verse, meticulously showing what is meant in terms of performance by spontaneous improvisation. Read sensitively, the Folio layout is remarkably supportive of the actor.

A different feature of the layout also intimates details concerning performance and that is the use of adjacent columns of text at certain moments. The most complex of these occurs in the 1640 text of *Bartholomew Fair* (3.5.144–57) where Cokes has his purse stolen by Edgworth while listening to Nightingale's ballad. Edgworth's movements around Cokes and Cokes's constant removal of the purse from his pocket to see whether it has been stolen or not are indicated at first by the use of marginal glosses. At the climactic moment, however, the lyric of the song, the thief's trick with the straw that enables him finally to get his hands on the purse and Winwife and Quarlous's observations on the scene which they are watching from within the crowd are laid out in three distinct columns side-by-side on the page to indicate their simultaneous performance (see Plate 1, p. 75).[11] Cleverly the commentary of the two gallants draws the audience's attention to Edgworth's action as the song continues to Cokes's delight; it is an intricate moment of visual theatre but Jonson has meticulously directed the focus of the audience's gaze so that they can not only follow the theft but also the cunning handing over of the purse to Nightingale. What is also notable about the way the episode appears on the page is the way Winwife's final comment ''Fore/God, he is an brave fellow; pity he should be detected' spills over from the columns (where the text of his dialogue with Quarlous and Grace is printed in a smaller typeface to allow it to fit the available space alongside the song and the stage directions) leaving the last phrase isolated in the same-sized typeface as is generally deployed for the dialogue. The remark 'pity he should be detected' is a direct challenge to an audience's moral codes and the sudden isolating of the line suggests that it should in some way be privileged by the ensemble of actors in a way that properly registers with an audience despite the mêlée that follows the conclusion of the ballad. Winwife, Quarlous and Grace have themselves been spectators of the action involving Cokes and Edgworth as have the audience; the episode is complex since it invites admiration for Edgworth's expertise and a certain comic release in his gulling of an evident fool; but the action is a criminal offence (the punishment for such a theft in Jacobean London was vicious) so what does delight in the episode reveal about the morality of the spectators both onstage and off?

Jonson is in fact to build on this intricate and challenging strategy by offering us shortly a second theft, which on this occasion Quarlous actually instigates because of his appreciation of Edgworth's skill. Chance puts him in the role of spectator on the first occasion; but in the second instance he determines the action, and so his watching the theft at Edgworth's invitation, which again involves the gulling of an ass, Cokes's tutor, transforms the nature of his role to that of *knowing* spectator and that invites a more disturbed response still from the audience. Do they watch now with the same degree of amusement or are they not more self-conscious about the degree to which being a spectator involves a measure of participation in the event? The comedy here reveals a sharp even dangerous edge, pushing an audience to interrogate the moral nature of their engagement with the play. Meticulously, Jonson's strategies with textual layout define the heightened degree of ensemble acting that is required in the first theft so that a subtly controlled focus is maintained throughout what is a boisterous crowd scene. It is essential that an audience attend to this specific focus closely, if they are themselves properly to be situated later within the thematic strategies that Jonson is to develop. The burden, then, is on cast and director to engage the audience in a specific way but Jonson has found the means textually to convey what the technical demands of staging the scene must involve. The layout insists upon ensemble acting of considerable virtuosity. When, however, twentieth-century editors lay this episode on the page sequentially with the dialogue interspersed with italicised stage directions (even if a device is invented like G.R. Hibbard's in the New Mermaid edition[12] so that the comments of Winwife and Quarlous are presented in brackets to suggest they ought to be performed across certain lines of Nightingale's song) the dynamics of the staging are no longer immediately, or indeed clearly, apparent. The 1640 text shows how what should *seem* to the audience a realistically staged crowd scene must in fact be physically choreographed and vocally orchestrated with a careful precision.[13]

One final point will substantiate my view that the 1616 Folio can be read as both a literary and a performance text: the case of the unidentified voice in *The Alchemist*. In the first scene of Act 2 Mammon brings Surly to the house to have him view the alchemical experiments. Mammon expatiates for his friend's benefit on the joys awaiting the possessor of the philosopher's stone, concluding with the keen injunction, '*be rich*'; then, turning his mind to Subtle hard at work for his benefit, he calls out to him; immediately an unidentified voice replies 'Sir./He'll come to you, by and by' (2.1.25–6). The accompanying stage direction in the 1612 Quarto and again in the 1616 text reads '{WITHIN}'; the speaker is not identified. Editors since Gifford in 1816 have consistently assigned the speech to Face; and generally in addition set the lines such that his words are separated out from Mammon's peroration which the voice interrupts but which immediately continues in full flood. The Folio text sustains its pattern of preserving the verse lines and only the stage direction indicates a discreet speaker shouting from offstage. The next burst of dialogue from Mammon reveals that the 'voice' is possessed by one Lungs, Subtle's 'fire-drake' (laboratory assistant) and factotum. 'Lungs' does not make an appearance for nearly eighty lines of text, when the audience perceive that this servant is Face in disguise. By not identifying the voice Quarto and Folio provoke and sustain a trick with the reader identical with that which at this moment is played on the audience in a performance.

Till now we have seen Face only in his role of Captain with dashing beard and uniform suitable for the part. Subtle by contrast we have seen in and out of his magic robes as magus adapting his persona in various ways to suit first Dapper and then Drugger when they come to him as clients; but we have as yet no experience of Face's multiple role-playing. Later in 3.5 when an impatient Mammon disturbs the trio's fairy scam put on for Dapper, Face talks to him through the keyhole as 'Lungs' and it is clear within the context that the actor has here to shift character and voice to be rapidly by turns a fairy for Dapper, Face to his colleagues, and the factotum for Mammon. Clearly there is to be a distinct voice for 'Lungs' but the precise identity of this 'Lungs' when his ancient, husky voice is first heard 'within', is kept secret from us audience. We have no knowledge that this is Face in yet another disguise, so it will come as a calculated surprise when he appears as the factotum, sweaty, ragged and (seemingly) weary with attending to the scientific apparatus, with a new bizarre costume we have not seen before and a carefully chosen voice to go with it. When he last left the stage (1.4.9), it was on Subtle's instruction: 'Face, go you, and *shift*'. 'Shift' is a wonderfully ambiguous word: it can mean to arrange, put in order or generally manage matters; to change (in the sense of altering one's clothes or appearance); to get out of the way, elude or evade another person (often with connotations of subterfuge); or simply to withdraw or depart. All are possible here; and so how the word is to be interpreted depends entirely on subsequent events.

By working this surprise on the audience during a performance, Jonson skilfully prepares for the Face-actor's spectacular round of shape-changings as the play evolves. When we finally see him in his manifestation as Lovewit's clean-faced butler, Jeremy, we are left marvelling at this consummate actor but also unnerved by his seemingly endless capacity for transformation. In the closing moments of the English version of *Every Man in his Humour* when Brainworm, another shape-changing servant, throws off a disguise to reveal his identity to his master, Kno'well, the latter expresses his astonishment at the completeness of a transformation which has repeatedly tricked him: 'Is it possible! Or that thou should'st *disguise thy language so*, as I should not know thee?' (5.3.81-2) Clearly for Jonson disguise was *total*, a complete inhabiting of a new persona: clothes, posture, voice and, where necessary, accent and a distinctive vocabulary. Face's transformation into Lungs is wholesale; and the trick that Jonson plays on the theatre audience involving the unidentified voice is a dramatic strategy that brilliantly establishes his point. It is the completeness of his many disguises that subsequently will assist Face/Jeremy to elude blame or punishment.[14] To deconstruct in detail this moment in both text and performance is to appreciate the architectural strengths of Jonson's dramaturgy. It is noticeable that in the Folio text when Surly appears in disguise to spy on the household and unmask the rogues, the fact is announced immediately in the accompanying marginal gloss: '*Surly like a Spaniard*' (4.3.20–1) which implies the audience should see through the disguise immediately; there is no attempt here to build up a strategy to surprise the reader when later he reveals his identity to Dame Pliant and then to Face and Subtle. Surly, for one thing, is not a master of the art and mystery of disguise: that he is quickly discomfitted once he announces who he is and his motive for transforming his appearance, serves to augment our relish of Face's expertise and the cool nerve that is clearly requisite if the ruse is to succeed. With that unidentified voice '*within*' Jonson was manipulating readers like his audiences into a strategy whereby they can begin to appreciate the extent and brilliance of Face's impersonations involving his body, voice and appearance, about which the whole comedy revolves. To identify the voice as Face's (as modern editors invariably do) is to have readers miss one disturbing aspect of *The Alchemist*: that, call him what you will ('Face', 'Lungs', 'Jeremy'), that particular character has no fixed identity but is all role play, a master at evasive duplicity, a *shifter* in every sense of the word. Again: the Folio text reconstructs an effect scrupulously designed for the play in performance, and does so in a way that reveals to an actor approaching the role of Face a great deal about the particular demands of the part. If modern editors were prepared to read the Folios as not only literary but also performance texts, then actors might find the plays more immediately accessible and a spur to their creative invention. Whether one attempts a literary or a theatrical reading of the plays within the 1616 and 1640 Folios, the texts (through the subtle combination of stage directions, marginal glosses and overall layout upon the printed page) continually assert their performativity. To apply the term 'stage direction' in its conventional sense to Jonson's plays as Gurr does is to miss the wealth of material relating to performance that the texts contain.

Notes

1 See p. 18 (my emphases).

2 Poel mounted such a production on his Fortune fit-up stage at His Majesty's Theatre on 20 April 1910. For a detailed discussion of Poel's work, see O'Connor 1987; and for Barker's involvement with Poel's enterprises and his eventual criticism of them which markedly influenced his own subsequent staging of Renaissance drama, see Mazer 1981.

3 This was the subject of a second lecture that Andrew Gurr offered the Reading conference on 9 January 1996. It was entitled 'Jonson's Stage Directions'. This paragraph draws on the substance of that lecture and the discussion it subsequently provoked. In pursuing his argument that Jonson's texts are aimed at understanding readers, Gurr made special reference to the title page of the 1631 Quarto of *The New Inn* with its description of how the play 'was never acted but most negligently play'd by some, the King's servants. And more squeamishly beheld and censured by others, the King's subjects' in 1629, 'only now at last [to be] set at liberty to the Readers, his Majesty's servants and subjects, to be judged'. Gurr is not alone in this view of the Folio versions of the plays as literary artefacts: in that otherwise exhaustive study, *Ben Jonson's 1616 Folio* (Brady and Herendeen 1991) no contributor investigates the Folio in relation to performance, to the Elizabethan and Jacobean theatre, or to printing conventions in respect of playtexts in the Renaissance. It is a serious omission.

4 See, for example, the surprising arrival of Envy rising from under the stage to forestall the speaker of the Prologue in *The Poetaster*; the emergence in haste (and armed) of the Prologue proper to halt her disappearance; the emblematic picture of him standing with his foot upon her head before he allows her to 'sink'; and finally the revelation of Ovid at work in his study composing a poem. The Ghost of Sylla similarly '*rises*', reveals Catiline '*in his study*' designing plans for his insurrection, then '*sinks*' as Catiline rises to speak his opening soliloquy. Volpone commands the revelation of his treasures within seconds of the play's start. It is interesting that this device is abandoned by Jonson after *Catiline* in 1611.

5 Peter Barnes stated this while giving an illustrated lecture-workshop on Jonsonian comedy at the Reading conference on 10 January 1996.

6 A significant change in the number of characters present onstage is designated by a new scene division. Sometimes the name of a single character arriving late into a scene is set at the heading of the scene but at some distance along the line from the names of the other characters present to indicate her or his subsequent arrival '*to them*'.

7 Herford and the Simpsons, vol. 3: xiv.

8 This was during a panel discussion at the Reading conference that was reporting the findings of several small groups who had been discussing ways of opening up the Jonsonian repertory.

9 No edition of the play published since Herford and the Simpsons repeats Jonson's way with lineation; all editors split the verse lines in the manner described here.

10 John Nettles and Simon Russell-Beale both made this comment in discussion with Richard Cave at the Reading conference. It was the subject in part of Peter Barnes's workshop and the discovery of the cast from Border Crossings Theatre Company who investigated scenes from *The Poetaster* with the director, Michael Walling. Pace was a major preoccupation for Sam Mendes in the later stages of directing *The Alchemist* (see pp. 79–85). Interestingly Nettles and Mendes both commented that once that pace was found, it was not noticeably deviated from throughout a run of performances: both *The Devil is an Ass* and *The Alchemist* sustained a near-identical running-time at Stratford throughout the particular season in which they played.

11 The columns are particularly accentuated in the text of the second Folio as they are separated by a grid of clearly defined lines.

12 See Hibbard 1977: 93. Not one editor since Herford and the Simpsons exactly copies the layout of the Second Folio for this sequence; most simply break up the song with passages of dialogue for Quarlous, Winwife and Grace. Few are as inventive in how they present this as Hibbard. Michael Jameson (1966) and Eugene M. Waith in his edition of the play (1963) give first the stage direction concerning Ezekiel's movements and then print song and simultaneous dialogue in adjacent columns, but keep the last phrase of Winwife's speech well within the column structure so that it is not privileged as in the 1640 Folio. Though Helen Ostovich in *Ben Jonson: Four Comedies* (1997) imitates the layout in columns of the scene referred to below concerning Doll's fit of talking in *The Alchemist*, she totally ignores the layout of this sequence from *Bartholomew Fair*.

13 A similar point can be made about the layout of the scene where Doll goes into her 'fit of talking' while pretending to be Lord Whats'um's learned sister. The 1616 text lays out her bizarre disquisition in 4.5.25–32 and Face's anxious talk with Mammon about what exactly brought on her manic state in two adjacent columns of text printed in a smaller typeface from the general dialogue and appends the marginal gloss at l.25 '*They speake together*'. There is to be a divided focus of attention in other words with all three characters talking at once: Doll in an increasingly hysterical monologue, Face and Subtle keeping pace with her so as to create a mounting volume of sound that is soon to bring an irate Subtle onstage. When these columns are broken up as they tend to be by many modern editors and Face and Mammon's dialogue is presented on the page *after* Doll's speech, the potent farcical dynamism of it all is lost sight of. It is not necessary that the audience hear every word (it's bizarre nonsense any way); the rising crescendo of speech is what should *tell* in performance. The 1616 text indicates to an alert group of actors what the pace and effect of the episode should be immediately; the sequential layout of the modern edition, even if prefaced by the stage direction '*They all speak together*', suggests a more orderly style of performance and a slower pace so the farcical potential has to be found by actors intend of being instantly obvious to them. (To be fair to modern editors, the Second Folio of 1640 for reasons of economy does print this scene sequentially in one long column so that the gloss '*They speake together*' here implies that Face and Mammon simply confer. But that is no reason for modern editors to follow the 1640 as distinct from the 1616 Folio which Jonson himself supervised in the printing.) Most but by no means all editors of the play since Herford and the Simpsons reproduce the layout in columns of the 1616 Folio.

14 Without exception editors since Herford and the Simpsons have identified that voice 'within' as Face's.

2   Visualising Jonson's text

Richard Cave

The issue of visual spectacle in Jonson's plays is problematic. 'Spectacle' for Jonson himself increasingly came to mean scenic theatre and the mechanics required to accomplish its marvels within the court masque; and, as his relations with Inigo Jones became strained, Jonson's pronouncements against visual effects and against those 'spectators' whose concept of theatre in his view extended no further than delighting the eye and the fancy became ever stronger. He began marking his preference for *auditors* as the ideal receivers of his drama. Certainly in his masques the spoken and sung texts have a profundity of import often accompanied by a delicacy of wit and elegant compliment that require attentive listening: the verbal artistry is sophisticated, pointed and challenging. Delight is present, but it is the delight of an urbane mind relishing the exercise of its learning, insight and scruple. Jonson clearly saw his texts and libretti as giving his audiences informed access to the visual splendours: his words taught how properly to read the visual dimension of the masques and so pass beyond a mere engagement with the eyes to an understanding of the symbolic intentions of the spectacle. But this was expensive court theatre; the popular theatres were a decidedly different world; and it would be wrong to apply Jonson's strictures about spectacle which derived from his work at court to his plays for more public spaces and deduce from his increasingly angry observations about masques a lack of concern for the visual potential of drama. The visual dimension of plays staged at the Globe, Blackfriars, or the Hope would be of an order different from what is implied by 'spectacle', being more preoccupied with a creative use of stage-space; and here, I would argue, Jonson demonstrates a remarkable expertise and inventiveness.

On the whole Jonson makes sparing use of the varying stage-levels for dramatic effect. The trap is deployed for Envy in *The Poetaster*; while the understage area twice gains a vivid dramatic life in *Catiline* when '*A grone of many people is heard under ground*' at line 315 in the opening scene. An upper level is required in several plays: for the parody of the balcony scene from *Romeo and Juliet* when in Act 4 of *The Poetaster* Ovid bids farewell to Julia as he goes into exile; for various scenes in *Every Man out of his Humour*; to meet the requirement that Cicero appear suddenly '*above*' at the close of Act 3 of *Catiline* to identify and frustrate his would-be assassins; to enable Celia to watch the mountebank scene from above and drop her handker-chief at the crucial moment of Corvino's return; and for Tub's first appearance when called from his bed on St Valentine's Day in *The Tale of a Tub*. That level is used more creatively in *The Devil is an Ass* when Wittipol in Act 2 courts Frances Fitzdottrel through the window of his friend Manly's upper chamber which fronts the Fitzdottrels' house across, we are to suppose, a narrow street; and again in Act 4 of *Epicoene* where the Collegiates with Trusty and Epicoene are required to look down on Dauphine indulging in sadistic horseplay with Daw and La Foole, each of whom is hiding in a closet but comes forth to undergo his punishment. This last arrangement allows the audience full view of a divided focus of action: the farci-cal violence on the main stage accompanied by suitable dialogue is watched in silence from above by the Collegiates who in mime must express a growing sexual excitement at this display of Dauphine's macho vigour, since the development of the action in later scenes when they come severally to court his favours needs to be strongly motivated in this episode. This use of the stage architecture allows the audience full view of the ten actors who are involved in this scene, where the responses of all ten are to have consequences in the remainder of the play and therefore must be fully registered. These instances, however, are few in number when spread throughout some seventeen plays.[1] Where Jonson is consistently at his most innovative is in his ability to create a powerful visual dynamic upon the main stage by exploiting the dramatic possibilities inherent in its very spaciousness.

The episode where the Collegiates watch Dauphine acting out what is to all intents a play is a characteristic metatheatrical device in Jonsonian comedy, drawing the theatre audience's attention to the way plays in performance may be received as a means to make them conscious of their own responses at that given moment. His plays abound in situations where one group of characters closely observes another group who are quite unconscious of being under surveillance. Quarlous, Winwife and Grace studying the play in which Cokes is robbed of his purse and later Quarlous watching Edgworth steal the marriage licence out of Wasp's box have been commented on above. In both instances the performed episode becomes more than conventional playing for the theatre audience, since their powers of interpre-tation have been heightened by watching an onstage audience reach their own conclusions about what has been seen and heard. The action of the theft in both instances has been framed, distanced, estranged to some degree from the quality and tenor of the rest of the play, as the conventional demarcation of stage and audi-torium is erased: the playing space has a divided focus and, disturbingly, the nature of the response that is asked of the theatre audience to each is different. The device requires each audience-member both to engage with one point of focus onstage and almost immediately by relating to the other focal point to deconstruct that engage-ment to perceive how personally it has been motivated. Properly submitted to, the strategy offers a measure of self-discovery: it is a lesson about the subjective nature of perception. The stage is used in a visually exciting way to provoke insight into both the multiple ways in which one may read performance and the degree to which any one reading exposes the perceiving self. In *Bartholomew Fair* much of what occurs once the action moves to the fairground is seen by Justice Overdo as a play presented to his watchful gaze and ripe for his judicious interpretation. He is an ass and his readings consequently absurd; Quarlous is an opportunist and his readings are continually adjusted to suit circumstance and his own best advantage. From his privileged position as spectator Quarlous reads with cynical accuracy and so, when he comes to act himself in the guise of Troubleall, it is to gain the hand of a rich widow and to place both Grace and Overdo under a longstanding obligation to him.

Jonson evolved this highly sophisticated use of the spatial dynamic of the stage for metatheatrical interrogations of his audiences from very simple beginnings. In *Every Man out of his Humour* Jonson frames each act of the play with discussions between two critics (one of discerning judgement, the other a prey to fancy and convention); they take Asper, the presenter of the play, at his word when he bids them 'liber-ally / Speak your opinions, upon every scene'(Grex 1.154–5). Seated onstage with the wealthier members of the audience, they are conspicuous throughout the action, but in this instance the theatre audience can choose whether or not to watch them during the play proper. The potential for a divided focus of attention is there, but is not insisted upon as in the episodes from *Bartholomew Fair*: a spectator's sense of the visual dimension of the play in performance need not include the two critics for long stretches of time. The idea of reading the performance is not therefore taken back into the world of the play as it is with Quarlous and Overdo and shown to have social and moral consequences.

This integrating of the metatheatrical strategy into the stage action begins with *Sejanus*, where in many scenes the main plot involving Tiberius and his court is framed by a group of dissidents led by Arruntius who comment sardonically on what they and we are required to witness, evaluating character, deciding how to interpret ambiguities of word or deed and voicing a fierce political and moral dis-gust with the gross duplicities that pass as policy. Through asides to the audience Arruntius builds up a degree of complicity and so the reading of stage event with which he encourages them to be complicit is one coloured by covert sedition; just how dangerous such views can be is enacted forcefully onstage when Silius, one of Arruntius's associates, is pressured by Tiberius to commit suicide on the grounds of treasonous behaviour.[2] The audience is trapped in a moral dilemma between siding with an establishment that is evidently corrupt or joining league with a dwindling band of threatened rebels. The terrifying tenor of Tiberius's Rome, with its cohorts of spies, flatterers and go-getters, is precisely realised in terms of the audience's relation to the stage action. This divided focus with its constant demand that one attend to what one sees with the utmost concentration because of the dan-gers inherent in interpretation and judgement brilliantly prepares the audience for Jonson's daring strategy in the last two acts where Tiberius moves against his one-time favourite, Sejanus, and brings about his demise while apparently offering him yet greater liberties and power in Rome. The brilliance of it lies in the fact that Tiberius manoeuvres everyone into a position where he can confidently leave the city yet still effect his triumph over Sejanus *in absentia*. Little in this play is what it appears on the surface; and the device of the divided focus in which so much of the public action is framed by the watchful chorus of rebellious spirits fine-tunes an audience's powers of perception with expert skill. The dramaturgy deploys the visual dynamic of the stage to effect a searching examination into the nature of political power that is experiential rather than simply presented.

The final scenes of *Sejanus* show Tiberius casting the remaining characters to play out roles in a scenario of his devising which he watches from a distance with evident relish at this display of his absolute power. In a less tyrannical mould this becomes the tactic of Volpone and Mosca and of the venture tripartite: in both plays the gullers act within the scenarios they create but the better to observe the success of their schemes. They fuse in their own persons the functions of actor and spectator, which, as in the case of Quarlous, continually poses a challenge to the theatre audience about their own chosen function within the performance and their motive for preserving distance from events which are actually criminal while gaining entertainment in the process. The visual dynamic in these episodes, drawing attention as it does to the predatory watchfulness of the trickster characters, heightens, renders self-conscious and so deeply problematises the whole experience of being a spectator for the audience. The seemingly simple act of viewing is transformed by Jonson's dramaturgy into an ethical challenge. Long before the gaze became a theorised issue of considerable complexity, Jonson was devising the means to deconstruct for alert audiences the psychological processes involved in reading the visual systems of performance. What he would appear to be denying audiences is the right to experience theatre as escapist and yet his devices for achieving that end are always wittily conceived.

This is especially true of *The Devil is an Ass* which begins with a clever factionalising of the theatre audience: the stage sweeper by way of Prologue requires those spectators wealthy enough to sit onstage for the performance not to take up so much room with their fine clothes and antics that they constrict the playing space for the actors and so limit everyone else's enjoyment. This immediately makes a certain section of the audience and their modes of self-display the focus of attention and object of the remaining spectators' gaze. What are their motives in choosing to be so conspicuous? If they want to be exhibitionists, then Jonson has given them their hearts' desire. Not long into the play we encounter in Fitzdottrel a character who longs to extricate himself from the plot so that he can get along to the theatre to join these onstage gallants, display a newly acquired cloak of great value, hiss the actors and generally make a disturbance that will draw the audience's gaze to himself; and the performance that he longs to disrupt, we discover, is that afternoon's showing of Jonson's *The Devil is an Ass*. Fitzdottrel would witness a play that is designed to expose his own folly, greed and corruption and yet he would go there primarily to be seen and so feed his own egocentricity. How much of what he watches will he understand? It is a merry conceit to bring home to audiences that for all its farcical exaggerations the play is about their own world and that how they choose to relate to the satire played out onstage is a reflection of how they relate to their society. Given the sharks abroad in the world of the play like Meercraft, Everill, Gilthead and Tailbush, watching is seen to have its necessary responsibilities, not least in terms of one's self-protection: the whole plot resolves itself around the need to ensure that Fitzdottrel's wife outwits his stupidity in ways that will keep her future financially secure without compromising herself morally and emotionally. When we first meet her she is seen as the silent object of Wittipol's gaze (Fitzdottrel allows the gallant to woo her for a set number of minutes and at a set distance in return for the fee of a splendid cloak). Wittipol next meets her at her window, where he begins to bridge the distance between them – the marginal gloss to this episode in the 1640 Folio reads: '*He grows more familiar in his courtship, plays with her paps, kisseth her hands etc.*' (Herford and the Simpsons, 2.6.71) – as the voyeuristic gaze is subtly replaced by attempts at possession. Always Frances is the object of his attentions. When she finally addresses him later in the play (4.6), it is to appeal out of her subjectivity to his understanding; she insists he engage his imagination in her predicament and perceive the realities of her social situation; and shows him the financial and moral implications of being seen by her husband (and by implication by Wittipol as her would-be lover) as merely an object for his use. She requires and trusts him instead to be her *friend*. In both these extended strategies Jonson is revealing why it is imperative to distinguish between *looking at* and *seeing*. The one is an operation of the eyes, the other calls for an integration of the whole self. Subtly Jonson has taught us how to read the importance that the visual sustains within his dramaturgy.

Accepting Jonson's strictures as extrapolated here opens fresh insights into the function of visual effects within his plays. Many seem to exploit the sheer size of the Renaissance stage. It becomes noticeable, for example, how frequently Jonson's text or directions require a passing of one or more characters over the space. Twice the discussions of Arruntius and his friends in the opening scene of *Sejanus* are interrupted by first Drusus, heir to the throne, with his attendants and then by Sejanus himself, accompanied by his circle of sycophants. Each time the passing over is subjected to comment by the onstage chorus of senators: Drusus's character is cause for some disagreement between Arruntius and Silius, the one sees him as riotous and headstrong, the other as growing daily into an agreeable maturity; but the passing over is swift and only Drusus's body language and physical carriage can leave an impression with us. Sejanus's appearance causes Silius to draw our attention to 'the stoops,/The bendings, and the falls' (1.175–6) of the favourite's entourage. His passage over the stage is arrested by a short interpolated scene in which Sejanus is approached by a suitor seeking 'a tribune's place' for a friend; but Sejanus's eyes are all the while searching the space for sight of Eudemus, whom as we later discover, he wishes to suborn to his intention of getting access to Livia, Drusus's wife, to further his ambitions for the imperial throne. The two processions are markedly different in tone and enable Jonson to effect a rapid exposition of the current political situation under Tiberius. Drusus is seen by us briefly; but we perceive that he is the object of Sejanus's close and envious surveillance; and, so objectified, is quickly eliminated. That Drusus's presence is differently read by Silius and Arruntius encourages us to attempt our reading of his character, which in turn encourages us to note the degree of bias in Sejanus's interpretation. Once again our attention is focused on the dangers and difficulties of reading appearances in this society and that is a theme which is to weave inexorably through the action, culminating in Sejanus's ominous failure to read accurately either Tiberius's removal from Rome or Macro's prompt arrival there.

In a wholly different mode Cicero's passing over the stage again and again in the final act of *Catiline* brings death to every house beside whose door his progress is halted. One by one he visits the homes of the conspirators and on their appearance consigns them to death; the pattern of approach, the summons to the man within, his appearance, the reading of his sentence and his departure under guard to the execution being prepared for him is relentlessly repeated for Lentulus, Cethegus, Statilius and Gabinus. In the presence of the Senators and of Caesar (who is suspected of being implicated in Catiline's threatened coup) justice is seen to be done; the ritual quality of the episode ensures that there is no intimation of private vengeance on Cicero's part as the deaths are exacted; he is to the last the depersonalised representative of a state recently under threat but now making a bid for freedom and stability. The ritual enables us to view each of the condemned men in turn and note the tenor of their acceptance of death: Lentulus speaks of the irony of fate and chance; Cethegus abusively sneers at his judge; the remaining two attempt a stoic indifference. The whole protracted sequence (so quick to read and yet requiring a careful gravity and stylisation in the acting) subtly prepares our responses for Petreius's long ensuing account of Catiline's death in battle which we are required to imagine in the mind's eye and in a manner that will ensure that we feel Cato's response, 'A brave bad death'(5.688) is the most fitting judgement. Each of the conspirators' deaths is emblematised as an apt summation of their several lives. Cicero's ritual passing across the stage symbolically enacts the return of order and the due processes of the law to the state which Catiline's rebellion had set at hazard – a time of danger which at the start of Act 4 had been equally powerfully evoked by visual means, when '*Diuers Senators passe by, quaking, and trembling*' to the astonishment of the Allobrogian ambassadors: 'Can these men fear? who are not only ours,/But the world's masters?' (4.1–2). The *public* consequences of the rebellion and its suppression are demonstrated by the simple device of these contrasting passings over the stage.

A further example of a passing over the stage which gives the audience access by a powerful graphic image to the thematic preoccupations of the drama occurs in *The*

Magnetic Lady (3.3) where the opening stage direction reads: '*Rut. Lady. Polish. Keepe, carrying Placentia over the stage*'. Everyone believes at first that the girl has taken fright at the fisticuffs that broke out between Ironside and Sir Moth at Lady Loadstone's dinner party. The dialogue that accompanies the image of Placentia being carried over the stage focuses our attention on her frail condition as in a sweat and fainting. Later we learn that Placentia has 'fallen again, / In a worse fit than ever' (3.5.74–5) and by the end of the act that she has been delivered of an illegitimate child. The midwife, Mother Chair, summoned to assist at the birth, is required to administer a potion to Placentia that promptly restores her to full strength so that she may be seen confidently walking about the house and so dispel gossip and rumours. Even her supposed aunt, Lady Loadstone, is deluded into believing Placentia to have been maligned. As Polish assures Mother Chair, she has 'done a miracle' (5.2.15) as Placentia appears onstage with a quick step and upright carriage. The contrasting images of Placentia's posture (one sickly and physically collapsed; the other a picture of vibrant health) not only add to the complications of the plotting but also highlight one of the thematic concerns of the play. Much of the surface action of *The Magnetic Lady* is bound up with finding suitable husbands for Lady Loadstone and her niece in conformity with patriarchal expectation (a widow and a virgin, both inheritors of sizeable fortunes, should in terms of such a value system be well matched) but this resolution to the plot is continually frustrated by the efforts of the female servants of the household, Polish, Keep and Chair, who play on men's expected fears or preferred distance from the mysteries of childbirth and such women's matters to shape the situation to their own advantage. Placentia's transformed appearance and the remarkable change in how she makes a passing over the stage is one manifestation of their special power.

A yet more sophisticated use of the device is to be found in *Volpone* (5.6.8) where Volpone, now disguised in the habit of a Commandadore, intercepts first Corbaccio and Corvino, then Voltore, and then his two earlier victims again as they are attempting to effect a passing over the stage on their way ostensibly to the court of law. For all the size of the space, they cannot escape Volpone's attentions as he adds to their bitter frustration by saluting them repeatedly as the heirs to a fortune they have just learned has been bequeathed to Mosca. (Mosca indeed passes over with ease at one point in the habit of a Clarissimo to add to their envy and chagrin.) All his victims' attempts to recover a proper dignity as becomes their station in Venetian society are undermined by Volpone's refusal to let them pass on their way; wherever they turn, he reappears to block their path. It is a remarkable *physical* conceit offering a visual parallel for the way that psychologically wherever they turn in their anguish the three gulls are trapped by awareness of Volpone's duplicity and their own consequent absurdity. There is no escaping the realities of their condition: they are everywhere an object of trickery and exposed to scorn; and Volpone, playacting in yet another disguise, is there to triumph in their adversity. The stage action now has a dark, manic aspect with its emphasis on the victims' desperation and Volpone's overly zealous teasing. Volpone has lost touch with the moral discipline that controlled his discomfitting of the three suitors earlier in the play and soon he is himself to be publicly discomfitted. Here Volpone can direct the action to his own ends, but it is the last time in the play that this will be possible. Once in the court he loses his mastery over the shaping of events, and largely because he has made the wrong choice of costume for his current impersonation: an officer of the court has no power in the presence of patricians; and there he has now to dash frantically from character to character in an effort to save himself. The physical use of the stage in the episodes that lead to the play's conclusion expertly prepares us for Volpone's exposure and disgrace.

With the masques the transformations were scenic and effected to delight the audience; in the last two examples drawn from Jonson's plays transformations occur but more startlingly within persons: Placentia is refashioned as (apparently) a whole, healthy and marriageable virgin; Volpone recreates himself as a servant, while Mosca struts past every inch the born patrician. While the first transformation affects posture and gait (the very ability to walk), the second is achieved in both instances through costume and an apt accompanying manner of address and (in Mosca's case) deportment. Costuming is in fact a highly potent visual signifier in Jonson's theatre: from the overdressed courtiers of *Cynthia's Revels* to the intricate shape-changings of *The Sad Shepherd* his plays feature costume, as defining gender, status, background or personality, as central to his dramaturgy. Often his plots are resolved around the disrobing (or as he prefers to call it, the uncasing) of a particular character: Brainworm; Volpone; Epicoene; Face/Jeremy; Overdo, Quarlous, Win Littlewit and Mistress Overdo; Wittipol; Pennyboy Canter; Pinacia and Pru, Laetitia and her parents, Lord and Lady Frampul (formerly Frank, the Host and the Nurse); Sir Hugh; and Maudlin the Witch. What is remarkable in such a list is the variety of thematic purposes such games with the significance of dress serve. Costume becomes the site for a number of interrogations about identity. When Volpone finally reveals himself in the courtroom, for example, it is to show us the angry, impulsive, overly superior patrician who has been fitfully intimated behind his earlier impersonations. Overdo pretends to be mad Arthur and by the time of his disrobing has shown himself to be, if not mad, then ridiculous; Quarlous impersonates a mad man, Troubleall, and, under cover of an antic disposition, has devised a series of strategies which will trouble a number of individuals whom he has cunningly inveigled into his debt (Overdo, Grace and through her, Winwife, Dame Purecraft and by implication her Puritan associates). Win and Mistress Overdo for all their superior, middle-class airs have with promises of fine clothes, the attentions of gallants and the pomp of a carriage been lured into decking themselves as whores; and in the speed of their undoing, we marvel at their vacuity. It is as if in these instances the stripping off of attire brings us to the core of a character we have till now only guessed at. Noticeably Face never uncases in this way: when he finally slips out of Face's uniform it is offstage and when he reappears it is in Jeremy's livery as butler; the core of him ever eludes detection, which is why he thrives while Volpone fails. Three of the plays deploy costume for more complex thematic ends that confront issues of gender and these merit more detailed study.

Wittipol in *The Devil is an Ass* dresses as the Spanish Lady the better to have access to Frances Fitzdottrel and to get the measure of her husband and his circle of cronies. Once she appeals to his honour and friendship, the disguise enables him to thwart Meercraft, who is robbing Fitzdottrel of every penny he possesses, and so safeguard Frances's dowry and her subsequent financial security. So corrupt is the world of this play (even Satan is disgusted by its excess) that, to survive and define for himself a degree of integrity, Wittipol must resort to the strategies and impersonations that previously characterised Jonson's criminal tricksters. Disguise enables him to make a moral stand against Fitzdottrel and Meercraft and in this instance it is noticeable that he tricks them by exploiting the male gaze. He appears as a woman before them and a woman who is an authority on the lotions and potions that best keep a female attractive in male eyes; 'her' expertise and allure utterly seduce Fitzdottrel till Wittipol can manipulate him at will and win him away from Meercraft's control. Yet the charisma and all the Spanish Lady's learning in the mysteries of the toilet table is a highly inventive scam, which succeeds because Fitzdottrel is wholly the dupe of his own chauvinist assumptions about a pretty face, a glamorous frock and a winning manner. He is infatuated by an image but knows no more of the reality that is the Spanish Lady than he seriously knows his own wife. In the opening act of the play Fitzdottrel considered that he could best display his own manliness by the ostentatious wearing of a cloak at the public theatre; now he considers that a dress makes the disguised Wittipol the acme of womanhood. When Wittipol throws off wig and dress to reveal himself, it is not he who is morally exposed by Jonson's satire but Fitzdottrel for his dangerously limited powers of perception. Costume and how its social or gender signification is read within the world of a play allow Jonson to investigate the nature of perception in considerable depth.

In *Epicoene*, for example, there are fifteen named characters, all of whom are onstage during the final scenes; six of them are identified as female and are dressed accordingly, yet such were the conventions of the theatre at the time that all fifteen actors present are in fact male; the female characters have been constructed within the tiring-house in terms of clothing, make-up, wigs and through the artistry of the performers in terms of posture, mannerisms, vocal timbre. Throughout the play Jonson draws attention to the idea of the constructed nature of what one might term an individual's public persona. The play begins with a trio of gallants discussing and in part scorning the elaborate processes involved when a woman makes up her face and dons her wig and the striking differences between this projected image of the self and the private reality. Later Mistress Otter overhears her husband, far gone in drink, describe to his male companions how she puts herself together of a morning and takes herself apart at night 'like a great German Clock' and reveal where about London she shops for her false eyebrows and teeth. The men adopt a tone of superiority; but, since they set the standard in acceptable female beauty, their criticism and want of charity rebound back on them. That Mistress Otter falls upon her husband and overpowers him in the ensuing fight undermines all his pretensions to authority over her and exposes him for the liar, cad and cowardly ass that he is; she shames and *unmans* him totally. All the men are seen in time to fall far short of the urbanity which they pretend shapes their lives, values and responses. Even the gallants' satire at the expense of the other characters, male and female, seems, as it is sustained scene after scene, to cover a deep-rooted insecurity about their own condition.

At the end of the play Dauphine suddenly uncases the most beautiful and gracious of the six women revealing Epicoene to be a boy meticulously disguised, and trained like an actor to *play* convincingly at being female. Dauphine has constructed a woman and passed her off successfully in polite society. He has done this cynically for his own ends which involve securing an inheritance, and his triumph over Morose, his uncle and, as Dauphine intends, his benefactor, neatly resolves the plotline. But the uncasing of Epicoene carries more resonances central to the play's themes than that tidy resolution contains: Jonson has relentlessly interrogated the nature of gender as distinct from sexuality, showing the extent to which contemporaneous definitions, premises, prescriptions and expectations bear scant relation to his characters' experience. Most of them resist easy categorisation, since the Collegiates are seeking to adopt masculine freedoms and tones of authority while still cultivating a feminine appearance and charisma, and the men seem increasingly absurd and unmanly the more they try to embody set styles of masculinity. Embodying gender as traditionally defined imposes a strain on their lives; and there is a sense of shocked release when Epicoene proves to be neither the stereotype of the silent woman nor that of the shrill-voiced harridan but a boy who has effortlessly (if with some art) transgressed gender boundaries. The removal of a dress and a wig subverts all patriarchal inscriptions of what properly constitutes 'masculine' and 'feminine', exposing those inscriptions as constructs that compel people to *enact* gender. What should (or so it is claimed) be natural is shown in Epicoene to be clever pretence, a product of technical virtuosity, gifted playing, a living up to the conventional significations of a *dress*. By the final scene the visual disparity between Epicoene's costume with all that it signifies and the actor-wearer's exposed body with all that it too signifies brilliantly synthesises the thematic life of the drama into one memorable and challenging icon.

Equally exciting and provocative is the deployment of costuming in *The New Inn* to level a satirical attack against class consciousness. Prudence, Lady Frances's maid, has been elected queen of the festivities that her mistress plans by way of diversion with her entourage in the inn but the dress specially commissioned for her role has failed to arrive in time. On changing dresses with Frances to give herself the required appearance of superiority, Pru quietly assumes a remarkable authority, which as the sports commence, is seen to have less to do with power over others than shrewd insight into both their natures and their ambitions in life. In every way she lives up to the status implicit in her dress. Or would it be more accurate to see the dress as an outward manifestation of her inner worth? That question is soon answered with the arrival at the inn of the gorgeous costume originally intended for Pru to revel in as Queen. It is worn by Pinacia, wife of the tailor who made it, who is pretending to be the grand lady to help her husband (dressed out as a footman) act out his sexual fantasy of copulating with his wealthy, titled clients. They are following a ritual they have evidently indulged in frequently before. Pinacia is the antithesis of Pru: she cannot convincingly play the role of lady, only a mannered caricature of what is required. That she commands no authority is evidenced by the speed with which she and her husband become an object of derision for the servants and a party of roistering drinkers who catch sight of them. Pinacia is stripped of her garb, which Pru assumes to look even more resplendently a queen.

That the one dress can look quite different when worn by two contrasting figures implies much about carriage and deportment but more importantly about inner grace and confidence. It is Pru who gives the dress its distinction; and Lord Latimer appreciates this fact: the change of dress brings Pru to his attention (whereas her dress as maid encouraged him to take her for granted as serving a particular function in Lady Frances's household; dress here signifying uniform) so that he begins to read her innate character closely which has found release through her garb as queen of the revels. She draws his gaze but to excite his understanding and sympathy, as she demonstrates such qualities herself through her conduct within the court of love, which is the form Pru insists the revels should take. He watches the movement of her mind and in admiration proposes marriage, valuing not her status but her inner worth and intelligence. Again Jonson invites the audience to perceive the psychological motivation underlying this aspect of his plotting by offering a parallel which also focuses on female attire and the male gaze. Lady Frances as an absurd whim has had the Host's son, Frank, dressed as a girl as part of the revelry; Lord Beaufort is increasingly inflamed by all the talk of love and fastens his gaze on the disguised youth with lecherous intent; he too proposes marriage and rushes his supposed bride off to church for a prompt wedding only to become the target of everyone's ridicule when, half undressing himself for the nuptial bed, he is informed of his wife's actual gender. By a twist of the plot it is revealed that Frank is indeed a girl dressed formerly as a page, but this serves only to excite Beaufort's snobbery at the thought of marrying a woman so far beneath his station; he threatens divorce until he learns the girl is titled and rich; then he is content to have her and bed her.

The absurdity of the plotting emphasises Jonson's satirical point: the absurdity of judging any partner as ideal exclusively in terms of what the male gaze alone reveals. Beaufort is trapped by his own superficiality; he knows nothing of the woman to whom he finds himself wed. Latimer's union with Pru by contrast is a marriage of true minds. A sophisticated argument takes for its mode of demon-

stration here a focusing on costume and the extent and potential limits of its signification when it is seen as a projection of the wearer's personality. In doing so,
Jonson presents in Pru a radical challenge to contemporary class distinctions and the
assumptions about worth that accompanied them. *The New Inn* is a highly subversive
play and one site of its interrogation of social attitudes is the male gaze and the patriarchal mind-set that generally (but not invariably) directed it. In pursuing the
ramifications of Jonson's argument the audience experience different ways of reading visually; to further that argument he deliberately problematises costume and
what it conveys to, or may be made to convey by, a viewer. Given such a complex
concern to determine the social and psychological ramifications of varying modes
of perception, it does Jonson a disservice to argue like Gurr that his plays lack a
developed visual dimension, that they are verbal constructs principally aimed at listeners. The visual has its distinct and creative place within Jonson's dramaturgy and
that place is not difficult to establish from his playtexts. By concentrating on costume, on actor–audience relations, and on spatial dynamics as defined by the
positioning of performers within the playing space, Jonson created a visual dimension within his plays that was rich in dramatic potential while observing the
relatively austere playing conditions of the public theatres of his time. His work
demonstrates the distinction between spectacle in the conventional usage of the
word as 'a show' and a refined visual sophistication that bears an organic relation to
a play's thematic agenda. One could justifiably argue that the plays offer audiences
exciting lessons in *seeing*. Always the focus of his visual effects is the actor's artistry
as shaper of meaning; and it is important that designers in the modern theatre
respect that focus and Jonson's ways of creating richness out of a seeming austerity.
Designing for one of Jonson's plays clearly requires a discipline that respects the
range and purposefulness of his visual strategies.

Notes

1 I have not included the fragments or the masques in this count, nor both versions of
   Every Man in his Humour.
2 One is tempted to speculate whether this was what led to the halting of the first performance of the play by the audience and to Jonson being required to explain the play
   before the Privy Council. The nature of the play's strategies is such that they lay *Sejanus*
   open to a highly radical interpretation. William Fennor's description of the body language of the lower-class members of the audience ('They screwed their scurvy jaws and
   looked awry') would suggest a profound unease at what they were watching rather than
   tedium; and their subsequent hissing an expression of political disquiet. The onstage
   death of Silius who takes his life with quiet stoicism is the only such death in Jonson's
   two tragedies (the deaths of Sejanus and Catiline by contrast are reported in detail); the
   presentation of this death adds to the sense of danger that permeates this tragedy in performance.

3 Designing for Jonson's plays

Richard Cave

'. . . this year there is a kaleidoscope of change and surprise, Jonsonian Venice being now staged with the utmost impermanence. For *Volpone* the box of tricks is lavishly employed; the Fox's earth vanishes, on the downward lift, into what moist celler-age may underlie the Grand Canal; Court House and Market Place slide in from the wings. A new designer, Malcolm Pride, has been given a free hand and acquits him-self most handsomely; congratulations . . . to Stratford's team of adroit stage managers. Nobody can complain of eye-starvation now.'

(Ivor Brown, 'Jonson on Avon', *Observer*, 20 July 1952)

'. . . Mr George Devine's production, with its sliding and sinking stages, [is] an engineer's dream.'

(Harold Hobson, 'Why *Volpone?*', *Sunday Times*, 20 July 1952)

'. . . at its first introduction in the Jacobean Court Masques the moving of scenes was intended to take place before our eyes; the mechanical marvels were an impor-tant part of the show. Mr. Devine and his designer restore this usage in full measure; and a present-day audience enjoys as much as its predecessors watching Volpone's bedroom sinking slowly down, while a piazza, complete with foreground beggars and background canal, slides in to take its place. It was Jonson . . . who led the opposition to this scenic theatre when the marvels tended to oust the words.'

(T.C. Worsley, 'The Fox', *New Statesman*, 26 July 1952)

'The play was introduced by music of a prodigiously abstract nature, but there was nothing abstract about the sets, which utilised very massively all the hydraulic tricks with which the Stratford stage is now equipped. To my mind these triumphs of engineering are the worst possible enemies of illusion. When Volpone turns out to have been sitting on a piece of funfair machinery that swings away before sinking through the floor, what hope has poetry; and when, in the middle of a conversation, he is swept slowly into the wings on some kind of escalator we are certainly not in Venice. Of Venice we were reminded briefly in a backcloth by Mr. MALCOLM PRIDE, a designer of promise who will no doubt learn to express himself more simply; but only to have the impression almost obliterated by two of his enormous buildings that seemed to be part of a municipal tramway as they rolled together and clanged against the buffers. It would be very clever if the stage could be made to turn upside down, but equally shattering to the innocent pretences on which all theatre depends.'

(Anon., 'At the Play', Punch, 30 July 1952)

The irony and sarcasm here are all too apparent: four critics were not amused (and they were not alone). Malcolm Pride's designs drew attention to his own clever ingenuity at the expense of actors and play (it is surprising how much space in these reviews is devoted to comment on the settings; it was rare in the 1950s for design to elicit much descriptive and critical observation). Looking over the photographs of Devine's production for the Memorial Theatre,[1] one can see immediately what was wrong: the stage in every setting is crammed with fussy detail. Pride deployed throughout a forestage from which two steps took actors up to the main stage beyond a proscenium arch. For the mountebank scene (2.2), for example, Pride created a central image of architectural pieces in the main space which focused to left-of-centre on the doorway to Corvino's house with (to its right and therefore almost centre stage) an oriel window overhanging the piazza at which Celia would appear. To the rear of this and to the right three steps led up to what one was to suppose was a quayside with a cut-out of a gondola, beyond which was a backdrop painted with a kind of overlay of appropriate Venetian palaces. To the right of this and parallel with Corvino's mansion was an arched entrance to a grand building with columned supports topped by miniature versions of the lions of St Mark's (see Plate 2, p. 76). Though Venetian elements are apparent to the searching eye, the overall effect lacks any sense of specific place and atmosphere because the assemblage of pieces is jumbled and devoid of visual rhythm. This is a preposterously fantasticated Venice from which it would be easy for an audience to sustain an amused distance; it is not a setting which Jonson's play can readily inhabit.

Against such settings costumes had to make a bold statement, if they were to assist the actors in establishing character. Yet again decorative detailing appears to have got in the way of clarity of definition. Celia (Siobhan McKenna), for example, was given a gown sporting a belt made of huge pearls, while more pearls were formed into a tiara and were spread liberally over her sleeves and skirt. What is the point, then, of Volpone seeking to seduce this Celia by proffering her 'a rope of pearl' of great value, 'each, more orient/Than that the brave Egyptian queen caroused' (2.7.191–2), when she is already positively dripping with them? Corvino is described by Jonson in his list of 'Persons of the Play' as 'a Merchant' and Volpone as 'a Magnifico'; there is a cunning strategy based on class distinctions underlying Volpone's seduction technique: he is tempting a bourgeois woman with the means to rival a patrician lady's ostentatious display. The social resonances of the moment are lost through Pride's crass design. Sexist glamour rarely has a place in Jonson's portrayal of women except as a means to satirise the wearer: richness of attire in *Cynthia's Revels* or *The New Inn* is emblematic of a distinguished *inner* worth. Pride's design for Celia and indeed his scheme for the whole production is frivolous in a manner perhaps befitting operetta, but that ill suits the subtler visual demands of Jonsonian comedy.

Since 1903 there have been thirteen productions of seven of Jonson's plays mounted by either the Memorial Theatre or the Royal Shakespeare Company.[2] Of these six have been staged initially in the Swan Theatre and two at The Other Place, the company's more intimate venues where design has to be both economic and disciplined by the particular nature of the playing space and its relation to the audience. Surveying the photographic evidence where it survives, one soon detects something of a tradition being established in respect of the designers' contributions, from which the only notable aberrations would appear to be two in addition to Pride's work on *Volpone* in 1952. J. Gower Parks designing for Robert Atkins's staging of the same play in 1944 set Volpone's bed on the forestage while a drop-curtain rose to reveal three scenic pieces, set against a predominantly curtained space, which changed to create varying locations: the central shrine-like display of Volpone's wealth was covered with a painted flat depicting either an image of Blind Justice for the courtroom scenes or a receding vista down an arcade for the piazza outside Corvino's house. Simplicity of design certainly allowed for rapid and efficient scene-changing. The problem was the opulently baroque lines of the painted work and the dazzling colours; it looked merely decorative, theatrical (without the purposeful metatheatrical challenges that Jonson delights in) and cheaply, cheerfully strident. As the reviewer for the *Royal Leamington Spa Courier* observed (9 June 1944): '. . . a too multi-coloured background detracted from the effectiveness of the actors'. Indeed reviewers write generally of what the chief actors appeared to have missed in their characterisations ('There should be a keen cutting edge to [Volpone's] villainy, an icy cynicism in his calculations. This astringent quality is hard to seek in Mr. Atkins's interpretation'[3]) which tended either to underplay the darker qualities of Jonson's satire or to go all out for caricature (Peter Upcher's Sir Politick wore a tweed cape over his doublet and ruff and the Jacobean line of his hat had been manipulated to emulate a deerstalker so that his performance continually evoked a manic Sherlock Holmes). The production had speed but little depth. One cannot but speculate at this distance whether director and designer were perhaps misled by reductive ideas about Jonsonian humours; it is significant that reviewers confronted by this staging felt a need for complexity of characterisation and did not dismiss the play as failing to offer it but chastised cast and designer for failing to realise such potential from the text.

The third example of aberrant design work was Timothy O'Brien's for Terry Hands's production of *Bartholomew Fair* at the Aldwych in 1969, where costumes and setting conflated periods in an effortful attempt to find contemporary relevance for the action (a supermarket shopping trolley appeared amongst the Jacobean market stalls, while a broken-down car, the then-fashionable mini, replete with red curtains, stood duty for Knockem and Whit's brothel). The problem here was the confusion of signs: in pausing to read their possible significance, one lost one's way in the intricate threads of plotting. The general distaste amongst critics for the self-conscious anachronisms of the design was perhaps best analysed by Irving Wardle (*The Times*, 31 October 1969) as militating against a prevailing sense of realism; instead in his view 'things happen . . . in the nature of a deliberate theatrical turn'. Again we confront the idea of there being a wrong kind of theatricality for a Jonsonian production: Gower Parks and O'Brien set up a relation between stage and auditorium which encouraged the audience to see themselves as merely spectators (and superior ones at that); the theatricality of these designs was not one that disturbingly intimated the ubiquity of performance and the performative in everyday life whereby Jonson creates an uneasy alliance between actor and audience. Design has somehow to acknowledge that dynamic within Jonsonian drama; and it is this purposeful theatricality which the tradition of designing for Jonson's plays at Stratford has addressed.

Benson's production of *Every Man in his Humour* in 1903 ran for but a few performances and appears in consequence to have used only stock scenery. When Ben Iden Payne staged the same play in 1937 with Wolfit as Bobadil he deployed (as was his consistent policy with Shakespearean revivals over his time at Stratford from 1935 to 1944) a permanent structure that he called his 'penthouse' setting, which was a stylised imitation of the overhanging penthouse on pillared supports that was the defining feature of Elizabethan theatres such as the Globe and Fortune.[4] This was constructed within the Memorial Theatre's proscenium arch; changes of scene were effected by the drawing or closing of curtains between the pillars. The whole idea for this scheme was inspired by the work of William Poel who staged numerous revivals of Renaissance plays from 1893 on what he called his Fortune fit-up (an easily erected imitation of its Elizabethan name-sake in oak, canvas and tapestried curtaining) in an attempt to reproduce the staging conditions of the Renaissance theatre. Poel had directed *The Alchemist* on a smaller version of his mock Elizabethan stage in 1899 (revived 1902) to considerable critical acclaim.[5] In both these productions what confronted audiences throughout was an image of theatre as the great stage of the world; it may not have been the theatre of their own day but it was an immediately recognisable icon with a specific range of associations that made it impossible for spectators to ignore Jonson's social and metaphysical interrogations of the nature of acting and performance. They were required to view a conscious *enactment* of Renaissance London and to participate in the creating of a historicist illusion. While this was not to share the experience of the original playgoer seeing *The Alchemist* in 1610, it had the beginnings of something approximate to that experience. A conscious delight in *acting* bridged the historical divide between 1610 and 1899 or between 1598 and 1937.

Chris Dyer designing *The Alchemist* for Trevor Nunn (The Other Place, 1977) proffered the simplest of settings comprising a plain plaster and timber background with a multiplicity of doors and hiding-places: it was at once a believable Jacobean

house, stripped (as Lovewit says it is) of most of its furnishings, and yet the archetypal structure for farce (see Plate 3, p. 77). More importantly it lacked visual
detailing (beyond a few alchemical and astrological charts for Subtle) so that the
extraordinary details of Jonson's dialogue could work on the audience's imaginations, encouraging them to create for themselves a sense of Jacobean London. The
effect of this in performance was to throw emphasis on Dyer's costumes where
design made its biggest contribution. Face, Doll and Subtle arrived appropriately in
their underwear and began dressing up as occasion demanded: they quite literally
recreated themselves before our eyes. Doll (Susan Drury) sported a lewd assemblage of bits of finery (chiefly ruffs, frills and nether garments) as more quean than
Queen of Fairy before the unseeing Dapper; then transformed herself into a bespectacled Jacobean bluestocking as Lord Whats'um's sister, her florid curls and pointed
lace cuffs offsetting an otherwise severe dress (clearly she was ransacking the late
Mrs. Lovewit's wardrobe!) and so her decline into a fit of learned talking was skilfully motivated. Subtle (John Woodvine) was exploring the camouflaging potential
of wigs: his prize possession being a lank, straw-coloured affair, which he wore
along with a leather loincloth and whip to turn himself into a hermit with a taste for
flagellation when giving audience to an adoring Mammon (Paul Brooke), who was
himself required to remove his shoes and don an alb before coming into the master's
presence. Ian McKellen's impersonations, by contrast, were effected with minimalist ease: permanently in trousers, braces and vest when not in role, he slipped
on a soldier's greatcoat and eye-patch as the Captain, leather apron and woolly bal-
aclava as Lungs, or waistcoat, small ruff and greased centre-parting as Jeremy. The
major changes were in bodily posture, gait and voice. This Face did not need the aid
of accoutrements like his companions, rather he could will into being a projected
role from *within*; it would metamorphose him completely, and elicit total credence. At once the three tricksters were differentiated and Face's supremacy as *actor*
established. Dyer's design schemes were wholly alert to the particular visual possibilities within the text and were directed at foregrounding the actors' artistry.

Simplicity was the keynote of Alison Chitty's designs for Bill Alexander's production of *Volpone* (The Other Place, 1983): a panelled screen the full height of the
stage ran along the back wall; its many doors opened out to reveal in a dull glim-
mering light all Volpone's treasures like a vast Renaissance cabinet of curiosities; the
backs of the doors, criss-crossed with tapes, were crammed with legal documents,
presumably the title deeds to estates willed to Volpone even as Corbaccio is intent
on doing now; later those doors swung silently open to reveal Nano, Castrone or
Androgyno voyeuristically studying the progress of first Lady Would-be's seduction
of Volpone and subsequently his attempt on Celia. They focused attention down-
wards on Volpone's bed, which was here merely a wooden dais covered with fox
furs which subsequently did duty as Scoto's stage in the piazza and the judges'
bench in the courtroom. The dais never left the playing space but was endlessly
adapted to changing locations: it was a stage within the main stage area, showing

how everyone (with the exception of Celia and Bonario and possibly at first Peregrine) was performing for personal gain. Volpone (Richard Griffiths) when we first saw him was a young, crop-headed patrician, who with rapid but elaborate skill plied the contents of his make-up box till he became a wizened, ailing dotard. We had to guess at the realities that lay behind the prepared fronts with which the remaining characters entered the scene. Rarely has the short episode between Lady Would-be (Gemma Jones) and her maids been so telling as in this production where she upbraids them for not properly attending to the dressing of her hair: there was the customary tetchiness but it masked the anxiety of a woman bent at all costs on sustaining a chosen image of herself that required meticulous and unremitting attention. This was the first touch in a complex characterisation that sought to define Lady Would-be as an aspiring parvenue: she talked breezily of books she clearly had not read, since when she actually opened them she was prudishly shocked by their contents and, worse, by their illustrations; she carefully assumed a cut-glass aristocratic accent but her Cockney vowels kept slipping through; and she talked of Platonic love and of encountering dangerous passion with reason, but all the time she was insinuating herself into Volpone's bed. Nothing was certain about this woman; everything was pose; and it was no surprise that she could be gulled into supposing the young man in her husband's company was a woman in disguise, acting a male persona (the hilarity lay in her utter bewilderment when, on attempting to undress Peregrine, she *felt* the truth and discovered that he was decidedly the man he appeared to be). It was a brilliant creation, sensitively attuned within the confines of the individual role to the larger strategies that permeate Jonson's play; but made possible by the clarity of Alison Chitty's design scheme which encouraged audiences to read *Volpone* from the first in a full awareness of its metatheatrical resonances. Again we find a designer creating a playing environment that invited the cast to find comedy in psychological complexity by exploring the gap between the characters' projected roles and their actual social selves. There was both comedy and pathos in consequence when Sir Politick struggled to play at being a tortoise when his social life suddenly turned menacingly nasty; but the episode posed an interesting question about the degree to which role play in the other characters was motivated by a like desire to escape from contingent realities. The subplot of the play was meticulously meshed into the main action in this production, providing in Sir Politick and his lady a commentary on everyone else's *need* to act. The setting unobtrusively supported the thematic drive of the production.

The six most recent RSC productions of plays by Jonson have all been staged initially in the Swan Theatre, which Sue Blane, one of the first designers to work in the newly opened space in 1986, has described as 'built for Jonson more than Shakespeare' (Mulryne and Shewring 1989: 88). From the context as she develops this idea it becomes clear that what especially moves her to make this observation is the awareness that actors in a Jonsonian play need to have direct contact with their audiences. If that intimacy is lost or compromised in any way then the comic momentum will suffer. She illustrates the point by referring to her own experience in working on John Caird's production of *Every Man in his Humour* (1986):

> The design . . . had at one stage, an idea of surrounding the edges of the stage with all sorts of objects, bonded together. What I hadn't realised was how much this would disturb the actors – this barrier between them and the audience. It wasn't very high, but it was enough to create a psychological barrier. The Company tried, very generously, to work with this at a preview. Then they asked if it could be taken away. I think they were probably right. The stage needs to be totally accessible.
>
> (Mulryne and Shewring 1989: 89)

This is a significant discovery, not least for illustrating how and why a designer must be alert to the dangers of imposing schemes which set at risk the particular technical demands that a play requires of the actors. Her actual design scheme was minimalist: basic pieces of furniture (a bench, stool and bucket for Bobadil's quarters) or simple set pieces (a signpost to indicate a suburban roadside location on route to London). Otherwise she left the playing space bare within the wooden structures of the Swan itself and suspended these scenic objects above the rear of the stage, whence they were pulled down as the action required their use. It was as if we were situated in the lumber room of history and so our perception of the past became literally a construct before our eyes; as we gave it imaginative credence so we as spectators became complicit in the construction: we helped shape the meaning of the drama.

Most of the subsequent productions of Jonson in the Swan have respected the shape, texture and atmosphere of the building surrounding the thrust stage. Blane, for example, designing for Caird's production of *The New Inn* (1987) continued the line of the first-level gallery into the stage area to the audience's left before bringing it down in the form of a grand staircase to a central raised platform from which stairs descended in all four directions to the main stage-floor. This was believably the stairwell and entrance hall of a country inn but the platform also sustained the effect of a stage-within-the-stage. On this Pru sat enthroned to supervise the revels and the Court of Love (which left the stage free for Lovel to traverse as he searched inwardly for the substance of his passionate disquisitions); from it Lady Frampul's entourage could survey the baiting of Pinacia as if in the courtyard below; and on to it the characters could severally be drawn in the final act as the various unmaskings, discoveries and revelations took place, as if to stress the deliberate theatricality of this series of possible closures to the play (Cave 1991: 168-71). The fact that inn setting and auditorium were seemingly of the same golden wood and seamlessly integrated in one enveloping design facilitated that accessibility that Blane argues is central to an experience of Jonson in performance. Again Blane had created an environment in which we as audience were caught up imaginatively in the creating of the dramatic illusion while remaining conscious that it was a constructed illusion, an attempt to mediate between our present-day sensibilities and what, within the limitations of that awareness, we can try to understand as being the sensibility of the Caroline age.

Kandis Cook similarly worked with the lines of the gallery fronts at both first and second level in creating her setting for Danny Boyle's production of *Epicoene* (1989), continuing them to cross the stage area making two bridges above the main playing space; the brick wall was exposed to the rear of the stage exactly as it is in the aisles surrounding the seating in the auditorium. The only decorative feature was some curtains reaching the full height of the stage on which were printed a 'long view' of Jacobean London; these were visible at the start of the performance and served to distinguish Clerimont's house in Act 1 from Morose's where the remainder of the play is situated. Anthony Ward's setting for Sam Mendes' production of *The Alchemist* (1991) virtually reproduced that created by Chris Dyer for Trevor Nunn in 1977 but deploying the various doors existing in the Swan leading from backstage on to the thrust; the main difference being a vast hall door centre-back (see Plate 4, p. 78). Essentially the set comprised five doorways; a table and three chairs; two benches placed either side of the forestage; and the trap: the result was wholly functional, a working place, a laboratory where the tricksters could conduct their experiments into the gullible imagination; but it was also clearly the Swan as familiar playing space so the metatheatrical dimensions of Jonson's comedy were evident from the start. Both schemes threw the visual focus on to costuming. Here Sue Blane is a useful guide: she argues that what is required is 'clothes rather than costumes' in the conventional sense of the words: dress designed 'to keep the social distinctions between the characters, and to make them distinctive, without making them too fantasticated' (Mulryne and Shewring 1989: 87–8). Cook fell into the trap of creating costumes which caricatured the wearers. Sir Amorous, for example, sported a short jacket decorated with tiny loveknots, which also defined his ample codpiece, and a lop-sided hat brim-full of lilies and all in shades of salmon pink and pale orange. The Collegiates were monstrously bewigged with hair teased into all manner of baroque shapes. The costumes offered a judgement on the characters, which severely limited the actors' powers of comic invention: they had to act up to the implications of their dress and were not free to develop the degree of complexity noted earlier in performances such as Gemma Jones's Lady Politick. We were in the world of carnival and masquerade but without the searching political commentary such a world may be made to convey to the modern mind; instead the designer's response to *Epicoene* was damagingly flippant. Ward's costumes for *The Alchemist* were both more disciplined and more creative: Mammon, for example, wore a slashed Jacobean doublet but made from modern city suiting. All the clothes had a recognisably Jacobean line but were sewn (or in the case of the tricksters' garb, deconstructed) from today's materials. This allowed a play of comic analogies to resonate in the audience's response without constricting the actors' artistry or confining their interpretation of their roles. It was too a frankly historicist approach, admitting the degree to which our perception and reading of Jonson's characters must inevitably be determined by our contemporary experience.

The setting for *The Devil is an Ass* (1995) by Bunny Christie departed from this pattern to some degree in not attempting to reproduce any structural part of the auditorium; but a dominant visual feature did continue the line of the first gallery and this was a row of miniature buildings suggesting the skyline of Jacobean London. The action on the main stage was therefore to be construed as situated in the underworld, both in the sense of hell and of crime; the characters with their mud-spattered clothes seemed to be struggling to drag themselves by any means to hand, devious or honourable, out of a prevailing filth. It was a powerful metaphor that helped to give a frenetic urgency to the action and a dark menace to the comedy. There were some changes to the design when Matthew Warchus's production moved to The Pit at the Barbican. At the Swan Fitzdottrel carried in a cloth painted with cabbalistic geometrical designs which he laid out on the ground as he began his conjuring of the devil; but in London there was a floorcloth reproducing these images of concentric circles covering most of the stage. To fix the centre in our awareness, he placed a statuette of Satan there as prelude to his invocation; later he would fix his wife, Frances, in this precise spot to be wooed by Wittipol who, in keeping the required distance from his beloved, had to tread a path around one of the painted circles. The demonic seemed to permeate every aspect of human exchange in the play. Interestingly this design concept had come from the staging at Stratford of the episodes in Lady Tailbush's salon (see Plate 6, p. 138) where the seating was arranged in a tight circle around a central table on which Pug was made to stand when being interrogated about his proficiency as a servant: we watched the devil being tempted, beaten and physically examined by the ladies of fashion – a man the focus of women's prying gaze and predatory fingers (an experience that leaves Pug longing to refresh himself in the fires of hell). By the time the production reached The Pit this patterning of the stage action in circles had been incorporated into the earlier sections of the play creating a subtle visual unity to the various episodes: it was as if the characters were trapped in a vortex and being drawn hell-wards. When Frances begged Wittipol to rescue her from the encircling horrors by becoming her protector rather than drag her further into the mire by tempting her to adultery, the pathos and desperation of her predicament were profoundly moving: the production had found through its patterned staging a way of endorsing her independent moral insight. Frances is the moral centre of Jonson's play and director and designer had found the means to invest her role with that status in the perceptions of a twentieth-century audience.

Where in 1969 O'Brien had overwhelmed stage, actors and play with too elaborately profuse a design, Tom Piper designing *Bartholomew Fair* in the Swan for Laurence Boswell (1997) opted for an extremely minimalist approach. We were situated firmly in the 1990s; the first act at the Littlewits' home was played on the forestage with only a preposterous hostess trolley to indicate Win's taste and pretensions; the screen that divided off the rearstage was raised as we entered the fair to reveal simply an arrangement of doors around an industrial waste-bin from which Overdo emerged to confide his schemes for detecting 'enormities'. Lanthorn had no booth; instead he emerged startlingly from the trap throwing back the flooring to expose (attached to the undersides) mountains of toys, dolls and bric-à-brac. It was an expertly timed surprise; and later, as expertly, the device allowed him to 'disappear' rapidly from view after he had sold his whole stock to an over-excited Cokes before the latter could properly lay claim to his property. The fair itself was evoked with the utmost economy by a mere line of light bulbs suspended individually on lengths of flex almost to the stage-floor at the division of rear- and forestage; this arrangement could swing out over the forestage and turn like a carousel; it evoked a multitude of associations of fairground, maypole, circus and carnival (there were strong overtones of the Notting Hill Carnival throughout the production); when first seen it conveyed all the magic of a child's delight in such occasions, exactly in tune with Cokes's response; later as night fell, the lights cast lurid and threatening shadows about the theatre as adult desires began to reveal a darker, sullied heart to that seeming innocence. Again the design concept perfectly kept pace with the transformations being worked in Jonson's text, while allowing for an uninterrupted flow of event.

Certain recurring principles of design for Jonsonian drama can be detected from this survey of stagings of the plays by the Royal Shakespeare Company. What appears most significant is the decision increasingly to play Jonson in small, intimate spaces, which is directly opposed to the policy pursued with Jonson by the National Theatre, where productions have consistently been mounted in the Olivier, the largest of their playing spaces. John Bury designing for Peter Hall's production of *Volpone* (1977) even stressed the vastness of the playing space by conceiving a precise image of three elegant arches (sometimes fitted with green or white doors to suggest various interiors) that spanned a marble floor patterned in concentric circles. Though aesthetically pleasing, it seemed at odds with the Venice that Jonson's dialogue conjures up in an audience's imagination. As an environment for the action it was too clinical, ordered, geometrically exact for a play that derives much of its comedy from disease, physical decrepitude and processes of ageing; moreover it in no way supported the metatheatrical strategies within the text. The lack of intimacy tended to invite quite broad acting from the cast except when the plot situation brought a small group within the confines of Volpone's bed which allowed for a sharper focus and more detailed playing.

As if learning from this experience, the next two NT productions contrived means through the design to bring the acting right to the forefront of the Olivier stage. Richard Eyre decided to update his staging of *Bartholomew Fair* (1980) to the Edwardian period which allowed William Dudley to fill the rear of the playing space with a ferris wheel, roundabout and numerous tents; this effectively required the actors to work far downstage while a sense of crowded activity could be maintained beyond. Characters could come readily into view for a sequence then merge back into the crowd; the production had both realism and pace in consequence. Richard Hudson manipulated the spatial vastness of the Olivier to his advantage by staging Matthew Warchus's production of *Volpone* (1995) on a revolving set that opened into a sequence of small, darkened rooms or confined exteriors which brought the play decidedly close to the audience; he achieved, too, a powerful overall symbol in that image of a revolving world within which the characters seemed to be trapped while racing for the spoils (the whole performance began with the entire cast pursuing a breathless and terrified Volpone round and round this maze of spaces like rats in some bizarre laboratory experiment till they hounded him to his bedchamber where he woke from a nightmare to greet the day). Again the setting allowed the cast to keep up a relentless pace and sustain a degree of intimacy with the audience despite the size of the theatre. It afforded the audience also a means of reading the production symbolically: there was always a sense in that menacingly revolving edifice that the whirligig of time would soon bring in its revenges and that, as the initial nightmare intimated, Volpone knew this at some deep psychological level, which brought a chilling desperation and savagery to his scheming before time should run out on him. (The production ended by cutting the epilogue; instead we saw Volpone being raced by guards from the court through these seemingly endless passageways to be shackled in prison in a cell where Mosca already lay whipped and unconscious.)

This design scheme raises an important issue about the degree to which settings can profitably make a visual statement that encourages a particular reading of the performance. This has tended to become common practice in designing for Shakespearean plays in recent years, but what works with Shakespeare in terms of performance will not necessarily work for Jonson's comedies. Hudson's work tended subtly to invite one to read possible metaphors into the visual environment he created but it did not insist on them; and, most importantly, while affording a means to release the darker tones in Jonson's satire, it did not limit the actors' contribution in shaping meaning, which may occur with too bold a design statement. The dangers accruing from a restrictive design concept were apparent in William Dudley's setting for Bill Alexander's staging of *The Alchemist* (Olivier and the Birmingham Repertory Theatre, 1996): reviewers reaching for images to evoke its effect write of the Mad Max films, Heath Robinson, *Gormenghast* and contemporary gothick chic. It seemed to be welded together from an assortment of scrap iron (as if Lovewit's house were constructed out of the metal goods the tricksters have stored in the cellar awaiting 'projection' or casting as dollars), mostly bits of defunct cars that had been amassed and then twisted to form porches, spiralling stairs, looming walls, all of it vaguely suggesting the plan of the London underground which was also reproduced on a curtain with the stations all named (for those close enough to read) in Latin. This was a grand, postmodernist statement but, as reviewers complained, it in no way evoked Jonson's plague-ridden Blackfriars nor any specific social world in which Jonson's satire might flourish; it registered only the designer's whimsy. It is worth comparing it with Mark Thompson's design for a permanent setting for Nicholas Hytner's production of *Volpone* (Almeida, 1990) which piled a similar mass of gilded objects (chiefly crates, chests and trunks) on a stage flooded with water so that Volpone seemed enthroned in his bed on the heap of his ill-gotten gains which were slowly deliquescing into some Venetian canal. It was a powerful image that, like Hudson's design, allowed the angry edge of Jonson's moral vision full expression. The precariousness of Volpone's world and its smelly corruption were given a sensual immediacy: the stage-picture symbolically defined greed as a psychological disease, which only in his downfall was Volpone to perceive. Like Hudson's this was a metaphorical use of design that opened up spectators' imaginations to possibilities of interpretation but ones that were precisely attuned to the imagery and moral urgency of Jonson's text. Thompson's artistry was put at the service of Jonson's. The design had a needful practicality too in that sightlines at the Almeida, especially from the circle if the production is confined to the stage-floor, are not good; by raising the action as the design required in its execution to achieve a steeply raked performance space, then a genuine closeness to the action was shared by all spectators.

Thompson's was a design scheme that was attempting to mediate between Jonson's vision and the audience, creating an environment which shaped a particular tone in which to read the performance but not in a way that limited the actors' own creativity. By contrast William Dudley's setting for *The Alchemist* was often the first aspect of the production that reviewers chose to discuss, as if its bulky stolidity remained at the forefront of their memories. Michael Coveney (*Observer*, 22 September 1996) was virtually alone in praising the set as superbly representing 'the engine of farce'; yet one could respond that the creating and powering of that engine is properly the actors' job. Michael Billington (*Guardian*, 18 September 1996) thought the design 'dwarfs, and sometimes even obscures, the actors', while Sheridan Morley noted that its vast dimensions and strange angles required the actors to be so continually on the move that 'they seem forever to be out of breath and on their way to yet another clambering session for no apparent purpose other than to convey a sense of movement and activity to what is otherwise a curiously lifeless evening' (*Spectator*, 19 October 1996). Moreover its fussiness overwhelmed the imagination with detail where audiences need to become increasingly aware of the power of the imagination to create fantasies out of nothing: here those fantasies were overly materialised and so the comic impetus of *The Alchemist* was suppressed. It is the spiralling of over-heated minds that should astonish, delight and shock audiences, not arabesques of wrought ironwork. Jonson himself worked on the barest of stage spaces and his tools were his actors' trained bodies and voices. The best designs for his plays in the contemporary theatre would appear to be those which respect these facts as a *given* and submit to its refining discipline. Sue Blane significantly chose with her two Stratford commissions to create a simple scenic environment and then focus her attention on the costumes; and she relished the six-week rehearsal period which enabled her to get to know the company so that she could build her costumes for them as she came to understand the actors' developing performances. Looking back, she considers this pattern of priorities as 'crucial' (Mulryne and Shewring 1989: 87); and, in stating that, she demonstrates her respect for the actor's artistry as a necessary discipline on her invention. Given such a principle in operation, what kinds of artistry are best supported by such a discipline? Is there a particular technique for acting in Jonson?

Notes

1 These are to be seen in the archives of the Shakespeare Memorial Theatre in the Shakespeare Centre Library at Stratford upon Avon. All the reviews of Stratford productions cited in this chapter and in Chapters 4 and 5 are also to be found at the Centre Library in the scrapbooks that make up part of the archive of the Shakespeare Memorial Theatre and the Royal Shakespeare Company.

2 *Every Man in his Humour* (1903, 1937 at the Mermaid Theatre and 1986 at the Swan); *Volpone* (1944, 1952 at the Mermaid Theatre and 1983 at The Other Place); *Bartholomew Fair* (1969 at the Aldwych Theatre and 1997 at the Swan); *The Alchemist* (1977 at The Other Place and 1991 at the Swan); *The New Inn* (1987 at the Swan); *The Silent Woman* (1989 at the Swan); and *The Devil is an Ass* (1995 at the Swan).

3 The review is from the *Birmingham Post* for 6 June 1944.

4 For a full account of Iden Payne's work at Stratford, see Brock and Pringle (1984: 55–79). Payne himself described the penthouse setting as dividing 'the main stage into four sections: the *middle stage* beneath the roof, is the largest area; the *forestage*, a fairly narrow, apron-like area, lies in front of it; two *side stages* extend on either side of it, with a door giving onto each from the tiring house' (Brock and Pringle 1984: 57–8).

5 See O'Connor 1987. The account of Poel's production of *The Alchemist* can be found on pp. 60–3.

4 Acting in Jonson – a conversation with John Nettles and Simon Russell-Beale[1]

Richard Cave

'Cast your Eye on the *Abel Drugger of G[arrick]* and the *Abel Drugger of C[ibber]*. I call the simple, composed, grave Deportment of the former Comic, and the squint-ey'd grinning Grimace of the latter Comical. The first obtains your Applause, by persuading you that he is the real Man. The latter indeed opens your Eyes, and gives you to understand, that he is but personating the Tobacco-Boy: But then to atone for the Loss of the Deception, you are ready to split with Laughter, at the ridiculous Variations of his Muscles. It may indeed be objected, that this Conduct destroys all Distinction of Characters, and may as well become *Sir John Daw* or *Sir Amorous La Foole* as honest *Nab*.'

(Samuel Foote, 1747)[2]

'Simon Callow and Tim Piggott Smith are fine actors – I admire them both very much. Nonetheless they didn't work for me in *The Alchemist* because they seemed to remain resolutely actors: I never believed in them as people. I wasn't convinced they belonged in the world they said they were of. Simon has immense mimetic skills (all those different voices, brilliantly done) but I wanted him just once to say to me: 'I can do this, and this, and this, but *this* is who I really am; I'm the rogue from down the road who's momentarily got lucky.' And actually all Simon told me was that he was Simon Callow, who is a marvellous actor – which is only part of what I wanted to know.'

(Genista McIntosh, 1997)[3]

Two hundred and fifty years separate these two comments, yet in both these instances a similar distinction is being drawn between a performance where the actor inhabits the role and one where the focus is more on the actor's technical brilliance, which rather than serving the demands of the role is therefore to some degree at the expense of the role. Theophilus Cibber was clearly ridiculing Drugger by making the part a vehicle for a display of stock-in-trade antics. Callow is criticised for using the role of Face for a bravura exhibition of his accomplishments which engages only with the surface requirements of the part rather than imaginatively entering *inside* the character in ways that would encourage an audience to engage its imaginative sympathies too. Cibber and Callow instruct their respective

audiences precisely how to read and judge the roles they are playing; the performance does not in either case become an imaginative journey into the psychological
potential of the role undertaken jointly by actor and spectator. The actor in both
cases trades on a known stage persona, which keeps to the forefront of the audience's awareness his status as *actor*. It might be supposed here that this would be
markedly in keeping with Jonson's metatheatrical strategies within the plays, particularly respecting Callow's interpretation of Face. But Jonson's method is to trap
audiences into a sudden (often deeply metaphysical) perception of the extent to
which performance and role play permeate all aspects of human exchange; he is not
inviting audiences to see his play as an escapist fantasy designed to reveal the actors'
expertise. It is not until we meet Face in the final act as Jeremy that we appreciate
how consummate an actor Face, the *character*, really is. If the actor invites us to
admire his personal excellence at carrying off the mechanics of the part from the
moment we first meet Face, then the increasingly sinister and challenging aspects of
Jonson's portrayal are never properly registered: it is a difference between display
and discovery (and *discovery* was a favoured term for Jonson). *Acting* for Jonson
meant *impersonation* to the fullest degree; none of his disguised characters is ever
detected till they choose to reveal themselves and then it is the totality of the disguise (voice, accent, vocabulary, dress, manner, deportment, posture) that is
commented on; admiration for the metamorphosis is invariably coloured by awe and
shades of fear. Tiberius would not be the dire threat to everyone's security in Rome
if his acting were overt: it is the total credibility of his performances that lures his
victims to disaster. It is essential for Polish's design to resolve the action of *The
Magnetic Lady* to her advantage that Placentia appear *healthy* of body and mind to
Lady Loadstone's intense scrutiny. The truly ridiculous figures in Jonsonian comedy
are invariably those like Bobadil or Overdo who cannot sustain their chosen role;
the mask slips and reveals the sorry truth beneath. Callow played a man juggling
with masks; but the masks were too clearly apparent, revealing not perhaps a sorry
truth but an overly self-conscious actor beneath.

The remarkable similarity between Foote and McIntosh's observations across so
large a gap in time underscores how there is no tradition in our theatre for playing
Jonson. If there were, then would Callow have been saved perhaps from repeating
Cibber's mistaken approach? The lack of a tradition was the starting point for a discussion with Simon Russell-Beale and John Nettles (the one at that time playing
Mosca, the other Meercraft) about acting in Jonson. Both agreed that in one way the
absence of a tradition helps contemporary actors coming afresh to Jonson's roles:
there is not the need as with Shakespearean parts of engaging with all the academic
commentaries on them and the line of actors whose impersonations have preceded
the immediate production, which can create a danger in Simon Russell-Beale's
view where 'actors produce not performances but glosses on their predecessors'
performances. There's such a pile-up of information about a play . . . you've got to
go and get more and more obscure, more and more exotic'. Arguably the want of

a tradition assists actors in another way: Jonsonian academic criticism for many decades, taking it must be admitted the cue from Jonson himself, has tended to overplay the line on characters-as-humours. It is a line that can quickly make for shallow performances in which caricature rather than character prevails (which in part is Foote's criticism of Cibber).

There is a problem here, since (in Simon Russell-Beale's words) a Jonsonian part generally 'doesn't warrant an excessive amount of vertical digging' and that can be an issue for a Stanislavski-orientated actor. John Nettles elaborated on this point:

> There is no time in Jonson or Renaissance drama generally for method acting, working oneself into the emotion of a line; that's how to lose the necessary *drive*. [Such an approach] makes for ponderous acting which is endemic in the contemporary scene; and it is very salutary to have a director [Matthew Warchus] who says 'No: don't pause there. Trust the lines; say it on the line; think on the line; use the word, not what you feel in your gut and say it immediately and don't think about it before you say it'. And this introduces a very welcome rapidity of delivery and then the glory of the language becomes apparent. You start to surf on the language; it's beautiful when that happens.

Since most of Jonson's characters live by their wits and are desperately thinking on their feet in the face of changing circumstance, this clearly is sound advice to get at that 'drive', which Nettles sees as essential in Jonson's plays, resulting in characters that in his view are 'wonderfully public theatrical people, tremendously vital, and *available*'. While agreeing with this, Russell-Beale went back to his comment about 'vertical digging', anxious not to give the impression that what was wanted was broad acting: 'I wouldn't want you to think that they [the characters] don't have delicacies which you can enjoy playing'; and he illustrated this idea with reference to the moment when Volpone returns from the first of the scenes in the lawcourts and, sickened by it all, feels 'an extraordinary amount of fear' or to Mammon as 'dreamer as well as being a greedy man' ('greed thoughout *The Alchemist* is tempered by visions of loveliness').

So what kinds of complexity ought an actor to seek out in these plays? Harold Hobson's review of Ralph Richardson's Volpone is instructive here: Hobson (*Sunday Times*, 20 July 1952) found the whole performance lacking in 'spring, elan, or attack' and characteristically began searching for an explanation for this:

> Now the reason why Volpone is not suited to Richardson is an honourable one. It cannot be too often repeated that this actor has received a revelation: he knows the simple goodness of the human heart as does no other player in the British theatre. Whatever is kindly, loving and tolerant he can portray with a moving pathos that is always saved from mawkishness by its wit and humour. He can also, with a cruelty quite startling, reveal these qualities when they have

turned sour. The hatred of his Dr. Sloper in *The Heiress*, for example, was a hatred that Richardson sympathised with and understood, because this hatred for the unhappy Catherine was only love for Catherine's dead mother turned inside out. It was this fact that enabled Richardson to give that superb performance which was exactly like a skilful surgeon deliberately choosing to perform a cruel operation without anaesthetics.

But there was never any goodness at all at the foundation of Volpone's avarice and lechery. The man was evil from the start. There is nothing in Volpone on which an actor like Richardson can catch hold. By an intellectual effort Richardson understands the part, but he does not sympathise with it. His performance is therefore never more than a careful commentary, instead of an uprush of the soul.

A danger might have been to push the performance towards melodrama, playing outright evil in as theatrical a fashion as possible; but Richardson opted for light comedy at the cost of the savage satire that invests much of the role and the play.

On the issue of complexity, John Nettles offers an insight into how his performance as Meercraft in *The Devil is an Ass* took shape in the early days of rehearsal:

When I started playing Meercraft, I played him as highly camp and very successful . . . and he [Matthew Warchus] went out and had a coffee and came back and shouted a lot at me and said: 'No! No! That's not the thing to do. Look for the points at which the guy is weak, look for where the failures of the character happen, where the fissures in the facade occur and see why that happens and see what level of desperation the man exists on'; and that approach – going against what appear to be the obvious characteristics as displayed in the text – enriched the characterisation. Similarly, for example, with Fitzdottrel, who's a lunatic in many ways (David Troughton plays him), Warchus said: 'Well, look for the moments of pathos, the moments of actual cleverness or wit: they are there, set apart from the buffoonery which is very evidently there.'

'Going against what appear to be the obvious characteristics displayed in the text' is perhaps not fair to Jonson: Meercraft's aplomb has definite cracks in its make-up; his confidence is continually compromised in the action by Gilthead, Everill and Wittipol with Frances and Manly; such moments give us a new perspective onto his seemingly endless supply of exuberance; his dynamic energy is the correlative of an indomitable instinct for survival. There is a subtextual life to Jonson's dialogue which is focused on both what lies behind the *front* characters like Meercraft assume and why that particular front has been adopted. Most of his characters have carefully constructed a public self; panic strikes whenever the construction is revealed (when Volpone uncases, Wittipol defrocks himself as Spanish Lady, Dauphine undresses Epicoene or Beaufort discovers he has no idea whatever about who precisely he has married – boy, girl, whore or virgin aristocrat). The panic afflicts not only the exposed but often more devastatingly those imposed upon. This is where Jonson's metatheatricality is at its most searching (for characters in the drama and for his audiences) when he insists that all recognise the extent to which life in society provokes the manifold duplicities which might today be labelled the performative. Warchus's directive to John Nettles goes right to the heart of Jonson's moral aware-ness and Nettles is convinced that Warchus's continuing success in directing Jonson's plays derives from the fact that he is 'very clear about the moral universe Jonson wishes us to inhabit'.

Simon Russell-Beale revealed that Matthew Warchus gave a rather similar direc-tion about going against the apparent grain of the part to him too in the early stages of rehearsing Mosca. He had come to the role after playing recently a line of Machiavellian types: Shakespeare's Richard III, Ferdinand in *The Duchess of Malfi* (and he was soon to play Iago for the RNT too). Warchus, he noted, responded to his Machiavellian qualities but did not wish to feature them at the expense of a partic-ular shape that he, as director, was choosing to give the production:

> He [Warchus] wanted Mosca *not* to pre-empt the end of the play and he didn't want the Mosca which I instinctively thought was right (but which I now think is wrong) – a Mosca who knows he is on to a winner very early on in the play. He said: 'You mustn't make the mistake of thinking that; and you mustn't make the mistake of thinking that Mosca's always in control because, although he's very clever, he makes one fiendish mistake half-way through the first half of the play and so you mustn't assume that he's faultless.' I think that was a very good note: it means that, when Volpone finally makes him his heir, it is only then that Mosca thinks, 'What do I do with this piece of information?' In other words he [Warchus] wanted to make it a more improvisatory role, less tunnel-visioned. The scene with Corvino (where Mosca persuades him to offer Celia to Volpone) is just dazzling and quite rightly Mosca comes out of it saying, 'I'm in love with myself, I think I'm absolutely fantastic. I really am a genius'; and then immediately he makes his big mistake of inviting Bonario for no reason at all to come and hear his father disinherit him. That's when it all begins to go wrong. So Matthew was very keen on that shape, on Mosca making a mistake; and then the mirror of that late in the play is when Volpone says 'Give out that I am dead . . .' and Mosca thinks his whole livelihood is about to go down the drain and so he must do something in order to preserve himself; and luckily Volpone makes the mistake of saying, 'I'll put your name in as my heir'. And then, and only then at the beginning of the fifth act does Mosca go: 'Right: this is it. This is the final showdown.'

Warchus, in other words, responded to a particular aspect of Russell-Beale's stage persona which recent roles had been evolving but chose to keep it in abeyance to the point where its upsurge took audiences by surprise. Technical accomplishment and previous stage experience are not being welcomed as matching the summary requirements of the interpretation, but developed in ways that extend the actor and make his performance rewarding. In both these instances we find a known way with a character being jettisoned in favour of an approach that required a searching investigation of the role and a consequent point of discovery for actor and audience. Simon Russell-Beale is right to describe this as finding the 'delicacies' within a role.

Matthew Warchus also allowed his appreciation of Russell-Beale's Machiavellian qualities to influence the particular dynamic he was building into the ensemble work between Mosca and Volpone, played by Michael Gambon. The initiative came, however, from an observation by Gambon about how he viewed his own role:

> What Michael has done is very interesting, because he has reversed the roles in an odd sort of way. Scofield was magnificent: grand, aristocratic and cold; and so Ben Kingsley (as Mosca) was very definitely the subservient partner. Michael said: 'I just see Volpone as this great child who wants to eat things, he wants to have lots of sex and lots of drink, and when he doesn't get his way he sulks.' And so Matthew used my Machiavellian qualities and Michael's *innocence*.

Gambon's was indeed a Volpone who became dangerous only when he did not get his way and there was a remarkable child-like quality about his handling of the mountebank scene, where he took the idea of improvisation literally and played games with the text, doing his own free rendition of the lines in a plethora of bizarre accents. Volpone is the con-man *par excellence* in this scene and the liberties taken with the text served to show how absurdly gullible his listeners were. The total enjoyment of role play Gambon demonstrated here and throughout the opening scenes made the surfacing of Volpone's dangerous nature as he loomed a big bear of a man over a cowering Celia the darker and more frightening. That the visit to the court reduced this Volpone from delight in his acting to naked terror at the absolute need now not for a style of light comedy but for sheer *verismo* (a terror that sent him relentlessly to the comfort of drink) made for a psychological development in the characterisation of considerable complexity. That the Machiavel in Mosca surfaced at just this moment when Volpone was suddenly seen as vulnerable suggested the extent to which the dangerous edge in Gambon's Volpone had kept Mosca till now in absolute thrall to his power. Behind this man's playful, childish *front* lurked a truly sinister psyche. The balance of the power structure in this relation of patrician and servant was constantly shifting which brought not only impetus but subtleties of motivation to the onward shaping of the plot.

The conversation began to revolve around one particular issue: the need for actors to ignore restrictive interpretations of Jonson's concept of humours and go for complexity, search for the 'delicacies', the anguish or the danger lurking behind the projected public image that the character has constructed and find the motivation for the development of the role within the plot in the cracks that start to emerge between the self and the persona. For John Nettles the explorations have to go on in the rehearsal room till the potential of a character is thoroughly known and then in performance 'the trick is to conceal . . . Do not spend all your golden pennies in one fell swoop in the first scene' so that the audience become sensitively attuned to hints, intimations and steadily themselves go on the journey the actor encompassed in rehearsal, allowing the unwinding of the plot to reveal the character's full nature. Only by the close of the play should one come into an awareness of the essence of a particular role. However funny the result, this is to create character not caricature; even when the public image projected by a role is itself a caricature, there should always be that sense of a different life behind the revealed self.

Perhaps in terms of a tradition, this is a discovery that earlier generations of actors had made in playing Jonson: the critic of the *Daily Telegraph* (7 August 1937) reviewing Ben Iden Payne's production of *Every Man in his Humour* particularly noted how 'Geoffrey Kenton, rejecting perhaps wisely the broader farce of Kitely's improbable jealousies, gives the part dignity as well as comedy', while Ivor Brown (*Observer*, 7 August 1937) singled out Donald Wolfit's Bobadil as 'admirable alike in swagger and humiliation. The battered, crestfallen creature which Bobadil becomes was grandly realised. One felt that the whole of the man's body as well as his spirit had dwindled and fallen in'. Earlier still the reviewer for the *Morning Post* (22 April 1903) watching Sir Frank Benson's revival of the same comedy was clearly surprised by the 'delicacies' Benson himself found in the role of Bobadil:

> Gaunt, lanthorn-jawed, half-starved, he makes in his tattered martial attire a most striking and fascinating figure, and the malign geniality of the braggart's disposition, his grim sense of and even pride in his own poltroonery, his sardonic condescension towards the dupes on whom he sponges and over whom he has by his lies gained an absurd ascendancy, are brought out with a humour and a finish for which one was scarcely prepared.

He continues with an observation about H.O. Nicholson's 'admirable' Brainworm: 'As the sham soldier he was almost too good, too natural that is, for an impostor.' The critic expected a disguised character to signal the fact to the audience, but the actor played true to the text where Knowell is astonished when the impersonation is finally revealed. In the world of Jonson's comedies, successful impostors are convincingly *natural*; therein lies their success; they do not show their hand till they are confident it is to their advantage to do so.

Asked what the pleasures and rewards are for the actor playing Jonson both John Nettles and Simon Russell-Beale immediately recalled the exhilaration that comes when a production finds the right momentum (as Nettles expressed it:

'Once you start you are on a rise'). Nettles went into the point more deeply: 'If you can combine speed with clarity then you are on to a good thing, it seems to me, with Jonson . . . You've got to take people on this tremendous rollercoaster of a ride and (as Meercraft says) if you fall from your gallop, you are lost.' He likes playing in the Swan because it is for him a 'fast theatre'; 'in the Swan you can flick it to the audience'. Russell Beale recalled that 'the forward thrust [of *Volpone*] came actually quite early and it just got faster and faster'. Both men in consequence worked to maintain an absolute textual clarity, partly because both Meercraft and Mosca are the engines of their respective plots and, given the sheer impetus of the action in both plays, plot-forwarding lines have to be clearly stressed. In the interests of that clarity both actors disciplined themselves to resist all manner of comic business, feeling that to indulge such invention would be a sign of 'panic', a 'walking away from the text because you don't trust it'. Laughter is Nettles's 'chief pleasure', though again a discipline is necessary: 'keeping up the tension, not relaxing after eliciting laughter is a major technical problem with Jonson.' Above all there is the delight of freshness: 'The glory of doing Jonson is that people don't know what's going to happen. The joy of surprising people merely with the narrative is inexpressible.'

Genista McIntosh is of the belief that 'Jonson wrote with a sense that the performers would relish the experience that he was giving them'. Nettles and Russell-Beale have markedly proved her point. This discussion began with the assertion that there is no tradition of playing in Jonson as there is in Shakespeare. By closely studying the discoveries made by some performers such as Garrick in the past and honouring the experience of actors such as John Nettles and Simon Russell-Beale today, the possibility of shaping a flexible tradition becomes viable. Connections and discriminations will have to be made and, most urgently, in ways that capture the imagination of future performers. Enough experience is to hand to help determine a discipline and technique, providing it is not so determined that it restricts the creativity of the individual player. It is evident from all this that the future of such a tradition of acting in Jonson depends also on a certain style of directing.

Notes

1 This interview with the two actors took place during the Reading conference on 11 January 1996.
2 Cited in Herford and the Simpsons, vol. 9: 231–2
3 Genista McIntosh in interview with Brian Woolland and Richard Cave.

5 Directing Jonson

Richard Cave

'The fiercely satirised world of London low life in 1614 has its historical interest if played straight and securely. But to introduce a jazz combo, a shooting stick, a supermarket wheel basket, a derelict mini and modern dress passion seems to me to abolish any historical interest at one blow. At the same time it might be possible to make the piece amusing in a wild way by sheer ingenuity of invention. This, I fear, has not proved possible in Terry Hands's treatment. The actors are given their heads and for the most part overdo things to a point where we felt that all artistic direction and economy have been thrown to the winds. Occasionally a point is amusingly made. More often the point is lost in an unorchestrated uproar, the overacting which assails opera choruses when they are not curbed. It is all so energetic and raucous that what should be salient details fail to stand out.'

(Philip Hope Wallace, *Guardian*, 31 October 1969)

'It will no longer do to put it on as a great romp in which anything will pass muster as long as it fetches a laugh. Mr. Hands has spared us nothing, but the chief weapon in his armoury is the anachronism. Anything out of period, he seems to think, is bound to make a point . . . And surely we must believe in it to some extent. If all we see in front of us is a bunch of familiar actors having a sort of end-of-term rag, why should we side with one camp or another?'

(B.A. Young, *Financial Times*, 31 October 1969)

' "What is't you lack, gentlemen? What is't you lack?" So runs the cry of the stall-holders at *Bartholomew Fair* in Smithfield in 1614. I can answer that question at Terry Hands's fair in the Aldwych in 1969. You lack, gentlemen, a style, you lack a purpose, you lack comprehensibility, audibility, even visibility. Ultimately you lack faith in Ben Jonson's ability to say his piece without being boring.'

(Peter Lewis, ''Tis a fair mix-up', *Daily Mail*, 31 October 1969)

The reviewers were virtually unanimous in deeming Terry Hands's production a fiasco; and yet disasters can prove instructive and it is worth looking closely at what these critics severally imply about Hands's failings in attempting to direct Jonson. The imposition of an idea about the liberating effect of anachronism had failed properly to take root in the interpretation and to become a consistently worked image; an interpretation in other words had been imposed upon the action so that Jonson's own subtext had been suppressed. Clarity was lost for want of a well-defined narrative taking its way confidently through the maze of plots and subplots. The actors had no sense of where the thematic heart of the play might lie from which they might sense the pulse of their individual interpretations. Easy ways to a laugh were encouraged, seemingly at the expense of Jonson's carefully built-up strategies, suggesting a lack of confidence in the text to make its points securely which in its turn argues a failure to find a particular rhythm for the performance that all the cast would acknowledge and work together to sustain. Because there was no perception of the way Jonson's comedy is structured, there was crucially no recognition of how important orchestration of effects is in his drama together with good ensemble work and within that a sense of focus. It is instructive to compare these complaints with the observations that John Nettles and Simon Russell-Beale make about working with Matthew Warchus. They independently reveal how achieving vocal clarity, an attention to structure and a dynamic rhythm were imperatives for both productions and how the text was searched in rehearsal till it began to yield up insights into how to reach these goals. Then there was Warchus's deft handling of actors to release a certain inwardness in the appropriation of their given roles: the directorial cues that challenged their first thoughts about interpretation, invited them to look deeper and to release their invention in ways that would extend their own personal techniques so that getting to inhabit the roles would be a discovery with particular rewards. Most importantly, both actors talk appreciatively of Warchus's handling of ensemble, the getting to a shared sense within the cast of the pacing appropriate for the production and finding how to sustain that degree of energy without losing 'comprehensibility, audibility, even visibility'. Warchus possessed with each production an acute sense of *focus*.

Frequently in Jonson's plays we find instances of multiple action within the playing space which require an acute sense of ensemble amongst the cast if the audience's attention is to be directed at any given moment to a necessary point within the constantly shifting centre of interest that makes up the larger stage-picture. They must register the significance of the individual parts the better to understand Jonson's purpose in uniting these into a carefully structured whole. To take an example from *Bartholomew Fair*: in the sequence where Cokes gets his purse stolen while listening to Nightingale's ballad, the gull and his property are the main centre of comic interest, and yet at this moment the stage is crowded with an audience of fairgoers delighting in the ballad-singer's performance. We have to be aware of Ezekiel's every movement about the crowd, his several approaches to Cokes, his initial failure to seize the purse, his eventual success and the trick whereby he cunningly passes the hot property to Nightingale. However, those movements have to be so choreographed that they can *plausibly* be interpreted by Overdo in his guise as Mad Arthur as proof of his belief that Ezekiel is an honest youth of some promise, while Overdo's concentration on Ezekiel's proximity to Cokes must be such that it in its turn can *plausibly* be assumed later to be proof that Overdo is himself the actual thief. Meanwhile Quarlous, Winwife and Grace are coming into ever more intimate relations. Mistress Overdo is ostensibly there as Grace's chaperone and as protector of the naive Cokes but she becomes so taken up in her enjoyment of the song that she fails adequately to see what is happening to either of her charges. Grace's intimacy with the two men is strengthened into a kind of bond by their amused detachment from the rest of the crowd, by their precise observation of how Cokes is robbed and by their complicity in relishing his discomfiture. Eight actors in independent groupings within the crowd must be shrewdly observed by the audience not only in respect of the immediate comedy but also in preparation for future developments in the plot. Yet to suggest that their attention is demanded by plot interests alone is to risk losing an awareness of how important the scene is in developing the characterisation of all eight roles. This sequence asks for ensemble acting of a very high order.

So too do the various trial scenes at the conclusion of *Volpone*, as the defendants sit virtually silent while their accusers plot and counter-plot, assert and then deny themselves with startling rapidity to the confusion of the three avocatori. In the first such scene all goes well since Mosca is in control of the situation and gives everyone suitable directions as to how to behave. But when Volpone enters in disguise and begins to give alternative instructions and to vie with Mosca as stage-manager of events, all hell breaks loose and the stage-space threatens to be overwhelmed with anarchic action. Yet Jonson requires the antics of the three gulls, Corbaccio, Corvino and Voltore, to be motivated largely by asides tossed to them *sotto voce* by either Mosca or Volpone. The extent to which all three have become manipulable puppets is darkly comic; but there is also the growing desperation of Volpone's contest with Mosca that will result in his 'uncasing', which causes everyone to be exposed as absurd. Bonario and Celia in their total innocence are the only still point in a madly swirling world that inexorably draws itself into a vortex as Volpone reveals his identity: stunned silence and stillness affect everyone but the two defendants who are at that moment joyfully released from the horrors that threatened to overtake them. The patterned counterpointing of the action in this sequence is breathtaking in performance for the sheer rapidity with which it must be played and yet no detail within that rising crescendo of activity must be lost by the audience: verbal and visual clarity are crucial throughout it all. Furthermore the pacing must be such that one still can register the mounting rage in Volpone that is making him increasingly a dangerous and wilfully destructive force, as he at last begins to recognise Mosca's superior skills in controlling others. Within the wild farrago an audience must not lose contact with the precise psychological oppositions that fuel its development. Here is at once savage satire, psychological analysis and a searching moral vision with metaphysical resonances: and an audience must be guided to respond to the action on all those levels, while still finding the sheer pace with which those insights are communicated utterly exhilarating.

Equally demanding in terms of the controlling of focus are the scenes where Pru stages her court of love in *The New Inn*. Lovel has two long disquisitions on the art of love and the high virtues it promotes in genuine lovers; fascinating and intricate though his platonic arguments are, they do not occur within a dramatic stasis; instead the stage world invites an audience increasingly to test ideas against actualities, generalising ideals against the variety of human experience. The very discussion of the topic inflames Beaufort who casts an appraising eye over 'Laetitia' (the disguised page-boy, Frank) to whom he begins to make ardent advances. Pru is ever watchful to protect Lovel's interests with her mistress and so is keen to judge Lady Frampul's responses to his words; she is increasingly vexed by what she believes is mere feigning of passion on Frances's part. This encourages the audience to watch Lovel and Frances attentively to test whether they should share Pru's interpretation of what is going on or whether they should judge Frances as developing a genuine regard for Lovel. Pru's anxiety and scruples begin to bring her to Latimer's notice, who warms to the inner beauty these qualities define in her. Three love relationships come into being before us: one based on physical attraction (Beaufort and Laetitia), one on learning and the eloquent expression of fine feeling (Frances and Lovel), one on generosity of impulse and moral insight (Pru and Latimer). The proceedings are viewed with a degree of indulgence by the genial Goodstock (the full implications of whose name we have yet to discover) and with a forthright approval of the various developments which fits oddly with his apparent function as innkeeper. Subtly within the one situation of the court of love Jonson is preparing the ground for the complex plotting of the final act. Speech is juxtaposed with a changing visual impact that illustrates, challenges and contests Lovel's stated beliefs. His account of the psychology of love invites an audience to examine the psychological motivation of the mating games that are being played out before him but which do not shift the focus of his own attention from Frances, to whom in revealing his innermost self he is rendering himself wholly vulnerable. A different kind of vulnerability is being explored in the relationship that 'Laetitia' is at first unwittingly exciting in Beaufort: she is exclusively the object of his gaze. Pru meanwhile is drawing Latimer's eye, but less for how she appears than for what she is, what she says, how she cares about others. Frances appears mesmerised by Lovel but no one seems sure how to read her mind or feelings, least of all herself. Eye-contact in these scenes is of manifest importance to the evolving of the thematic life of the drama and, in performance, is often the best means to direct an audience's attention about the shifting points of focus. This requires a heightened degree of concentration in the players and a sense of ensemble which understands and respects the subtextual energies involved. Everyone onstage throughout Lovel's great speeches has a precisely defined function within the overall dynamic: the scenes are not just a vehicle for a star performer, however beautifully the speeches are delivered.

A different kind of ensemble direction is required in those large-scale scenes where Jonson begins to play challengingly with the tone as if to invite the audience to question more deeply the morality of what is happening. A good instance of this is the staging of the banquet that Ovid and Julia hold in *The Poetaster* (4.5) to which all invited must come dressed as a classical deity. At first, disarmingly, the diners indulge in witty banter about each other's impersonations, exploring how appropriate the choice of god or goddess might be for the several characters. Subtly the banquet declines into the beginnings of an orgy as certain of their friends, spurred on by Ovid and Julia as Jupiter and Hera, start to investigate the sexual implications of the specific roles they have adopted. Suddenly Augustus invades the stage with his guards and his advisors. He expresses profound shock at the impiety of the scene before him; threatens to kill his daughter, Julia; interrogates each of the diners about their motives for choice of costume and intentions in attending the feast; and then awards appropriate degrees of punishment for them all, culminating in his decreeing Ovid's exile from Rome as perpetrator of the scandal. Twelve actors at first take the stage for the feast, to be joined by a further six (together with the soldiery) when Augustus enters. The banquet requires each of the twelve actors to establish a comic caricature within the compass of the role being played throughout the main action. The anarchy of the feast and of all attending it is then held up to question by the actions of Augustus, whose threats are to be registered as a serious danger to the prevailing mood of comedy. The scene ends with Augustus voicing his decision to honour only those artists whose art is the product of a disciplining of their strong passions and spirit. Art that tends to indulgence and excess, such by implication as Ovid's stage-managing of the banquet, is held up for scrupulous moral examination. This is one of Jonson's earliest strategies that seem designed to encourage an audience to question what motives underlie their desire to laugh, if laughter is to be seen as expressing complicity with what occasions the mirth. Cleverly an audience is disarmed by wit, intellectual energy and invention as the feast proceeds, only to have those responses investigated as wanting in moral rigour. This is not a puritanical expulsion of comedy from the stage, but an attempt through stagecraft and dramatic artistry to interrogate the nature of comedy and its different styles and to discriminate the varying qualities of response it might provoke in audiences. Jonson in other words is not so much castigating audiences for being undiscriminating or lax as encouraging them to recognise the moral potential of experiencing performance. The surprising shift in tone requires careful handling by cast and director so that the strategy behind the surface action becomes accessible. Again this requires ensemble work that attends as much to the subtextual implications of event as to the staging of the event in itself. A director must secure a shared understanding of these implications by the cast, if the audience is adequately to appreciate their need too to participate in the construction of meaning within the performance. So much of Jonson's metatheatricality seems directed at this particular aim.

An equally sophisticated attention to tone and ensemble work must obtain in the closing act of *Sejanus*. The senate meets in Tiberius's absence but is required to listen to a lengthy letter from him that relentlessly focuses in on Sejanus himself. As the letter unfolds through its careful patterning of seeming praise and thinly disguised blame, the hearers are made wholly unsure of how to respond, which is reflected in the way the sycophantic senators alternately shift their places either towards or away from Sejanus. This anxiety to be seen to do whatever best reflects Tiberius's will provokes scorn and amusement in Arruntius and his circle; yet they must be guarded in their elation, since, as is all too apparent to the audience, their number has been severely depleted since the start of the action as either Tiberius or Sejanus has picked off various members of the group, one by one. This bitter comedy of action focuses attention on the still presence of Sejanus, waiting, in ever-deepening despair, to know his fate. He, whose words for so much of the play have shaped and controlled the action, is now noticeably silent, rendered utterly impotent by dread as the full implications of what he has lost are brought home to him. How ought the audience to respond to his predicament? How ought the actor to play (or perhaps it would be more appropriate to write 'mime') this scene? Jonson gives no indication of what would be appropriate in either case. To what degree should we see Sejanus here as a figure of pathos, since he is shortly to be brutally savaged by the mob once Tiberius's full displeasure with him is known? How the actor uses the focus that is directed on him here is his and the director's choice. But however he chooses to play the climax of the scene, it will always be contested by the action going on around him. The director must attempt a most sophisticated tonal balance so that all the various responses to the emperor's letter are registered by an audience. Such is the absolute power of Tiberius in Rome that he can stage-manage this whole scene without being present in person to ensure he achieves his will; he can handle everyone within the scene like puppets as they act out his whim to their personal confusion. If absolute power chooses to represent itself as malign, then everyone under that power is robbed of integrity of response and with that their dignity. Does one view this world as tragic or as absurd? Only questions obtain for characters and for audience. Jonson's dramatic artistry demands a complex staging which requires the audience to share the moral and political impotence that the emperor creates in Rome *experientially*. That is to know the full horror that is Tiberius. It needs expertly controlled ensemble work for the complexity of the sequence to register its implications to the full.

Virtuoso ensemble work is also required to negotiate the complexities of tone that obtain in the concluding scene of *The Devil is an Ass*. At first we see Meercraft and Everill instructing the Eithersides, Tailbush, Ambler, Trains and Pitfall how to read the body of Fitzdottrel as possessed by demons. Fitzdottrel at the tricksters' prompting then gives a hilarious demonstration of 'possession' (he speaks in tongues, his belly swells, he sings wanton songs and has visions of being pricked with a pin and of devils coming to dine on his person). It is all nonsense, except to the all-too-gullible onstage audience whose superstitiousness quite gets the better of their perceptions and common sense. When Frances arrives with Wittipol and

Manly and they laugh at all Fitzdottrel's playacting, they find themselves attacked as the agents of witchcraft. All that saves them is the arrival of the turnkey from Newgate and the news that Pug was indeed an actual devil who has spectacularly returned to Hell, leaving most of the prison in ruins amidst a great stink of sulphur. Fitzdottrel, now free of the familiar which he conjured to attend him, decides to end his masquerade and confesses the extent to which he was counterfeiting. But his wife, Frances, is still not clear of suspicion: her arrival with two male companions Fitzdottrel decides is visible proof of adultery, until Manly speaks in her defence and sways public opinion. (For a second time in the play a man has to speak for her; before it was to talk of her supposed feelings; now it is to give voice to her rectitude and claim her dignity; noticeably it requires male endorsement of her worth – and from a character actually called Manly – before that worth carries social credibility.) The shifts of tone here must be deftly handled: the farce of the demonic possession is suddenly displaced by the vicious attack on Frances and her confederates, which Jonson requires a cast to sustain long enough for that attack and its implications to register fully (the capacity of Londoners for exploiting evil has to Satan's chagrin long since outstripped his powers of invention and this theme is fully endorsed by the stage action here). Relief of a kind comes with the arrival of Shackles and his tale of the disappearance of Pug and the plot appears now to be resolved, except this resolution leaves Frances isolated and still under attack and misrepresentation. That Manly must resolve the play fully in the way that he does is itself a reflection on a society in which Frances cannot seemingly defend herself in public, even though we know from an earlier scene that she can forcefully and persuasively express her intelligence and integrity in private with a man she believes she can trust (though, significantly, Wittipol is at that moment dressed as a woman when she pleads her case to him and trusts him not to take advantage of her vulnerability). It is a complex final scene in which Frances's attempt to secure the moral centre of the stage is repeatedly set at risk by the mad and vicious society she has to inhabit; though she is restored to her rightful place at the close of the play, it requires two male champions to effect the situating of her where she rightfully belongs. Still her goodness must remain an inward (silent) grace of temperament; it is not given social currency. Though the plot is adequately resolved, the conclusion so resonates with echoes of earlier scenes that it is anything but a closed ending. The metaphysical questions Jonson has posed throughout the action about how to determine contemporary manifestations of good and evil are fully explored as *questions* but remain largely unanswered. Frances is known to us, but her social predicament is still unsettling. The confidence to leave the play open-ended in this way requires some courage of a cast and director and it requires a finely developed sense of how the final scene is properly to be placed in relation to the dramatic structure overall. Judging how to achieve that placing nightly with changing audiences requires the keenest attention to company values in ensemble.

When talking with actors about playing in Jonsonian comedy, the conversation continually veered round to discussing the ideal kinds of help a director might offer in approaching such plays in rehearsal. In exploring the role of the director in staging Jonson's works the emphasis has continually been on the relation of director to actor and above all on the promotion of an integrated ensemble. Earlier what emerged from an examination of different approaches to the function of design in productions of Jonson's plays was a growing preference for functional settings that in large measure left the playing space bare the better to foreground the artistry of the actors in shaping that stage world peculiar to Jonsonian drama that hovers (often precariously) between precise social realism and private fantasy. Jonson in the theatre would appear on the strength of the more successful productions of recent years to invite a disciplined democratic collaboration in the processes of staging: a 'venture tripartite' between text, director and design team working not to gull or outwit but to serve the actors and the complex relationship they are being required to build with their audience. This may be why productions have of late worked best in intimate theatres like the Swan and the Almeida (or where, as with Warchus's production of *Volpone* in the Olivier, the design has created a confined playing space within a larger stage area) where there is not the pressure to make an elaborate or intrusive directorial or visual statement which risks overwhelming Jonson's intricate strategies. Always in our explorations we come back to the actors. Jonson, of course, had known and worked with one eminent director-designer, Inigo Jones, and had come with time to view the ambitions of such a functionary (as Jonson saw him) as highly suspect, particularly as Jones began to limit the autonomy of the performers in the masques, requiring them to serve his dominant master-plan. Jonson's masques were elegantly witty conceits that created contexts in which to foreground the performers' artistry, personal skill and physical perfection; for Jones the performers were the syntax necessary to shape the rhetorical flourishes of his grand statement, the means to his chosen ends. It was a reduction in status for the performers and for the dramatist whose artistry was placed at the service of their skill; and Jonson deplored the resulting change in the balance of relationships that had formerly made the creation of masques a truly collaborative art. Acting fascinated Jonson (as any of the plays reveals): acting as an art, as a recognised and skilled profession, and as a conceit that helped him define the pervasive infiltration of the performative into every stratum of social life. At the core of Jonson's plays lies this enduring passion. The more he analysed it, the more it intensified (there is no diminution of its strength in the last plays right up to the fragments that make up *The Sad Shepherd*). It excited his imagination, fuelled his invention and whetted his moral rigour. When in his old age actors betrayed that passion and trust in their staging of *The New Inn* and *The Magnetic Lady*, his rage and scorn were fierce against them, but his commitment to acting and to theatre remained unaffected. Jonson in the theatre, then and now, is (and always should be) about *acting* in all its manifestations:

It is so liberally professed! almost
All the wise world is little else, in nature . . .

(Volpone: 3.1.11–12)

It is appropriate to end with Mosca: in Jonson the truths that confound come not from the mouths of babes and sucklings, but invariably from the smiling lips of tricksters and parasites. The socially marginalised in his dramas know the world through and through and best reflect its nature. Actors in his day, even when under royal patronage, were after all still classed as rogues and vagabonds. Acting was aptly, then, the focus of Jonson's artistry; it should be our prime concern too in reviving his plays today.

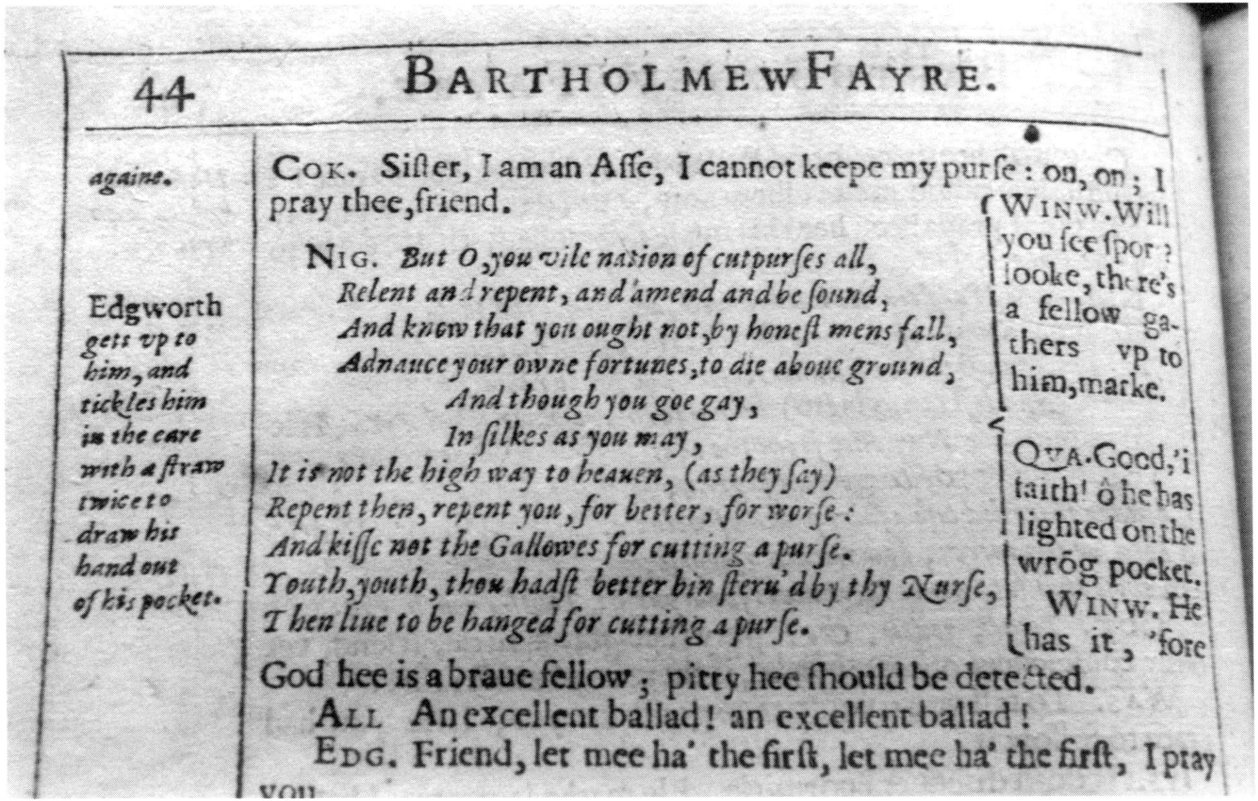

againe.

Edgworth gets vp to him, and tickles him in the eare with a straw twice to draw his hand out of his pocket.

Cᴏᴋ. Sister, I am an Asse, I cannot keepe my purse: on, on; I pray thee, friend.

Nɪɢ. But O, you wilde nation of cutpurses all,
Relent and repent, and amend and be sound,
And know that you ought not, by honest mens fall,
Aduance your owne fortunes, to die aboue ground,
And though you goe gay,
In silkes as you may,
It is not the high way to heauen, (as they say)
Repent then, repent you, for better, for worse:
And kisse not the Gallowes for cutting a purse.
Youth, youth, thou hadst better bin steru'd by thy Nurse,
Then liue to be hanged for cutting a purse.

God hee is a braue fellow; pitty hee should be detected.
Aʟʟ. An excellent ballad! an excellent ballad!
Eᴅɢ. Friend, let mee ha' the first, let mee ha' the first, I pray you

Wɪɴᴡ. Will you see spor? looke, there's a fellow ga-thers vp to him, marke.

Qᴠᴀ. Good; i' faith! ô he has lighted on the wrõg pocket. Wɪɴᴡ. He has it, 'fore

Plate 1 *Bartholomew Fair:* the Second Folio of the *Collected Works* of 1640, showing the layout of the text for the scene where Cokes's purse is stolen.
(By kind permission of the Library of University College, London: Strong Room Ogden A298.)

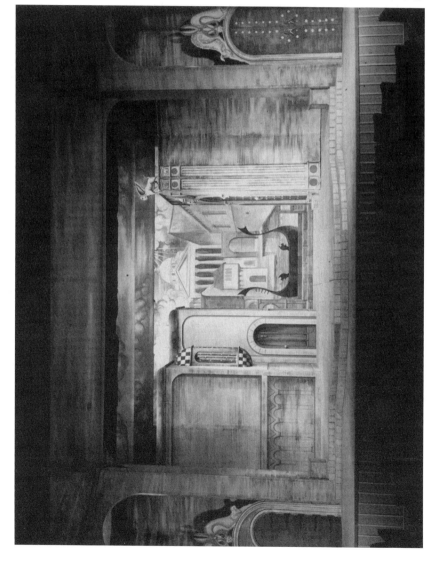

Plate 2 Setting by Malcolm Pride for the Mountebank scene from the 1952 production of *Volpone* at the Shakespeare Memorial Theatre, Stratford.
(By kind permission of the Shakespeare Centre Library.)

Plate 3 Model of the setting designed by Chris Dyer for Trevor Nunn's 1977 revival of *The Alchemist* in Stratford and London.
(Joe Cocks Studio Collection, by kind permission of the Shakespeare Centre Library.)

Plate 4 Anthony Ward's basic setting for Sam Mendes' revival of *The Alchemist* at the Swan Theatre in 1991.

(Joe Cocks Studio Collection, by kind permission of the Shakespeare Centre Library.)

Interlude I

Sam Mendes talks to Brian Woolland[1]

BW: I'd like to start by asking you how you came to Jonson, what baggage you brought with you?

SM: I think I brought rather a lot of negative baggage, which, I'm afraid, a lot of people do. 'Suffers in comparison to Shakespeare, second best to Shakespeare,' instead of it being as it is, instead of realising that it's just completely different; it's a totally original and different voice, almost as if he's writing a different art form sometimes; a completely different understanding of the theatre.

BW: Where did you first encounter Jonson?

SM: I think I saw a production of *Volpone* when I was at school – which wasn't done very well. I don't remember reading any. So I suppose my initial interest came at university; and, although I struggled with it, it grew from there. I approached it as a man of the theatre – not as a scholar. It's when you look at the theatrical possibilities of the texts that you realise what a genius he was. He bears the audience in mind a lot of the time, most of the time putting them onstage in front of themselves. I always had the feeling when I was doing *The Alchemist* that this was going on in a room down the road from the theatre: two doors away from the auditorium was this very same room. He plays on this all the time. His obsession with London led me into – not an obsession with London – but a great interest in London because he has such a strong feeling for it. When I started work at the RSC (I loved the Swan and I still do; I think it's a wonderful theatre) it seemed an obvious thing to do a Jonson in the Swan because there'd already been a tradition of it with *The New Inn* and *Every Man in his Humour*.

BW: Your perception of Jonson changed through exploring the text in rehearsal?

SM: Definitely. The first day in rehearsal, it was like the actors were reading a sort of Swahili text. I've never had such a terrible read-through in my life, and such an appallingly depressed group of actors – for at least a week – because it really is very difficult. Then suddenly something happens, something clicks: they begin to understand the rhythm of it and it becomes suddenly incredibly translucent, and very easily understandable. Structurally I think *The Alchemist* is very, very fine. The key to it lies partly in understanding that there's a rhythm not just in specific scenes but throughout the whole play; that there's a rhythmical mainspring to *The Alchemist,* as there is to all of his plays. If you tap it, if you can get on the back of it, it's remarkably powerful.

BW: How did you get to that?

SM: I showed the cast the set and said 'This is it; it's just you and these five doors and a table and a light bulb, and we have to make it happen in this space.' [See Plate 4, p. 78.] I think that's very easily understandable: you know that it's the play and what they do with it that's going to make it work. With Jonson it's much less appropriate to discuss 'motivation' than with Shakespeare or many modern plays. You have to get it on its feet very early, throw it around. I remember doing a very early run-through just to see what doors people had to come in and out of; and that's the way we had to work on it. We had to sort of decode it as a series of moves, a series of journeys, a series of stage shapes. The moment they were up on their feet and playing with each other they realised how alive the language was and how many options it gave them. I think it is very, very difficult to judge straight off the page.

BW: Had any of the cast played in Jonson before?

SM: David Bradley had played in *The Silent Woman.* He was confident that it would come to life eventually. And so was I, because I had seen those other plays – and I was astounded at how easily accessible they were to an audience.

BW: Can you talk a bit about the rehearsal process?

SM: I think one of the things you realise when you start working on it is that every character is given a different rhythm and you don't realise that on a first reading. For me *The Alchemist* is about the alchemy of making something out of nothing in an empty room; Face and Subtle creating something out of language itself. I deliberately set it in an empty room with nothing onstage but a table and the three people. It was up to them to make everyone who walks into that room believe it's what they say it is, to create the pictures in the minds of the gulls and in the minds of the audience. Within that linguistic alchemy they shape-change, they shape-shift the whole time – by changing rhythms; and they tend to change rhythm to suit the person that they're trying to gull. So when Subtle talks to Epicure Mammon, he talks as the person he thinks Mammon would like to see. And they role-play to each other. They do a wonderful one for Dapper – with Subtle as the Mystical Man and Captain Face, the Military Man. I had David Bradley putting out a ring of stones and chanting and smoking a joint, with Face (Jonathan Hyde) as the Captain complete with eye-patch and military get-up. Complete fantasies – which they pursue with utter conviction. But they need money, they are also starving. Acting becomes their livelihood . . .

All the time I was trying to find ways of making graphic the language. When Abel Drugger comes for a sign for his shop, for example, I gave David Bradley (who played Subtle) a little blackboard: he draws a bell (which is A BEL) then a little dog with 'GERRR' coming out of its mouth (DRUG-GER); and he turns around and tells him that's his sign; and of course Abel's absolutely thrilled. If you're going to have a sign, why not just draw it as you do it. Similarly, when he's talking about the cures for the gout and stuff like that: if you remember he had a little picture of Henry VIII with a bandage, and then Henry VIII without a bandage, and Mona Lisa with a smile – after she'd been cured of the gout. They're street-traders. You go down the Walworth Road now, round where I live, and you go down the market, and it's the same guys. They've got endless tricks. They're endlessly inventive. We spent some time talking to market traders. Because it's that sort of street nous that they use. You're looking all the time to try to find a way of demonstrating the artistry, with nothing, out of nothing. In the end they only had two or three bits of costume: Subtle had a turban to play the Mystical Man, and we originally gave him a beard as the conjuror, but we even cut the beard eventually, because it's too good a disguise. That's not the point: it's not about criminality, it's about gullibility; about the need to believe. The gulls believe that that room is what Face and Subtle say it is because they want to believe it is. They have to have something to believe in. That's why we had Drugger (who absolutely worships Face) gradually look more and more like him: he bought a jacket like Face's; and for his final entrance when he comes back with the flowers for Dame Pliant, for the brief moment he was on he had an eye-patch – looking exactly like Face. That's his desire to belong somewhere. That need to believe is what characterises them all – so you never lose sight of the fact that these people have got their dreams, and that the crushing of their dreams is a ter-rible thing. The portraits aren't heartless, they're not condescending and they're not patronising; and that's a very difficult thing to do.

BW: But Jonson is sometimes accused of being cantankerous and spiteful.

SM: I think that's in the gift of the actor – not being cantankerous and spite-ful. The moment you have it in the right hands it ceases to become two-dimensional, it ceases being patronising and they start to become loveable human beings.

BW: There's so much energy and vitality in those characters.

SM: Exactly. It's almost four years ago since I did it; but there are moments that linger in my mind which are for me pure Jonson – like when Face is being the Captain, and he's got the Roaring Boy, Kastril, and he's trying to teach him how to quarrel, and there's a lot of thigh-slapping and shoulder-punching and this sort of stuff, and Kastril is thinking 'God, this guy's *it*, you know . . .' and Drugger's just watching the scene. He watches them doing their RSC kneel with their legs up on the table sort of stuff and he thinks I'll try that – Kastril and Face are talking all the while – and Albie Woodington (who was fantastic as Abel Drugger) gradually, very slowly, put his leg up on the table but he was a little too far away . . . It really is the essence of character acting. I think it pushes you into finding those moments and exploring a character way beyond what appears on the page. Every time you see something hinted at in the text it's worth making it graphic. They talk about his teeth being yellow, for example, so presumably he's got terrible breath. So every time he turns towards anyone, they turn away. And there was a fly at one point. Everyone stopped because there was fly buzzing around his head because he's so smelly and disgusting. It's just pushing out to those logical extremes. Fortunately, I happened to be surrounded by a cast of like-minded individuals.

BW: It was a very long run overall, wasn't it?

SM: A very long run. The extraordinary thing was that when it hit its rhythm (which it did about the third or fourth preview) the timing of the show never changed. We have little charts backstage which graph the running time. *The Alchemist* ran at two hours twenty three minutes. For forty performances it never lost a minute or gained a minute. I've never seen anything like that in any of the plays I've done. It's always a minute or two either side. It was like clockwork. And they never stopped for laughs. Because actually they grew and grew. So although there was a huge response, they never actually played it. It was just one laugh after another after another. And that's in the writing. Just when you think 'Oh, that's the big comic dénouement', there's another one. There's the fairies, then there's the Queen of the Fairies, and then the Master returns; and then they betray each other.

BW: Could you talk a bit more about audience responses?

SM: It's a huge, cumulative, farce-like response. You realise early on, as Noel Coward says, that you have to sit on every laugh in the first act – in order to let it explode in the second half. Psychologically, Jonson's sense of what is right never deserts him. In rehearsals I literally used to gong people. I had a little drum, and I used to bang the drum when people paused too long. I know it sounds incredibly dictatorial. Well it was dictatorial. Deliberately so. Because when you pause too long you've lost it.

   The scene that was most difficult, funnily enough, was the Mammon scene with Doll Common because there were no jokes in it. By then you've had some of the funniest scenes, the audience is really wound up: they're rolling, everyone's laughing; and then suddenly you've got this scene which is the heart of the play. There's such irony in Mammon speaking the greatest, most beautiful lines in the play, pouring his heart out to a tart who's just making up the lines as she goes along; and he comes out with this fantastic poetry. It's a sad and very desolate scene. It was difficult because they wanted to make it funny. You've just got to let it be what it is. Maybe that's a flaw in the structure of the play. It comes slightly too late in the day; and the rhythm is built up to such a degree . . . It's a wonderful scene, but I think that rhythmically it always felt that it came a beat too late. Maybe I'm wrong about that, maybe my production just wasn't up to it.

BW: How did Joanne Pierce feel about playing Doll?

SM: I think she felt frustrated, yes, although she's the person who holds them together. There's a strange mutual attraction: you feel that Face and Subtle are flirting as well as Face and Doll and Subtle and Doll. Although she has that sexual pull, she doesn't have any gags – apart from the Queen of the Fairies (which is Doll's high spot). I know it sounds stupid, but she's not funny: she doesn't have the comic motor of the play. In fact, to a degree neither do Face and Subtle. The real comedy comes from the gulls; they do a lot of work. They motor the play. But I think she was frustrated . . .

You have to imagine you're working at Stratford in a very heightened atmosphere. You're working on a Marlowe, or a Shakespeare or a Jonson, you get a very clear idea with Marlowe or Jonson who you might end up down the pub with for a drink at the end of the day. You have no idea who it would be if it was Shakespeare. But you certainly know with Jonson; and you get the feeling that he'd be making remarks that weren't entirely PC down the pub. He's a lad. There's one side of him that's a lad, a beer drinker and a common man, a man of the people – in a way that Marlowe patently never was. Marlowe's cynicism and far more patronising attitudes to humanity are almost totally lacking in Jonson. Somehow there's a much, much bigger heart there: tremendous warmth and tremendous imagination, and such visual flair.

BW: How much of the play did you cut for the production?

SM: The cuts were very judicious, but I cut maybe twenty minutes. Mostly from what I call the catalogue speeches, which are the lists. When Mammon got going, or when Subtle got going, when they pulled away from the rhythm of the whole thing. To a degree it's like a musical score, like any farcical comedy is. You mustn't let things dwell too long. And once the rhythm is built up it can't stop. And that was why we didn't really change the set for the neighbours [the one scene set outside the house]. We couldn't work out how to design it. We thought we were going to have to bring on another set, or use gauzes or front cloths. In the end we just had a double hinged door so that in the last act there was a panel in the door that flipped so Face could walk out with an umbrella and walk straight back in through the same door and he was actually walking out of the house. The lights changed and he was outside; and the doors of the room were the doors of the adjoining houses, so it looked exactly the same but completely different; and when he went back inside again he did the same in reverse. Which always used to get a round.

BW: It was a wonderful device, because it was so simple, and so much in the spirit of the production. Did you update the language at all?

SM: I remember using 'three-card-trick' instead of whatever it is in *The Alchemist*. We made a few cheats. A couple of times we had to spell out changing metal into gold. Because otherwise the 'philosopher's stone' is lost on most people. But beyond that, once an audience got the initial conceit, just placing it was enough: once they understood what drives each of the gulls, it's very clear. Then you can play around with it.

BW: The Swan is a very intimate playing space. What happened to the production when it went into the Barbican?

SM: It wasn't as good – because the Swan is an exceptionally good theatre for those plays. Had we designed it for the Barbican we'd have designed a space that brought the action right down towards the audience. It was a bit cold in the Barbican; whereas in the Swan it was very warm because the theatre makes it warm. But I do think it's possible to do it at the Barbican. You just have to have the right sort of imagination; and focus it on the people and not on the set.

　　　The desire to fill the stage with scenic devices is the enemy of Jonson. It's perfectly possible to do it in a proscenium as far as I'm concerned, but you have to depend on the same things that you would depend on were you doing it in the Swan; and that is the empty stage and the actors. You've got to ask the audience to use their imagination. The moment you start building Ye Olde Worlde London with little houses on stilts, and everyone going round selling oranges before the curtain goes up – you know, cleavage acting – and a bit of mud on the hem to make it look realistic. That sort of stuff makes your heart sink. It's to be avoided at all costs. I think there's something of the conjuror about Jonson; and the enemy of that is not releasing the play, not releasing the imagination of the audience, making it terribly pedantic and straight. He's more of a magician.

BW: In spite of the realist elements in the texts?

SM: For me that's what releases it. What I like about Jonson's Blackfriars, his Smock Alley, is that they are at once very specific and yet they don't exist any more except in the minds of the audience. He uses reality in the same way that Ridley Scott does, or indeed Dickens. If you can create something that's a sort of cross between *Martin Chuzzlewit* and *Blade Runner*, then you're starting to get interesting. He uses reality in an incredibly heightened form. And it's very, very potent. He jams everything into a tiny little vessel. Words and places and images spew out at incredible speed. The man can turn on a sixpence. He's got far more interest in the real and the specific than Shakespeare ever had. But you've got to create a new Cheapside in the minds of the audience – a new tavern or a new shop or a new room or wherever it is – that sits somewhere between our time and theirs. In terms of scenic design and costume and the props that one uses, it should be possible to create a world that is somehow an amalgam of the 1990s and 1610.

BW: That was one of the most successful features of your production.

SM: That was down to Anthony Ward, the designer, who found a way of putting bowler hats with doublet and hose or even a pinstripe doublet and hose with a spotted tie for the Maxwell-like Mammon; and still making it seem like clothes rather than costume. Bits and pieces. It's in the details really.

BW: Your enjoyment of *The Alchemist* is obviously enormous; but how about programming other Jonson plays into the repertoire?

SM: You need wonderful acting from top to bottom and it's very difficult in a company outside the RSC or the National, the places that should do it – the RSC should do a Jonson every year. I think it should be a tradition. And there are lots that haven't been done. *The Tale of a Tub, The Staple of News, Sejanus* – these are the plays that should be done. *The Devil is an Ass* until this year hadn't been done for God knows how many years, apart from by Peter Barnes. And many more no doubt still to be discovered. I do think that there should be some sort of duty for the RSC to revive a Jonson every year. He is a great dramatist and he is genuinely – and unjustly – neglected.

BW: Why has Jonson been so neglected then?

SM: I think it's how they read. I think people get very frightened and put off by the density of local reference, and the incredibly dense texture of the language. He's not a spiritual or a mystical writer. He parodies mysticism and spirituality. There's something concrete and tough about him. Above all he's a man of the theatre whose works don't really come into being until they get on the stage. And then you realise what a magician he is. When you've done one [Jonson play] you're in no doubt about the greatness of the man, about how brilliant he is.

Note

1 Sam Mendes is Artistic Director of the Donmar Warehouse, where this interview took place on 4 January 1996. The interview was video-recorded and screened as part of the Reading conference. Sam Mendes directed *The Alchemist* for the RSC at the Swan Theatre in Stratford-upon-Avon (1991). The production later transferred to the Barbican.

Part II

Working with Jonson

Brian Woolland

6   Introduction

Brian Woolland

'Jonson would be as dead as most of the books about him without the one essential quality a playwright must have. On stage, his seeming heavy, clotted verse unfolds like a Japanese paper flower in water. It is a wonder and a mystery. He works in the theatre. In the end it is the only thing that really matters.'

(Peter Barnes)[1]

Or is it?

Jonson's plays themselves are a continuing testament to the essential interaction between theatre and education. Although his plays resist simplistic didacticism, all social satire has an educative, or an instructional function; and, just as theatrical form in Jonson's theatre is never static, so, too, there is a continuing exploration of educational method in his satire. There has always been a reciprocal relationship between theatre and education, in the broadest sense of that word. Jonson, Shakespeare and their contemporaries may each have used their classical sources rather differently, but all the English Renaissance playwrights were steeped in 'learning' (many of them writing for companies of boys drawn from grammar and choir schools). It seems disingenuous that certain of Jonson's critics (who themselves work in the academy) have focused on the contention that he occasionally appears to wear his scholarship rather ostentatiously.

For as long as plays have been taught in schools, colleges and universities, readings of those texts (from the page and in the theatre) have been profoundly affected by pedagogical method. For all the accreted mythology that Shakespeare's genius somehow sprung untutored from the nurturing soil of rural England, the production and reception of his plays (as both written and theatrical texts) is no less culturally determined than the unfamiliarity of the Jonson canon.

This section of the book examines the connections between particular kinds of educational approaches and rehearsal methods: those which are concerned with exploring dramatic texts in order to reveal their theatrical qualities; and which value students, actors, audiences and readers as active collaborators in a continuing process of making meaning.

In doing so it aims to confront and refute the reputation that Jonson is 'difficult' and to allay the panic that is often associated with studying and staging his work. It does so by identifying those characteristics of Jonson's plays that sometimes create a challenge to readers, by showing how they can be a source of pleasure and cele-bration both for readers and audiences; and by exploring the informing critical and ideological contexts within which Jonson is taught and produced (both with pro-fessional and with young, non-professional actors). It proposes that the English and drama curricula would be greatly enriched by the addition of more plays from the Jonson canon, suggesting that these plays are not only important in their own right, but that they also offer ways of teaching about theatre practice and about the-atre criticism, and that they provide a rewarding means of discussing the ideological nature of such criticism. Throughout this section, references to 'study' include academic textual analysis, practical workshop activities, rehearsal explorations and attending to the plays in performance.

The interviews with Sam Mendes and Genista McIntosh (see pp. 79–85 and 143–9) reveal that each was circumspect of Jonson – (bringing 'rather a lot of neg-ative baggage' to Jonson, as Mendes puts it). Their sense of wariness is mild compared with the almost pathological dislike (or fear?) of Jonson expressed in a recent review of *The Alchemist* for a readership of English teachers: 'If I had, on pain of death, to teach the play, I'd go for this edition.'[2] The reviewer's reaction is not unusual amongst teachers. It is revealing that both Mendes and McIntosh refer to Jonson's absence from school curricula.[3] What is also evident in these interviews is that each has grown increasingly excited by Jonson's work as they have become more familiar with it in the theatre. This notion that Jonson's plays only really 'take life' in performance is commonly held by most of the theatre professionals who attended the Reading conference and to whom we have subsequently spoken. Whilst Jonson's plays may demand a knowledge and understanding of theatre, there are also inherent dangers of allowing this position to become restricting. As both Mendes and McIntosh argue, theatre companies are understandably reluctant to programme large-cast Renaissance plays unless there is some level of certainty that they will attract an audience. One of the most likely constituencies within which any theatre seeks an audience for Renaissance plays is amongst those studying plays at A level. The corollary to this is that texts that do not get theatrical revivals are less likely to appear on A-level syllabi. Even at undergraduate level, lecturers will include plays on drama courses that are currently in production. The canon of Renaissance theatre available for performance is thus restricted. This restriction, though apparently pragmatic, can be traced back to the ideological contexts within which Jonson criticism operates.

Innovative artistic directors and theatre managers can, and do, programme lesser-known Renaissance plays, attracting audiences with starry casts and brilliant marketing; but the vicious circle can also be broken through education. It is our experience that Jonson's work is far more accessible to students (at sixth form and at undergraduate level) than is commonly thought.

'Teaching Jonson' can mean many things; but in the context of this book, where we are concerned with Jonson and the theatre, I would divide these into two different areas of study: teaching the plays (and/or masques) themselves, and *using* Jonson's plays to explore and examine other, related issues. The former is self-explanatory; the latter might include practical workshops on the written texts, theatrical productions of the plays and critical responses to the plays in order to examine theatrical issues, such as approaches to character and role, aspects of metatheatre, and the ideological nature of pedagogy and criticism itself.

Throughout our discussions and interviews with conference participants, theatre professionals, teachers and publishers, Jonson's work was identified as having certain distinctive qualities. Each of these characteristics is sometimes perceived as a 'difficulty', or more charitably as a 'challenge'; but the overriding sense was that many of these characteristics created 'obstacles' in the way of an appreciation of the plays. I note these distinctive qualities below, with a very brief indication of the way that each is sometimes represented as 'difficult' for readers:

- Language itself. In particular, his vocabulary and his use of the vernacular (frequently peppered with topical references to place and incident) tends to deny access to those without scholarly knowledge.
- Use of classical allusion and classical form. This relates closely to the use of language, but is more extensive than the surface of language, and is sometimes characterised as being deliberately obscure, even as a way of deliberately 'testing' a reader's erudition.
- Narrative complexity. The plotting is frequently complex and, furthermore, in many of the plays (perhaps most notably in *Bartholomew Fair*) there are multiple narratives which are difficult to follow when reading from the page.
- Approaches to characterisation. Characters are perceived to be created as types or as examples of 'humours' – in itself a puzzling concept for a modern reader.
- Comedy and use of comic form. It is sometimes argued that comedy is more socially specific than tragedy; and that much of Jonson's comedy is social satire which does not translate easily to the modern period.
- Theatricality. The plays are peculiarly dependent on production.
- 'Modernity'. The plays are frequently self-referential, metatheatrical and underpinned with materialist concerns.

I suggest that an approach to Jonson which sees these qualities as obstacles, or 'hurdles' to be jumped before one can get access to the 'true Jonson', is at best unproductive and at worst self-defeating. These qualities are indeed at the heart of Jonson's plays but they can offer immediate and lasting pleasures even to young students who are completely new to Jonson's work. This is not to imply that Jonson is 'easy' (the man himself would surely be most hurt by the suggestion) but rather to propose pedagogical approaches which revel in the particularities and peculiarities of Jonson's theatre, rather than apologise for them.

The pejorative tone in which reference to these qualities is made frequently derives from comparisons with Shakespeare; and many of the genuine difficulties associated with studying Jonson arise from perceived relationships between the two playwrights. It is as if Shakespeare sets the 'gold standard' by which all of his contemporaries are measured. Jonson's plays deserve to be seen and studied for themselves. This section of the book considers how this might be done.

I want to return briefly to the qualities identified above, to indicate more positive ways of looking at each:

Language

This is perhaps the most frequently cited 'challenge' in Jonson's work. Drama is essentially a multi-vocal form, but some drama is essentially more multi-vocal than others; and one of the distinctive features of Jonson's work is his ability to characterise through voice: through choice of vocabulary, dialect, speech rhythms. Jonson's 'erratic' rhythmic patterns are frequently carefully crafted signifiers of character and social situation. His theatrical language is a living language, in that it is language in use, language in a state of flux, language that is always active. In their different ways, for example, *The Alchemist*, *Volpone*, *Epicoene* and *Bartholomew Fair* all inscribe modes of improvisation into the written text.

Classical allusion and classical form

Critics (such as Edmund Wilson[4]) who have characterised Jonson as being a 'retentive' show-off, flamboyantly trotting out his learning are missing the point. It is the characters who speak in this way in the plays; and the use of classical allusion is (at least sometimes) one of many signifiers of voice. Jonson also uses (and then subverts) classical, Aristotelian models to structure his plays. Analysis of the structural forms is productive in itself and can lead to study of Plautus, Terence and Aristophanes.

Narrative complexity

The plays are certainly narratively complex; but this should not in itself be problematic so long as the story-telling is foregrounded. Students studying Shakespeare are at an advantage here in that retellings and simplifications of his stories abound. As Brecht frequently pointed out, however, Renaissance theatre was far more concerned with telling stories than many modern commentators (who dwell on the psychology of imagined characters) allow. Jonson's narrative complexity also includes multiple narrative (exemplified in *Bartholomew Fair*) and multiple conversations (as in *The Devil is an Ass*). The problem here is not that young people are unfamiliar with such dramatic strategies (the dramatic fictions they watch on television abound in them), but, rather, one of expectation: their experience of drama does not lead them to expect such techniques in 'classic' plays. In this sense Jonson is extraordinarily modern.

Approach to characterisation

'Those seeming "failures of characterisation" are not failures when the words are spoken and the character given flesh by an actor . . .'

(Peter Barnes)[5]

Close work on the plays reveals many of Jonson's characters to be far more complex than is commonly acknowledged. They frequently attempt to reconstruct themselves during the course of a play; and to see them as complex social constructions is far more productive than bemoaning their lack of psychological depth. But the issue here is also as much about 'identification' as with apparently 'two-dimensional' character types. Audiences and readers frequently don't know with whom they should identify when watching a Jonson play. Far from being a failing, this is the way the plays work: the 'difficulty' of identification is a deliberate theatrical strategy, a way of keeping an audience constantly alert as characters in Jonson frequently re-present themselves to an audience and to each other. As Margot Heinemann has noted when discussing Brechtian approaches to Shakespeare, 'Empathy in Shakespeare's theatre was "a contradictory, complicated and intermittent operation"'(Heinemann 1985: 238). The same is true of Shakespeare's contemporaries. Studying Jonson can be a revealing counter to that strand of Shakespearean criticism which focuses on the psychology of the individual at the expense of the social. It is, however, simplistic and inaccurate to ignore the subtlety of Jonson's characterisations – which are frequently psychologically remarkably truthful.

Comedy and use of comic form

'It seems to me that only laughter may have a future. So, one of the most important things about Jonson is that he is a comic dramatist who is still funny. Shakespeare's comedies may be poetic, even life-enhancing, but funny they are not. Who actually *laughs* at *Twelfth Night* or *Love's Labour's Lost* with a laughter that is still real and unrestrained and not tinged with cultural fear? We titter, if at all, because we have been conditioned to titter. The arbiters of taste dare you not to. Audiences once laughed at Sir Harry Lauder and George Robey, just as they once laughed at Toby Belch and Lancelot Gobbo. But no more; these characters aren't funny in themselves because they never were. Jonson's Face, Justice Overdo and Fitzdotterel were, and are.'

(Peter Barnes)[6]

'When you laugh [at a Jonson play], you laugh at the human detail of what you
see, rather than the working through of some sort of comic contrivance.'

(Colin Ellwood)[7]

Theatricality

'It seems entirely paradoxical that because Jonson's a great theatre dramatist he
should therefore suffer from not being performed in the theatre.'

(Genista McIntosh)

The paradox referred to by Genista McIntosh arises at least in part from the ideological weight given to the study of Shakespeare, and the fact that even with the
growth of Theatre Studies as an A-level subject, Shakespeare's plays are still studied
predominantly as written texts. Studying Jonson's plays demands thinking about
them as theatre: considering, for example, the ways in which characters are invested
with theatrical energy; the extent to which intra-dialogic stage directions are
embedded in the texts; and the ways in which Jonson's theatre, which has been so
often derided as predominantly verbal, works through complex juxtapositions of
oral and visual language codes.

Modernity

Whilst much theatre of the 'early modern' period has been a powerful stimulus in
the development of recent critical theory, Jonson's constant experiments with and
exploration of theatrical form (his use of metatheatre, his incisive examination of
social roles and character function, the self-referential discourse about what we
might now term generic conventions) can illuminate study of theatre of the modern
period.

The subsequent chapters in this section return to these qualities, examine them in
greater depth and relate the exploratory nature of teaching and learning about
Jonson in an educational context to theatrical rehearsal processes.

Notes

1   Extract from the text of Peter Barnes's illustrated workshop-lecture on Jonsonian
    comedy at the Reading conference on 10 January 1996.
2   *NATE* magazine, spring 1997. Review of Cambridge University Press edition of *The
    Alchemist* (in the Cambridge Literature series) by Bob Ford for the National Association
    of Teachers of English.
3   In the past five years the University of Cambridge Local Examinations Syndicate have
    regularly offered *Volpone* as an optional set text in their English Literature A-level. To my

knowledge no other Jonson play has been used as a set text by any other A-level board. Plays by Christopher Marlowe, John Webster and by John Ford, however, appear frequently amongst the texts set by several different boards.

4 Wilson's loathing of Jonson is far more revealing of the critic's own psychological make-up than it is of Jonson's. The following brief extract gives a flavour: 'When he is dirty, he is, unlike Shakespeare, sometimes disgusting to such a degree that he makes one sympathetic with the Puritans in their efforts to clean up the theater . . . Ben Jonson seems an obvious example of a psychological type which has been described by Freud and designated by a technical term: *anal erotic*' (Wilson 1963: 62–3).

5 Peter Barnes, op. cit.

6 Peter Barnes, op. cit.

7 Extract from Colin Ellwood's discussion of the workshop he ran at the Reading conference on 11 January 1996 (described in Chapter 7 below).

7   First encounters

Brian Woolland

'The first day in rehearsal . . . (of *The Alchemist*, and I would imagine any Jonson play) . . . it was like the actors were reading a sort of Swahili text. I mean I've never had such a terrible read-through in my life, and such an appallingly depressed group of actors . . . and then suddenly something happens, something clicks: they begin to understand the rhythm of it and it becomes suddenly incredibly translucent, and very easily understandable . . .'

(Sam Mendes)

There is a well-known quiz show on British television, *Have I Got News for You*, which involves teams looking at a group of pictures and guessing which is 'the odd one out'. Maybe one day the following might come up: Ben Jonson, Peter Barnes, Charles Dickens, Edward Bond, John Arden. The 'game' works on the basis that even though there are several possible answers, only one of them is 'right'. In this instance, for example: Charles Dickens because he wrote novels and the others are playwrights; John Arden because he lives in Ireland and the others live(d) in England . . . But no – the 'right' answer is never the obvious one; and Angus Deayton, the quiz master, is annoyingly revealed as the fount of idiosyncratic wisdom. Paul Merton, one of the contestants, usually mocks the very idea of the closed question, and so everything's all right – and, even if his suggestions don't get rewarded with points, he gets the best laughs.

Many students go through school either submitting to the determined correctness of their teachers and examiners or learning to survive (at least in their immediate social environment) by amusing their peers. Teachers of theatre and drama in particular know how rewarding it can be for a student to be able to delight their peers by entertainingly subverting the system. Many teachers of drama, however, pride themselves on being able to work collaboratively with their students for much of the time; they create questions to which there is no single right answer, and create situations which demand collaborative responses. Their pedagogical model is the antithesis of the authoritarian pedant parodied by Deayton. When it comes to teaching plays, however, the problem rears its head again but in a slightly different guise: how to overcome the intimidation of the text;

how to counteract the sense (often encouraged by traditional methods of studying dramatic texts as literature) that there is a 'right' way of reading any given text, that its meanings exist before each new audience approaches it. One of the implications of this notion that each text has pre-existent meanings is that all readers and audiences are thereby constructed as culturally homogeneous – which is as inappropriate an account of the diverse group of people who might study Jonson as it is of Jonson's plays themselves.

This chapter describes two workshop approaches to Jonson's plays: firstly, a series of four two-hour workshops on *The Alchemist* with lower sixth formers who had never encountered Jonson before; and secondly a one-off workshop given by Colin Ellwood on *The New Inn* at the Reading conference. The methods used for each play were designed primarily to address some of the issues that can arise out of 'first encounters' with a Jonson play on the page; and in particular, to overcome the sense of intimidation that so frequently accompanies approaches to Renaissance playtexts, and particularly Jonson's. Ellwood introduced his workshop by expressing his intention to treat it as a rehearsal:

> 'In an RSC rehearsal a great deal happens "below the surface". Actors do things which disguise the amount of work that they do subconsciously during rehearsals and consciously between rehearsals. One of the things I want to do here is to tease out those processes and apply them, as exercises, to *The New Inn*.'

This approach also informs the work on *The Alchemist* outlined below. Practical workshops thus become a way of revealing the many layers of a dramatic text; of exploring the theatrical qualities of a written text; and of making visible those processes employed by actors and directors which have become intuitive for most theatre professionals.

Critical practice

Too often discussion of practice and debates about theoretical criticism betray their mutual suspicions of each other. The workshops referred to below (and in Chapters 9 and 10, 'Contradictions' and 'The gift of silence') were developed as 'critical practice'. The term is not easily defined, but can be thought of as practical work in which theory and practice mutually inform each other. Critical practice is reflexive; a means of exploring 'conceptual issues . . . in concrete terms' (Lacey and Pye 1994: 21); it appraises practice in the light of theory, and re-examines theory in the light of practice. As such, it is particularly appropriate for Jonson's theatre – in which audiences and readers are constantly positioned to interrogate and reconsider their own relationship to what they are reading/watching.

The Alchemist

The Alchemist (1610) was chosen as the text for working on with groups of lower sixth formers because of all Jonson's plays, it is the one that they would be most likely to be able to see in production and is readily available in student editions. The students were all in their second term of a Theatre Studies A-level course at an urban comprehensive with a racially mixed catchment; the workshops took place in the school drama studio. The approach adopted in the workshops was to set up possibilities for exploring the text, whilst not letting the workshop participants become intimidated by it. The prime aims for the workshops were to encourage an attitude of excited curiosity about *The Alchemist*: its theatrical form, the characters and their functions within the play and use of language. The workshops were intended to open up possible meanings for the participant students, rather than teaching pre-existent meanings. The students should use the workshops to interrogate the play as actively as possible; and they should leave the final workshop wanting to read (or reread) *The Alchemist* and to see it (and other Jonson plays) performed in the theatre. Although the choice of play might have been reinforcing the self-perpetuating limitations of the canon, it was in repertoire at the Royal National Theatre at the time of these workshops.

The workshops

Before the first workshop started the students knew they were to be working on *The Alchemist*, but had not read the text, and were not given copies of the play until the end of the first of the four workshops.

The persons of the play

They began by looking at the list of characters. Working in small groups, they were asked to consider the title, to look carefully at the list of characters, and to use this information to speculate about the play. 'What do you associate with the names of each of the characters?' 'Given that the play has characters with names such as Face, Subtle, Dapper, Drugger, what kind of play do you expect it to be?' 'Note down any questions you want to ask.' 'Note down what you *might* expect from these characters'. They were asked to keep the (collective) notes that they made at this stage, to refer back to them and to develop/amend them as the work proceeded. This first set of notes was written on Overhead Projector acetates, so that each group's speculations and questions could be shared with others. A number of very interesting questions were raised: notably around the characters of *Face* and *Drugger*. Several students thought that *Face* might be a kind of mask and noted that the character list seemed to indicate 'types'. Some students wanted to know what the relationship between this play and commedia dell'arte might be (they had touched on commedia earlier in their Theatre Studies course). Several students thought *Drugger* might be the seventeenth-century equivalent of a dealer. 'Is he as shady a character as he seems?' 'How does Jonson's language relate to ours?'

The teacher's function in this exercise was to prioritise their questions, to focus each group's attention on specific questions as they worked through other material – aware of the sense of intimidation which teachers' knowledge can create. If a group can formulate their own questions, if they *want* to know about the material, anything they find out is likely to be far more meaningful to them than information received passively. The teacher's experience of the text was there for them to make use of. The overriding principle here was to arouse curiosity and keep it alive. The small groups then speculated about each character's behaviour/physical mannerisms (the teacher always trying to keep the intelligent guesswork as active as possible) and offered short presentations, which were effectively summaries of their *speculations* about the text.

The argument

The students and teacher read Jonson's *Argument of the Play*. The students then 'enacted' it, under the guidance of the teacher, initially using a series of still images and then simple movement. Students were encouraged to note any further questions they had at this stage about the play; and to note whether any of their earlier questions had been 'answered' or whether the questions themselves needed modifying.

Characters and their 'voices'

At this stage it might have been appropriate to look at the first scene of the play; but reading any play demands an identification of character and voice. As students become increasingly adept at play reading they do this almost subconsciously, but to facilitate the private reading that they will need to do between workshops and subsequently it is worth considering the voices of characters before they embark on their own private reading of the text. Jonson's ability to work to create different voices is one of the very qualities that is so attractive about the texts theatrically; and, paradoxically, precisely why they are so 'difficult' to read off the page for students who have never encountered them before. In the late twentieth century we have become used to naturalism as the dominant dramatic form. What makes Jonson doubly difficult is that we have also learnt to equate realism with naturalism. Jonson's realism is anything but naturalistic. His characters may use colloquial speech, but they never do so innocently; they use language; it is always at their service.

In small groups, students looked at a number of short extracts from the text. Each of these was chosen because it shed more light on a specific character. An example of one of these extracts is reproduced below:

DRUGGER arrives at 'The Alchemist's' wanting help. He explains to SUBTLE:

DRUGGER: . . . I am a young beginner, and am building
           Of a new shop, and't like your worship; just,
           At corner of a street: (Here's the plot on't.)
           And I would know, by art, sir, of your worship,
           Which way I should make my door, by *necromancy*.
           And, where my shelves. And, which should be for boxes.
           And, which for pots. I would be glad to thrive, sir.
           And, I was wished to your worship, by a gentleman,
           One Captain FACE, that says you know men's *planets*,
           And their good *angels*, and their bad.

                              (1.3.7–16)

The students were asked to prepare a reading of this extract, using every punctuation mark as a signifier of speech rhythm; and to find a way of using the text as an indicator of Drugger's vocal mannerisms. Each group was then asked to prepare a 'performance' of Drugger's 'speech' with Subtle present, making Subtle's silence an active agent in the piece. Drugger's discomfiture in the situation is at least in part a product of Subtle's silence. Every group's presentation was different. In one Subtle stared at Drugger, listening intently but inscrutable; and Drugger became more and more nervous. In another he took little notice of Drugger, apparently concerning himself with an arcane text, and only occasionally looking up quizzically. Whatever the specific stage business, Subtle's silence is as important as Drugger's speech; and is rich ground for exploration by students. The students looked at a number of other short extracts, in each case trying to find appropriate vocal mannerisms and speech rhythms through short practical exercises; searching the short extracts for intra-dialogic indicators of action.

    The short extracts were chosen to give insight into the ways that Jonson uses language to indicate how a character speaks; and the students were again asked to consolidate their understanding of the play by relating the new information they had acquired through the exercise to their earlier speculations.

Improvisations based on the opening of the play

Moving briefly away from the text itself, the small groups were asked to devise situations for improvisation which would loosely follow the following scenario:

A, B and C have made a plan which involves some kind of illegal activity. They are about to carry it out when A and B start to argue between themselves. Their argument rapidly shifts away from the pros and cons of the plan and becomes increasingly personal. C realises that their argument will prove disastrous and intervenes, attempting to get them both back on course.

The improvisations are played out; and the *structure* of each of the resulting scenes is noted. Where are the climaxes? *How* does the third character attempt to control the others – verbally and physically?

Realising the first page of the play

The first page of the play was then read aloud, and compared with the previous improvisations. This is a strategy for making the reading and interrogation of the written text as active as possible. Having read the text, it was noted that it is full of 'implied' stage action. In groups of threes, students enacted the scene as actively as possible. This was again followed by discussion about how this modifies thinking/expectation about characters/plot and the whole play.

Editing and performing Act 1, Scene 1

Act 1, Scene 1 is 199 lines long. One of the groups was asked to cut this down to about 75 lines. Having conducted this radical piece of editing, they then performed the resulting text. Such a radical act of editing forces students to read the text very carefully, to consider the shape and structure of a scene and of its theatrical functions. The edited text is not definitive, but the act of *editing for performance* becomes a way of getting to know a text very well. It is in itself an active interrogation of the text; and demands that they think about the play as theatre.

For all our reservations about the Shakespeare/Jonson binary, there are points of comparison which are potentially very positive: one of the great joys of working on a Jonson play is that he is not revered in the way that Shakespeare is. Peter Barnes, a latter-day Jonsonian (and himself a vastly underrated playwright), has 'edited' a number of Jonson's plays for performance. He is very clear that the published texts of his own plays are there for readers, and that anyone wanting to perform them should edit them. Barnes is convinced that Jonson himself expanded his own plays for publication. Although he says this is a 'hunch', it is well supported by scholarly research; in particular, Stephen Orgel has argued this case most convincingly (Orgel 1981).

At this stage the students began to work on the playtext 'proper'. They were keen to do so, prepared for some of the 'difficulties' and able to relate their reading of the text to their previous explorations and speculations. They had already begun to make the play 'their own' even before embarking on a reading of the second scene; and could see that putting any scene 'on its feet' would be likely to bring it to life and clarify meaning. They trusted the play, and trusted themselves as active readers.

The outcomes

Whenever I have worked on this play with sixth form students and undergraduates they seem to have found it not only interesting in its own right, but have been able to use their developing understanding of Jonson to inform other theatre work. They seem particularly stimulated by their first encounter with a great playwright whose characters *use* language in ways with which they are remarkably familiar: to baffle, to bemuse, to exclude, to impress, to intrigue. And what pleasure there is in seeing the contemporary parallels they draw: secondhand car salesmen, computer buffs, politicians – and teachers.

If the approach outlined above seems a little like a kind of detective game, it is a detective game which effectively subverts most expectations of the genre; a detective game in which any sense of finite closure (and definitive readings) is actively denied to the participants, in which the teacher's knowledge of the text is itself increasingly revealed to be speculative; which is as much concerned with opening up the processes of reading a theatrical text as it is about 'teaching Jonson'.

The New Inn

In the participatory workshop given at the Reading conference on *The New Inn*, Colin Ellwood adopted a method of exploring the text which at first sight seemed very different from that described above. He took on a dynamic role, organising the participants, actively intervening, using Jonson's own detailed argument to encourage the conference delegates/workshop participants to visualise the whole of the play up to the final scene. In small groups they created a series of still images of each of the scenes in the first four acts. Most participants had copies of the play; not all had read it. But the plot of *The New Inn* is complex and was unfamiliar to most participants; and the activity of creating the still images provoked even those who thought they knew the play well into an active interrogation of the text. With Ellwood's assistance the images were then refined. In some teaching situations the teacher/director's close knowledge of the play can be a constant reminder of the participants' own ignorance. In this instance the teacher/director functioned more as a resource for participants to draw on.

Having worked their way through the whole play, the participants then enacted the final scene, using a slightly condensed text. The large group was divided into small groups; and each small group was given a short extract from the final scene to prepare for presentation. The task was limited in scope, but enabled the participants to succeed in realising a version of the whole play in the space of a three-hour workshop. By working through the first four acts of the play in this fashion, Ellwood was able to focus attention on the final act and to examine the 'extraordinary range of levels on which the play works'. The achievement of Ellwood's workshop was to make this layered quality visible in a very short space of time. It made sense of the layers of disguise in the play, of the mechanics of the play, and of the emotional truthfulness of a play which is often perceived as narratively convoluted. In the discussion that followed the workshop it was noted that the play works by 'gently sending up the long-lost-foundling comedy whilst at the same time being psychologically real'. Colin Ellwood summarised this discussion:

> 'It works as comedy; it is warmly, benevolently, compassionately human as well as being parodic and hinting at darker things. What is so remarkable about the play is that these different elements do not get in the way of each other.'

Examining short extracts from the plays, exploring appropriate vocal mannerisms and speech rhythms, searching short extracts from texts for indicators of theatrical *action* offers a way of approaching the plays *as theatre*. To do so necessarily involves an acknowledgement of the extent to which received reputations can intimidate both actors and students, and demands an understanding of the innate theatricality of the texts.

Approaching the texts in these ways can overcome the initial intimidation that students might feel when faced with the unfamiliarity of Jonson. Giving students carefully selected extracts from the play in question arouses curiosity, provokes speculation, enables them to find their own meanings in it. This keeps the process of reading *active*, and encourages them to interact with the text. As a pedagogical strategy it is very close to the way that Jonson himself uses inductions and on-stage audiences. In the Induction (and Chorus) of *The Magnetic Lady*, for example, Probee and Damplay discuss with the Boy of the House the nature of what they have seen and what they want to see. Their speculation is entertaining and diverting in its own right, but it also encourages an audience to do the same and reminds it that watching a play is an interactive experience.

And the 'right' answer to the quiz? Ben Jonson. Peter Barnes, Edward Bond, John Arden, Charles Dickens have all actively championed Ben Jonson as our great 'unknown' playwright, and all acknowledge(d) a considerable debt to him.

8 Jonson as Shakespeare's Other

Mick Jardine

As the title indicates, this essay draws upon Lacanian theory with its central claim that 'the unconscious is the discourse of the Other' (with a capital O) (Lacan 1977: 171).[1] The main objective is to use this theory in order to take a fresh look at the well-worked area of Jonson's relationship to Shakespeare. In turning to the same topic recently, Richard Dutton acknowledges that the history of Shakespeare's ascendancy at Jonson's expense eludes easy explanation:

> We need to steer round the very potent constructions that . . . later ages have placed upon their relationship. No one has chronicled the process of those constructions more scrupulously than Sam Schoenbaum, though he has usually fought shy of cultural explanations as to *why* they should have occurred.
>
> (Dutton 1996: 140)

He himself contributes to the chronicling of what he calls the 'twisting' of stories of the two dramatists' rivalry to Shakespeare's advantage, but evasively concludes, 'Why that twisting should take place is a larger question than we can fully address here' (141). In returning once again to this still unanswered question it will be seen that this chapter depends upon aspects of poststructuralist theory to seek an explanation for the 'potent constructions' referred to above.

The argument which will be developed is that Shakespeare's cultural pre-eminence is posited upon Jonson's secondary status as a scapegoating Other to a Shakespearean 'centre' or ideal. Jonson's 'Otherness' is perpetuated by pressures from a Shakespeare-centred publication and theatre industry, together with broader politico-cultural phenomena, such as the National Curriculum. Although it can be plausibly argued that 'Shakocentricity' has been beneficial in putting early modern drama on the map, the danger is that it results in the relegation of early modern dramatists in general, and Jonson in particular, to mere points of comparison. The Shakespeare industry has acted as a sort of magnetic lodestone, pulling all into its sphere of influence, and criticism of early modern drama needs to take protective measures against this process, by examining the criteria upon which it is based, beginning with the question of where we place value and why, in relation to literature and its social role.

However, critics who wish to challenge Jonson's supplementary status in relation to Shakespeare are placed in a curious double-bind. On the one hand, in
coupling these names they perpetuate Jonson's supplementarity, by not granting
him independence. On the other hand, *not* to seek to understand the process by
which he has become the negative to Shakespeare's positive also risks continuation
of both the hierarchy and the dependency. This presents a particular pedagogical
problem also, as in a classroom situation the teacher has to wrestle directly with
the effects of the Shakespeare 'force-field', the enormous cultural weight which
assures his unparalleled primacy, together with, I believe, unparalleled damaging
consequences for the reception and reputation of another author – Ben Jonson. In
order to try to counteract this magnetic pull, a number of strategies can be developed to persuade a Shakocentric world of the need to see this as an ideological
rather than a literary phenomenon, and to be sensitive to the political implications
of constructing a literary 'pecking order' in which authors strive to overcome
belatedness.[2] One such strategy is to use the insights of poststructuralism regard-
ing the structuring power of binaries, alerting us to the probability that the
persistency of this particular 'S/J' binary indicates that these two early modern
dramatists have come to represent an ideological conflict of some considerable significance.

Jacques Derrida's work on the hierarchical binary oppositions underpinning
Western metaphysics (which he labels 'logocentricity') can serve as a helpful
explanatory tool, as can Hélène Cixous's application of this work to patriarchy.[3]
Space forbids a full account of Derrida's critique of Western metaphysics, but it will
help my argument at this stage to draw upon certain relevant parts. In Derrida's
words, 'metaphysics works by excluding non-presence', which it achieves by 'determining the supplement as simple exteriority' (Derrida 1976: 167). What Jonson
and Shakespeare criticism across the ages discloses is a process of alignment of
Shakespeare with logocentricity, by fashioning Jonson as a supplement, external to
the full presence of his rival and precursor:

> Speech comes to be added to intuitive presence . . . writing comes to be added
> to living self-present speech; masturbation comes to be added to so-called
> normal sexual experience; culture to nature, evil to innocence, history to
> origin, and so on.
>
> (Derrida 1976: 167)

While the Shakespeare industry has flourished as representative of the positive
terms (the 'natural', 'instinctive', 'normal' in Derrida's list), Jonson is doomed to
the status of negative Other. Hélène Cixous has shown how Derrida's insights can
be adapted to account for the operation of patriarchy, and the following analysis by
Toril Moi shows the relevance of Cixous's thinking to this chapter:

In a typical move Cixous then goes on to locate *death* at work in this kind of thought. For one of the terms to acquire meaning, she claims, it must destroy the other. The 'couple' cannot be left intact; it becomes a general battlefield where the struggle for signifying supremacy is forever re-enacted . . . Her whole theoretical project can in one sense be summed up as the effort to undo this logocentric ideology.

(Moi 1985: 105)

The project of this chapter is similarly to challenge the logocentric ideology in which Jonson has been caught up. For Jonson studies, which have tended to be suspicious of Theory, it must be maintained that such a theorised approach is not a distraction from the author and the plays, but that both can best be enlivened by attempting to explain and understand the corpsing of his corpus at the hands of the Shakespeare industry. Underlying this enterprise is the proposition that the hegemonic status of Shakespeare, together with the construction of Jonson as his binary opposite, has had, and continues to have, a corrosive effect on his theatrical as well as his literary reputation. Richard Cave, for example, notes that 'the list of revivals [of Jonson's plays] is short; its brevity is a measure of our cultural loss' (1991: 171). Hopefully, this chapter will contribute to an awareness of the need to view Jonson as more than a supplement to Shakespeare.

I recall being asked by a student in my first year of lecturing, 'Why is Dickens great?' a question which I thought of at the time as being both silly and unanswerable. I still think it is probably unanswerable, but no longer think it silly, and the question of value judgement in literature is a vital and persistent one, if kept in place by no other reason than the urgent desire of students to know why some works are studied/valued and some not, and to learn a discourse which would allow them to discriminate and justify their discrimination. The case of 'S/J' provides what I believe to be the most notorious and revealing example of evaluative discrimination in literary studies. I will set about justifying this claim by noting the way in which 'Brownie points' have been awarded or denied on the basis of a powerful mythology which seems to mediate between critic and text even when a biographical approach is overtly eschewed. I offer the following account of what I take to be a critical orthodoxy:

SHAKESPEARE: Of relatively humble, rural origin; he becomes a success, but is neither a swot nor a sycophant and manages to escape both the taint of commerce and sub-gentility, despite fears expressed in his sonnets. He earns a good living out of his genius and flourishes, apparently effortlessly, leaving it to others to worry about collecting his plays for publication. There is nothing in his biography to seriously stain his high reputation, not even the 'second-best bed' nor the hints of sharp business practice. He retires gracefully from the stage and lives in a rural retreat, benefiting from the paucity of information about his life, and leaving suggestive gaps for others to fill.

JONSON: Also of relatively humble (urban) origin, but his being forced into manual work gives him a chip on his shoulder and long-term aggressiveness. He, too, works his way up to become a success, but only by being a swot and a relentless pursuer of court favour, preferring to write for patrons rather than the market. His classical learning smacks of bookishness and effort, and he imitates rather than creates. Although, like Shakespeare, not a university graduate, he is awarded an MA by both Oxford and Cambridge, reinforcing the impression of bookishness. He is clearly not as close to the springs of Nature as his rural contemporary. We know enough about his life to be able to fix an image, with few gaps to fill, and his famed violent cantankerousness can be set against Will's reputed gentleness. He dies poor and neglected.

SHAKESPEARE: His views are elusive and intentions unknowable. No characters 'speak' for Shakespeare; he remains an enigma. He satisfies our need to proclaim 'natural' genius, elevating the author while denying authorial claims to control textual meaning. His plays are widely celebrated as 'open' texts, leaving us to fill gaps, to appropriate both him and his works so that Left and Right claim to be able to bind him to their colours, making him alternately 'safe' and 'subversive', the universal man for all seasons.

JONSON: He parades his opinions and intentions, seeking to promote the author at the expense of the audience. He craves closure and strives to leave his signature everywhere, fearful of misinterpretation, hostile to proliferation of meaning. It is as if he does his best to stop the critical industry feeding off him by cementing a consistent value system into place. It responds by keeping him and his preference for satire out of fashion. Thus, even while recognising his role in exposing the acquisitiveness of his early capitalist age, he is generally given up as a bad job by the Left.

SHAKESPEARE: He lends himself to later suspicion of commitment, polemic, set ideas or propaganda, and can be used to endorse the dominant political preference for avoidance of 'extremes'. Hence he comes to stand for moderation, impartiality, pluralism and even-handedness. He does not wear his political preferences on his sleeve, and could be said to be ungendered in his gentleness and openness, reflected in his positive representation of women. Perhaps he even gave Jonson his start in the theatre. His greatest modern biographer describes him as 'an innate gentleman' (Schoenbaum 1977: 255). As Prince Charles has recently observed, Shakespeare's plays are transcendentally universal, while managing to be so precisely particular that only Charles and Will could know what it is like to be a Prince of Wales (Windsor 1995).

JONSON: So firm in his stated beliefs that it seems every critic comes to Jonson with an assumption that he is in essence a 'conservative', being an apologist for an absolutist monarchy and a believer in the Great Patron ideal. He presents an image of straightforwardness and lack of sophistication on the level of content. He is malely aggressive, a masculine preference that spills over into his writing, where he reviles both social climbers and uppity women. Far from being grateful to the elder playwright, he is envious and hostile. If only he could have had a more liberal and open-minded world-view, he could have been more like Will. Despite dealing in types or 'humours' he fatally fails to achieve the universality of Shakespeare.

SHAKESPEARE: Although the soul of neutrality he also speaks on behalf of a distinctive way of life, which has come to be associated with England, in particular a Tillyardian, Arcadian England, non-political, ordered but without compulsion, positive but fair, bringing together in harmony a host of disparate opinions, united under a consensual banner of liberal humanism and democracy. As David Riggs puts it in his biography of Jonson:

> [In Shakespeare] lovers run off into the forest, madmen wander on the heath, outcasts find a world elsewhere, but journeys end in lovers' meeting. Longing for a return to those golden days, literary historians have castigated neoclassical plot conventions on the grounds that they were an aberrant intrusion of academic 'rules' into an inherently 'free' field of discourse.
>
> (Riggs 1989: 277)

Such democratic freedoms, rather than rules and regulations, is what free marketeers want, hence 'Shakespeare' has become the brand name to signify the free market. He lends his name to a county and almost to a country; his face appears on beer mats and credit cards as he achieves the status of a cultural icon.

JONSON: Suspiciously 'un-English', the 'Jonson' brand name has never taken off; he seems to offer us none of the reassurances that have been found in Shakespeare. In the hierarchised world of 'S/J' his name is associated with the negative pole in each of the binaries that have been constructed over centuries of literary criticism, which include:

- flat vs round characters;
- satire vs romance;
- rules vs freedoms;
- comedy vs tragedy;
- alienation vs empathy;
- London vs the universe;
- Classical vs Romantic;
- constructionist vs humanist;
- moralistic vs non-judgmental;

- laws vs nature;
- imitation vs originality;
- Art vs Nature.

To arrive at the above orthodoxy, reception of Jonson has had to be filtered through the lens of a set of critical values which are themselves drawn from a Shakespearean model. It is apparent from the Critical Heritage volume on Jonson that the process of demonisation was in evidence well before the nineteenth century. There is extreme antipathy from those promoting a Shakespearean model of writing, who often personalise the contrast in terms of rivalry between the two men, as in the following representative extract from Sarah Fielding and Jane Collier's *The Cry: A New Dramatic Fable* (1754):

> After Shakespeare had nourished in his breast this young and venomous snake, now grown to maturity, and warm'd by his friendly bosom, *Ben Johnson*, like himself that is, like one who possess'd so much of genius to make him grasp at the fame of having all, caught the ears of the multitude by sharp expressions against him, which he call'd humour, and I call spite, and endeavoured to throw all the obstacles he could invent in the way of *Shakespeare's* race to the goal of fame. But *Shakespeare* could never be provoked to return such paltry spite; he, like the strong mastiff, steadily pass'd by the whiffling cur, unheeding of his yelpings.
>
> (Quoted in Craig 1990: 448–9)

Craig himself makes some trenchant observations on the way in which Jonson's reception has been contaminated by his enduring binary relationship with his great contemporary, resulting in what he strikingly calls 'a life and death struggle in which only one mode of creation can survive' (Craig 1990: 20):

> The Shakespeare enthusiasts demanded rivalries and contests rather than any balancing of qualities: theirs was an exclusive, ideological fervour. The new atmosphere encouraged a Shakespeare hegemony and required a clearly identifiable enemy.
>
> (Craig 1990: 20)

It could be argued that this 'atmosphere', supported by 'ideological fervour' is long gone and that we live in more enlightened times in which the marginal has come into its own, as the principal focus in criticism of early modern drama undertaken by New Historicists and cultural materialists in the past two decades. However, this has not been my own experience as a long-standing reviewer of Jonson criticism,[4] which supports the conclusion arrived at by Richard Burt:

> Shakespeare continues to occupy a central place in New Historicist and Marxist

accounts of the theater as a social institution, while Jonson has often been relegated to the margins.

(Burt 1993: 79)

This is part of the more general marginalisation of Jonson criticism from the debates stimulated by the 'theory revolution' in English Studies. It seems that a by-product of the 'S/J' polarity is that a certain sort of critic, and a certain sort of criticism, have come to seem most appropriate to the 'conservative' Jonson, a further detrimental aspect of the 'deadly' binary. On the occasions when new historicist approaches have been applied, they have tended to focus upon the poems or masques or upon Jonson's relationship with the court and the patronage system. This approach links new historicists with the revisionist historians of the period, who also focus upon court circles and see involvement in faction as the crucial site of politics. As a result, Jonson is firmly placed within his milieu, while Shakespeare remains transcendent. Thus new historicism has failed to encourage a reappraisal of Jonson, rather it has confirmed the 'S/J' binary, by reinforcing the established image of Jonson as a conservative. Oppositional readings are not attempted, despite the reactionary new historicist safeguard of subversion being always already contained.

According to D.H. Craig (1990), 'In the twin struggle to establish more Romantic values, and to raise Shakespeare to a national idol, Jonson played a surprisingly prominent part' (79), but it is the contention of this chapter that Jonson's 'prominence' in this 'struggle' to raise a set of values and to secure pre-eminence for Shakespeare is anything but 'surprising'. Jonson had been so *constructed* as to occupy the secondary position in a fundamental binary, one which, as we have seen, has been identified by Derrida as the structural dynamic of Western metaphysics. The outcome has been so debilitating to Jonson's reception that I would argue that there is no other figure within the English canon whose reputation is determined to such an extent by a *relationship* to another artist.[5]

This crippling binary is most commonly summoned up in discussions of character transformation, related in Jonson to the inner workings of the market, rather than the inner workings of the human consciousness. His plays offer us little optimism that there exist powers to counterbalance market forces; short shrift is given to the power of love, so crucial in character transformation in Shakespeare. In Jonson the decentering of the subject appears as an adjunct of the market system, whereas Shakespeare is celebrated as restoring primacy to the self-fashioning subject, confident of transcending or controlling the economic forces which threaten subjectivity. While Shakespeare rises above the materiality of the professional writer's world, Jonson is perennially embroiled in and besmirched by it. What has particularly upset commentators is that the humanist ideal of the integrity of the self is seen as being threatened and this more than anything consigns him to the status of Other. As J. Bamborough puts it, as grounds for Falstaff's superiority (he 'engages our sympathy') to Bobadil: '[Jonson's] principle of Decorum left no room . . . for what makes human beings interesting' (Bamborough 1970: 34). Many critics have concluded that Jonson's apparent alienation from his audience is of a piece with this failure of humanity in his creative art. This 'alienation' would appear to place Jonson in the same camp as Brecht, as has been noted by Richard Cave (1991: 5), both playwrights receiving hostile liberal humanist critique from a value system based on Romanticism, with its privileging of 'feeling' over rational judgement as the defining feature of humanity. Judgement is, of course, central to Jonson's conception of art. For him, as many critics have noted, there can be no room for uncertainty with regard to an audience's response to characters onstage. Here, too, Jonson has become a predictable victim of ideological antagonism, with the ambiguity and openness of Shakespeare's plays being commonly preferred. It is not surprising that Jonson's reputation was at its height when Shakespeare's was at its low point, during the brief ascendancy of neo-classicism in the early eighteenth century, which soon gave way to a strain of humanist/ Romanticist antagonism to Jonson which has dominated ever since, as represented by Horace Walpole's judgement that 'Jonson translated the ancients, Shakespeare transfused their very soul into his writings' (Craig 1990: 489).

The persistence of this binary structure is best exemplified by an essay by Anne Barton entitled 'Shakespeare and Jonson', which can serve as a critical paradigm (Barton 1994: 282–301). Barton does not offer an overtly evaluative comparison, but the deadly 'S/J' binary haunts Barton's 'well-worn series of antitheses' (287). On the Shakespearean side are terms like 'forgiving', 'relaxed', 'cavalier', 'tolerant'; on the Jonsonian, 'punitive', 'moral', 'disjunctive'. Shakespeare is pro-woman, Jonson anti-; Shakespeare's characters learn from experience, 'becoming wiser and better', while Jonson's cannot, being trapped and 'fundamentally uneducable' (292–3). Ironically, Barton is a great apologist for Jonson and she heroically tries to dislodge him as Shakespeare's Other. However, this can only be achieved by discovering a Shakespeare hidden within him, by exposing those overlooked moments in which he comes closest, in her view, to his rival's brand image. This is the basis for Barton's well-known revaluation of Jonson's later plays, in which he comes to his senses, and tries to reproduce rather than resist the 'Swan of Avon'. Thus, in her discussion of *The Devil is an Ass*, she identifies redeeming Shakespearean elements where Jonson 'strikes out bravely in new and unexpected directions':

> Misstress Fitzdottrel behaves as though the real woman has agreed to feel and be guided by the sentiments her imitation has expressed. The theatre dictates to life, not because it is an agent of deceit, as it was in the hands of performers like Volpone, Face, or, in this play, Merecraft the projector, but because it has uncovered a hidden, emotional truth.
>
> (295)

The now familiar polarity is apparent; Jonson as deathly, Shakespeare as a life-force. Perhaps the most painful aspect of this myth-making is that not only are Jonson's plays to be viewed through critical parameters set by his contemporary, but his life is also. He is transformed into a Shakespearean character, but one who is unable to transform himself, as Shakespeare was, and has eventually to abandon the stage, his comic stream dried up and unable to write tragedies, because he had no 'untapped tragic potential left him to explore' (295). Late in life he returns to comedy, the story goes, now confronted by the triumph of the First Folio of 1623 and hence forced to seek to emulate Shakespearean comedy, 'to come to terms with its attitudes, and, up to a point, make them his own' (297). The late plays can be safely celebrated as breaths of Shakespearean life, characterised, predictably, by that most Shakespearean of dramatic features, *transformation*. 'These are people [not characters] capable of change' (301), is the rapturous celebration of late Jonsonian drama. Barton asks for a 'sympathetic reassessment' of what used to be called his dotages, but this can be achieved by collapsing Jonson into his 'great competitor', the late plays becoming simply a 'tribute' to Shakespeare's art.

Barton's acceptance of the 'S/J' binary reproduces a discourse within which Jonson criticism is immobilised. This is not to claim, however, that there have been no attempts to break out of this dominant paradigm. Tom Hayes, for example, has demonstrated that in characterising Jonson as an artist of 'contradictions', there is an alternative approach, which I believe offers a way forward. He identifies a concern with 'self-fashioning' as being at the heart of the Shakespeare–Jonson antinomy, drawing attention to the urgency with which Jonson tries to fashion an authorial persona repeatedly in his plays:

> The effect of all these efforts at self-fashioning – and they are all obviously *failed* efforts – is to remind us continually of his insecurity, of his neediness, of his *lack* of a secure selfhood. Shakespeare *never* inserts himself into his plays. And this has the effect of making us see him as an absolute transcendent ego, as a masterful consummate artist both of himself and of his plays.
>
> (Hayes 1992: 75)

This approach has the effect of 'modernising' Jonson, by focusing on the restless insecurity of the authorial persona rather than the allegedly 'fixed' characters of his plays. Western culture has resisted the view of the 'Real' which represents identity as fixed and predictable, and has preferred Shakespearean idealism, tolerating improbabilities as the price to be paid for a promise of identity in flux and freedom to change, to *choose* to change. This is a contrast noted by Gail Paster:

> In a Shakespearean play the absence of a narrator challenges the audience to produce meaning, to suspend disbelief and accept the scenes, characters, and

language as real; in a Jonsonian play the narrator . . . is given priority, and we are invited to accept this speaker as the authentic voice of the author. This has the effect of constantly drawing our attention to the fact that we are watching – or reading – a play.

(Paster 1993: 75)

Hayes, however, offers a way of deconstructing this typical 'S/J' binary and refashioning Jonson's texts as attempts to 'define a self that is always in progress, always shifting, always rambling, never fixed, never satisfied with itself, never finished' (74), while he argues that at the same time Jonson is 'founder' of what Foucault identifies as the 'author-function' in literature. Thus Hayes's strategy when confronted with Jonson's binary entrapment is to refuse either/or polarities and argue for both/and, as when he argues,

There is no easy answer to the question of whether or not these plays or masques reinscribe the patriarchal ethos or undermine it. Or, rather, the easy answer is that they do both.

(1992: 161)

The subject as 'free agent' and 'centre and origin of action' is, of course, the rallying cry of Western democracy and liberal humanism, while the 'constructed' subject is the nightmare vision of the modern French philosophy underpinning this chapter and of communism, the demise of which has been widely celebrated in Western democracies.[6] Again Jonson can be seen to be on the 'wrong' side of powerful binaries, his inferiority to Shakespeare apparently assured, as we have seen, before a word has been read or spoken on a stage. What has been received as the 'Shakespearean' character is, in political terms, a celebration of the centred self as opposed to the constructed self, and, as Peter Womack pointed out some time ago, 'the beginning of the sovereignty of character is marked by the end of Jonson's viability on the stage' (Womack 1986: 73).

Jonson's plays appear to be closer than Shakespeare's to the capitalist world that we recognise as our own, a world of atomisation, using what Peter Womack calls 'the individuating language of private property' (74), one constructed by powerful media influences, rather than kinship and social bonding based on love. As early as the nineteenth century William Hazlitt had complained about Jonson's characters being 'like machines' and hence lacking the moral dimension of Shakespeare's, and the reduction of humans to 'machine-like' automation is a common concern of the very cultures which accord pre-eminence to Shakespeare. Of course, it could be argued, on the other hand, that the great advantage of centralising Shakespeare in English in the National Curriculum is that it can be represented as celebrating precisely those national traits and values which are most under threat by the economic system which Jonson's plays more graphically depict. For the same reasons, perhaps, our theatres will continue to turn a blind eye to the relevance of Jonson for our own times, as such is the power of the binary logic discussed here that we are unlikely to abandon Shakespeare for a dramatist who shows us our favoured vision of ourselves as free agents collapsing into farcical chaos.

Whereas literary rivalry, as most thoroughly theorised by Harold Bloom, appears rooted in an 'anxiety of influence', with the latecomer striving to kill off the precursor in a classic Oedipal struggle, the 'J/S' opposition is of a different order. Jonson appears to have been used as a scapegoat traditionally has been, to purify and to take upon himself the crimes of the dominant group. Thus, in order for Shakespeare to enjoy an unequalled and unprecedented cultural precedence, Jonson has been formed into a receptacle of negatives. He never stood a chance! But rather than Jonson being transformed into a Shakespearean, as Barton attempts, deconstruction of such a potent and damaging (for Jonson) binary opposition seems to offer the best way forward to achieve a reassessment of Jonson. Such reassessment cannot take place from within the binary discourse analysed in this chapter.

We finish where we started, drawing upon Jacques Lacan. Peter Barry's analysis of Lacan's usefulness for literary critics is relevant here:

> Lacan says that the unconscious is the 'kernel of our being', but since the unconscious is linguistic, and language is a system already complete and in existence before we enter into it, then it follows that the notion of a unique, separate self is deconstructed. If this is so, the idea of 'character', which rests in turn on the notion of a unique separate self, becomes untenable. So a major consequence of accepting the Lacanian position would be to reject the conventional view of characterisation in literature . . . Hence a whole different reading strategy is demanded.
>
> (Barry 1995: 113)

Insofar as such reading strategies have failed to take hold, so Jonson remains firmly ensconced as Shakespeare's Other, unable or unwilling to tap into the universal life-force which shapes our humanity. David Riggs comments that,

> It is an irony of literary history that future readers not only accepted Jonson's claim about Shakespeare's 'natural' genius, but also turned it into an indictment of Jonson, the plodding and laborious exponent of 'art'. In the eyes of posterity Jonson's 'principle function', as Harry Levin says, 'has been to serve as a stalking horse for Shakespeare. Others abide our question, Shakespeare transcends it; and if you would understand, point for point, the limitations he transcends, go read Jonson.
>
> (Riggs 1989: 278)

This chapter has argued that it is necessary to demystify the ideological process of canon formation by which Jonson is reduced to such a 'stalking horse'. Jonsonians need to strive to seek to release him from his entrapment on the horns of a deathly binary, by refusing and refuting its terms; only in this way will his plays be given attention in their own right, relieved of the burden of being viewed as Shakespeare's Other.

Notes

1 Lacan's substitution of Descartes' 'I think therefore I am' by 'I am where I think not' (i.e. in the unconscious, where real selfhood resides) sets up an opposition between the orthodoxy in Western thinking, which this chapter links to Shakespeare, and an ex-centric Other, which it links to Jonson.

2 Harold Bloom's work on the agonistic relations between authors and their precursors is still the starting point for consideration of the battlefield of canonicity. See Bloom 1975.

3 See Derrida 1976: 165–268; and Cixous 1980: 245–64.

4 See *The Year's Work in English Studies* for the years 1987–94.

5 It should be noted, however, that Marlowe has suffered from a similar process. With Shakespeare established as the norm, Marlowe has been comfortably positioned to his left as the dangerous radical, whose flame blazed and burnt out, while Jonson sits on his right, as the dull classicist, courtly, contrived and conformist. M. Maclure's judgement on the critical heritage of Marlowe is that 'It is impossible that Marlowe will ever receive just recognition; he is quenched by Shakespeare.' See Maclure 1979: 22.

6 Linda Charnes argues that 'Shakespeare is the iconic guarantor of liberal humanism [and] . . . the humanist way of reading has been the academy's most successful export into the culture at large.' See Charnes 1996: 268–86 (here 281).

9 Contradictions

Brian Woolland

Mick Jardine observes that many critics have seen Jonson as a conservative with an obsessive desire to assert his authority over the authorship of his work. Theatre practitioners tend to take a very different line. Griff Rhys Jones's assertion that 'In Shakespeare there's nothing to live for if anarchy reigns, whereas for Jonson that's where life really has its foundations'[1] exemplifies the understanding of most of the practitioners we spoke to, who saw Jonson as a subversive radical. 'Jonson never writes about Kings and Queens, that whole moth-eaten hierarchy of privilege and incompetence, but about people like us, working people who work to live . . .' (Peter Barnes).[2]

It is tempting to conclude that the two (incompatible) characterisations of Jonson arise from different points of view: it is hard to see Jonson as an apologist for the Establishment when working on the plays in production – so much wit, insight and theatrical energy is invested in characters of the underclasses; but it is equally hard to see the writer of the non-dramatic poem 'To Penshurst'[3] as a subversive radical. Mick Jardine's sense of the ideological nature of the construction of Jonson as Shakespeare's binary opposite in criticism and biography is useful and revealing, but it must be added that it arises at least in part from the way that Jonson constructs himself through his own writing. He is a profoundly contradictory writer, and the danger of following these accepted 'lines' (either that he is a conservative or that he is a subversive radical) is that to do so flattens out the work and tends to deny contradictions within the plays (and many of the poems) that are inherent and central. In this context the following extract from *A Grace by Ben Jonson Extempore before King James* is revealing:[4]

> Our king and queen the Lord God bless . . . .
> God bless them all, and keep them safe:
> And God bless me, and God bless Ralph.

In *Brief Lives* John Aubrey noted 'The king was mighty inquisitive to know who this Ralph was: Ben told him ''twas the drawer at the Swan tavern by Charing Cross, who drew him good Canary' (Aubrey 1949: 179). However light-hearted the jest, Jonson's role in court seems not unlike the Norwegian god, Loki, who was a god of both laughter *and* mischief. That he could get away with it (Aubrey goes on to recount how the king was so amused by this 'drollery' that he gave Jonson 'an hundred pounds' for it) certainly indicates that Jonson was on excellent terms with the king, but to speak of God, the king and queen, himself and a tapster in the same breath is sailing very close to the wind – especially when one remembers that Jonson had twice been imprisoned (for his shares in the 'lewd' and 'seditious' lost comedy, *Isle of Dogs* and the seditious anti-Scottish satire, *Eastward Ho*) and questioned by the Privy Council on charges of treason relating to *Sejanus*. It is, however, its contradictory quality that makes the little poem so amusing. Flattening out or denying the contradictions is at best a simplification, but more frequently a denial of the way in which the plays work. Indeed the nature of laughter is that it is essentially contradictory.

In editing this present volume we sought – in a Jonsonian spirit – to allow different voices to be heard. Andrew Gurr's argument that 'Lovewit . . . is the exception to the generally moralistic rule of Jonson's comedies, that all the gulls are held up to ridicule for their foolishness while all the knaves are punished in a fitting way for their crimes' appears contested by Genista McIntosh's assertion that he does not judge his characters.

> Jonson comes at you much less obviously attempting to give you a message . . .
> In some way [he is] leaving you to come to the conclusions rather more for
> yourself than Shakespeare often is. Shakespeare is certainly ambiguous on occasions but it's perfectly clear that there are messages. In Jonson there's a less
> superior tone about what he's doing. When you get a good production of some
> of those plays, you come away thinking about human behaviour very actively.
> He's not judgmental. I mean in the end when Volpone and Mosca get their
> come-uppance, you feel that it's right and proper that they should because
> they've been ripping people off. On the other hand there is a bit of you that
> wants them to get away with it because he's given them such extraordinary
> intelligence and ingenuity; and you admire their human ability to make something of their lives, albeit criminally. It's very un-judgmental. I don't think he
> is a moraliser at all.

Could it be not only that both readings are available, that the two apparently contradictory readings co-exist, but that Jonson's theatrical method is to be essentially contradictory? Stallybrass and White have argued that 'Again and again, Jonson defines the true position of the playwright as that of the poet, and the poet as that of the classical isolated judge standing in opposition to the vulgar throng' (Stallybrass and White 1987: 67). They suggest that the published text of *Bartholomew Fair* marks a shift away from the polyphony of popular culture as Jonson attempted to stamp the play with the mark of the single authorial voice. But, just as Zeal-of-the-Land-Busy *tries* to control the puppet Dionysius, so Jonson strives to control his carnival. On the page the significance of Jonson's inductions and prologues may out-weigh the Bakhtinian carnival, but in the theatre it is the characters of the fair who live on because (whatever Jonson may or may not have intended) it is they who have the theatrical energy. The play presents us with a dialogue between the desire for authorial control and Dionysian release. Critics who suggest that *Bartholomew Fair* works against itself ignore the fact that Jonson is writing a play in which the char-acters of the Induction are themselves voices. The prologues to the editions of the plays supervised by Jonson himself may offer another voice, an authorial voice even, but that does not mean we should read that voice as definitively authoritative. The play could not be more explicit about the madness of admitting to but a single authority. Whatever Jonson's apparent intentions, *Bartholomew Fair* (and, indeed, many others of his plays) dramatise and theatricalise discourses about the nature of authority, authorship, control and justice.

The desire to create an image of a 'coherent' Jonson is counter-productive both in teaching and in rehearsal. An approach which attempts to seek out the contra-dictions, to play them up, is likely to expose the social context which creates them and to discover more of the humour in the plays. This might be seen as a Brechtian approach; and, although it is certainly an appropriation of Brechtian methods, it is not intended as some kind of assertion that Jonson was a proto-Marxist. It is, how-ever, worth noting the extent to which Jonson's theatrical methods are echoed by Brecht.[5] Certain aspects of Brechtian practice and Jonsonian theatre seem remark-ably similar: the perception of theatre as an educative medium; the individual seen as a social phenomenon; the emphasis in theatre on telling stories from which audi-ences might learn about their social situations rather than on feeling and 'sharing the inner life of characters'; making audiences as active as possible; making the famil-iar seem strange in order that it should not be seen as inevitable; shifting the perspective from a top-down to a bottom-up view of society. Margot Heinemann has argued that 'The acid test, probably, for a production that has assimilated the most important elements of Brecht's thinking is how it deals with the crowd, ser-vants and lower orders generally' (Heinemann 1985: 248). She then observes that too many contemporary productions of Shakespeare demonstrate a 'revealing con-tempt for "low" characters' (248). Whereas productions of Shakespeare can, and do, survive such attitudes, Jonson's plays do not.

This reveals a crucial difference between Shakespeare and Jonson – in that Jonson writes about the emergent middle class and the underclass, whereas the monarchy and aristocracy are at the centre of most of Shakespeare's plays. It also draws atten-tion to the frequent absence of a single protagonist in Jonson's theatre. This has contributed to the 'difficulty' facing students new to Jonson. Whose play is *The Alchemist*? Subtle's or Face's? *Epicoene* is certainly not the protagonist of *The Silent Woman*. Even *Volpone* belongs as much to Mosca as to the old fox himself. And although *Bartholomew Fair* is a wonderful play to explore in a workshop situation, it is notoriously challenging to read – not least because it constantly denies us the security of a single character's point of view from which to see the events of the fair. Genista McIntosh referred to Jonson's language as 'wonderfully demotic'; the same might be said of his theatrical structures, which of themselves reveal much about the social construction of character.

Adopting the Brechtian strategy of seeking out examples of contradictory behaviour at the heart of the plays can expose important discourses within them. Consider the following examples from *The Alchemist*:

- The 'venture tripartite' needs to work as a group to succeed, yet each member is fiercely independent and competitive.
- In Tribulation and Ananias, Puritanism is inextricably linked to enterprise; and in Mammon, altruism to narcissism.
- The finest is basest.
- Face has no name; and yet he is the only character in the play to be given a 'normal' name.
- Lovewit does nothing; and wins all.
- The promise of transformation tendered by 'the alchemist' transforms nothing. The only real transformation in the play is effected not by the alchemist, not by the venture tripartite, not even by Lovewit the absentee landlord, but by the virtually silent Dame Pliant who transforms Lovewit, making him 'seven years younger' (5.3.86).

This is a far from exhaustive list. Close analysis of any of them, however, will take students to issues at the heart of the play. The first of the above opens up an exploration of the relationship between collaborative action and individual action; the first scene of the play grounds this struggle firmly in its social context. The second leads to an examination of Jonson's treatment of hypocrisy, which might be a useful way in to consideration of the play as social satire.

The third and fourth might take students to analysis of the language games at work and the relationship of these games to issues around the social construction of identity. Drugger and Kastril are desperate to construct themselves, or, perhaps more accurately, to reinvent themselves: Drugger to know how to arrange his shop (and himself) so that he can be a successful shopkeeper; Kastril to know how to talk, how to dress, how to act so that he can be the sort of person that he wants to be. They need instruction. Face offers it; able as he is to change his personality to suit the demands of the moment. This is how you survive. Subtle may be the fount of all (arcane and spurious) wisdom; but Face is the teacher. As a brilliant improviser, he is also an excellent listener, able to 'read' the gulls with insight and precision and give them back what they think they most want. The image is all. Drugger wants to acquire the outward signs of a successful shopkeeper, Kastril the signs of being a 'Roaring Boy'. That he is not a roaring boy does not enter into his thought process. The assumption by Kastril is that in order to become what he wants he has only to wear the appropriate behaviour mask. The implication is that 'Character' can be acquired and the signifier is everything. Face would have promised that Subtle could turn plimsoles into Nike Air Soles if only Kastril had known what to ask for (the Greek god as brand name would surely have been a stock in trade for Subtle had he ever imagined that the business of choosing footwear might one day challenge *chiromancy* as an arcane art). The gulls believe implicitly (because they desperately want to believe) in the transformative power of the venture tripartite's language. 'This ready acceptance of what seems for what is leads inevitably to a fantastic mangling of language, and the fools usually reveal most tellingly the inadequacy of their views of reality by their insensitivity to words . . . By and large Jonson's fools, both great and small . . . cannot understand metaphor' (Kernan 1959: 182–3).

Richard Wilson – with close reference to Roland Barthes (1982) – has argued that 'The generation of '68 learned what Saussure propounded: that men and women are not primarily economic beings, but talking animals, created by and in words' (Wilson and Dutton 1992: 2). Jonson's fools may not understand metaphor, but they most certainly do understand the power of sex and property (even if they are not adept at dealing with either) and if one of the sites of contested power in *The Alchemist* is language (and the appropriation of language), then another is Lovewit's house itself; and ultimately the play can be seen as a struggle between language and property.

I will devote the rest of this chapter to a more detailed analysis of the last two contradictions that I listed above – both of which reveal the implicit interaction between the transformative powers of language, sex and property. It might seem curious to argue that the central site of struggle in *The Alchemist* is the house, given that Lovewit does not return until Act 5, but the *possibility* of his return is trailed in the opening scene of the play when Subtle interrupts Face:

> Who's that? one rings. To the window, Doll. Pray heav'n
> The master do not trouble us, this quarter.
>
> (1.1.180–1)

In theatrical terms the imminence of the master's return not only 'raises the stakes' (to use a Hollywood term), but also focuses our attention on one of the central concerns of the play: the concept of property and ownership. It is worth noting here that fifth-act catastrophes are common in Jonson, and are more far-reaching in their effect than straightforward last-minute twists of plot. In almost every instance they substantially affect our reading and understanding of the meaning of the play(s). The structuring of Colin Ellwood's workshop[6] at the Reading conference enabled participants to focus on the final act of *The New Inn*, not only because the final act demonstrates the multi-layering of meaning within the play, but because understanding this sense of a 'layered' text is so central to understanding the play as a theatrical text. Perhaps the most obvious example of this is in *Epicoene*, where the sensational revelation of Epicoene as a boy should not only make the audience gasp, but also make us reflect on the sexual and gender roles of all the characters in the play. The effect of the shock ending of *Epicoene* is to make visible to an audience what is normally invisible, the construction of gender roles. A similar turn occurs in the greatly underestimated *The Magnetic Lady*, where in the final moments of the play Placentia (hitherto thought to be an extremely wealthy heiress and the eponymous 'magnetic lady') is revealed to be the daughter of the housekeeper, Polish. This late twist (or 'catastrophe' to use the classical term with which Jonson himself describes the play's final act) confirms that the play's central concern is the commodification of women and appears to suggest that sexual attraction is itself a social construct.

In *The Alchemist*, the return of the master at the end of the fourth act to assert his 'rightful' ownership of the house has often been seen as problematic. Lovewit does nothing but takes all, including Dame Pliant. It might be seen that this is a final twist in the satire against romantic comedy; but relating the 'catastrophe' to Jonson's methods elsewhere would suggest that Lovewit's taking possession should be seen as central in reading the play. In this context I want to consider Andrew Gurr's prologue, *Who is Lovewit? What is he?* which opens the present volume, and enables us to place *The Alchemist* firmly within the socio-political, the economic and the institutional context of its own first production.

The challenge that the chapter offers is twofold: first, that the exact meanings intended by Jonson cannot be reproduced in the late twentieth/early twenty-first century; and, second, that this play (and others of Jonson) are 'so securely of his age' that they 'are not for all time'.

The Alchemist dramatises a continuing struggle between cultural power (situated in language) and economic power (situated in wealth, property and social status). Subtle, Face and Doll construct themselves before our eyes; and they do so without recourse to elaborate alchemical mechanisms. They change themselves and they weave their alchemical spells by language and by dress. They are able to fool the gulls because they understand the ideology of each of their victims; and they adjust their language accordingly; they construct themselves according to the needs of the situation; they change – not in the profound metaphysical and/or psychological sense that is sometimes claimed of Shakespeare's characters, but in a material sense and for material gain. This is what they have to do in order to survive; and this is what the play makes clear. Andrew Gurr's revelation about the 'application' of Shakespeare to Lovewit draws attention to the social and economic relationship between Lovewit and Face. It is an absentee landlord whose return enables him to share in the profits of the operation. This creates a challenge for present-day theatre performance of the play not simply because a modern audience is unlikely to know the historical context of the play's original production but because directors (if they are to offer readings of the play that take account of this context) have to find ways of playing Lovewit that clarify his opportunist collusion in the exploitation of the gulls; and make explicit that 'ownership' and 'shareholding' in the house in which the gulling takes place is potentially as important as the gulling itself.

I do not intend to propose specific theatrical strategies for focusing an audience's attention on Lovewit's house as a site of contested power, but rather to suggest that the issue is one which is well worth examining with students – not least because it would enable a teacher to introduce students to some of the analytical tools and methods of cultural materialism,[7] and encourage them to approach Jonson's plays in this spirit of active negotiation and interrogation, provoking such questions as: How might a contemporary theatrical production of the play take account of a cultural materialist analysis? How might our knowledge of the specific conditions of production referred to by Gurr affect our reading of the end of the play?

Stephen Greenblatt has noted: 'This absorption – the presence in the work of its social being – makes it possible, as Bakhtin has argued, for art to survive the disappearance of its enabling social conditions, where ordinary utterance, more dependent upon extra-verbal pragmatic situation, drifts rapidly towards insignificance or incomprehensibility' (Greenblatt 1985: 33). One of the questions that is raised by Jonson's dialogue (peppered with colloquialisms and vernacular references) is whether it remains dependent upon 'pragmatic situation' or has 'absorbed' its 'enabling social conditions' to the extent that the use of language reveals the social. In all our conversations with practitioners the sense of text as live and active was pervasive; and I am convinced that Gurr's research, far from restricting possible meanings, opens the play by focusing on Lovewit's socio-economic role.

The last of the contradictions listed above, which notes that Lovewit's marriage to Dame Pliant will apparently reverse the ageing process, may be a throw-away line on Face's part; but we know Face well enough to know that even his most light-hearted quips are always psychologically acute: they will find their target, because the target wants to be found. Furthermore, the comment links Lovewit to Mammon. In Act 2 Mammon has clearly stated clearly what his aims are in visiting the alchemist:

> The perfect *ruby*, which we call *elixir*,
> . . . Can confer honour, love, respect, long life,
>   . . . In eight, and twenty days,
> I'll make an old man of fourscore, a child . . .
> . . . I mean,
> Restore his years . . .
>   (2.1.48–55)

In Act Five, there is a remarkable coda to this as Lovewit echoes:

>   . . . if I have outstripped
> An old man's gravity, or strict canon, think
> What a young wife, and a good brain may do:
> Stretch age's truth sometimes, and crack it too.
>   (5.5.153–6)

The connection that this creates between Lovewit and Mammon is worth pursuing in that, at the very least, it is a marker of common desire. I am not proposing specific readings of the plays, but rather considering particular approaches to studying/rehearsing the plays that are likely to be productive of meaning. Using this approach with students – seeking out and analysing the contradictions, playing them out in workshops, and relating them to historical research (including Andrew Gurr's essay) – has been very productive with my own students, who have used the work to develop sophisticated arguments about specificity, equivalence and 'application' in modern productions of Jonson and his contemporaries; and have, at the same time, found that this approach, which is grounded in textual analysis and realisation, has given them a substantial grip on theory.

Frank Lentricchia has written that 'Ruling culture does not define the whole of culture, though it tries to, and it is the task of the oppositional critic to re-read culture so as to amplify and strategically position the marginalised voices of the ruled, exploited, oppressed and excluded' (Lentricchia 1983: 15). Students found that working on *The Alchemist* along the lines outlined in this chapter, and attending closely to issues of voice substantially affected their readings of plays by Jonson's contemporaries, including Shakespeare. In particular they felt that the distinctive qualities of Doll's voice and her essential participation in the 'venture tripartite' made the absence of the voices of the prostitutes in *Measure for Measure* very visible. But that's another story.

Notes

1 Griff Rhys Jones, in the programme notes for his 1985 production of *The Alchemist* at the Lyric Theatre, Hammersmith.

2 Extract from the text of Peter Barnes's illustrated workshop-lecture on Jonsonian comedy at the Reading conference on 10 January 1996.

3 'To Penshurst' – a eulogy to the Sidney estate and a harmonious way of life in which all human beings and all creatures know their allotted place in the social frame – was published in *The Forest* (1616).

4 The poem can be found in Ben Jonson's *Ungathered Verse* no. 47. Herford and the Simpsons date the poem to shortly after 1617. The full text of the poem reads:

> Our King and Queen the Lord God bless
> The Palsgrave and the Lady Bess,
> And God bless every living thing
> That lives and breathes and loves the king.
> God bless the Council of Estate,
> And Buckingham the fortunate;
> God bless them all and keep them safe
> And God bless me, and God bless Ralph.

5 This provokes the question of why Brecht adapted Shakespeare, Marlowe and Webster and not Jonson. Because he didn't feel that Jonson needed adapting? Because he didn't like Jonson? Or because he didn't encounter Jonson? Translations of Jonson into other languages are few and far between.

6 Described in Chapter 7, pp. 102–3.
7 Cultural materialist analyses lead to readings of texts which take account both of the cultural and material conditions of production of those texts and acknowledge the cultural position of the reader. Renaissance theatre was *and is* a site of cultural production. Because culture is 'a material determinant of history' it is in itself a site of ongoing struggle. Cultural materialism is multi-disciplinary, in that its analyses make use of historical research, philosophical debates, etc. Cultural materialist critics perceive themselves as oppositional, in that they reveal social processes and social structures, making the invisible visible.

10 The gift of silence

Brian Woolland

'No, let us mark, and not lose the business on foot, by talking. Follow the right thread, or find it.'

(Probee in *The Magnetic Lady*, 4.Chorus.19–20)

Jonson's reputation as a playwright is as a writer who loves words. In this section and elsewhere in this volume we have argued strongly that to be fully appreciated his plays need to be seen in the theatre or studied as theatre. This is at least partly because the apparent nonsense, the notorious lists, the nonce words, are examples of active language use; language used creatively as an active agent by characters who purposely wish to baffle and bemuse, to intrigue and intimidate, to distract and confuse.[1] Jonson's language *is* difficult sometimes, his local references are sometimes obscure, but this should not conceal the fact that some of the problems associated with reading the texts from the page are a product of specific pedagogical and critical methods.

For many students, their only previous knowledge of Renaissance theatre will have been through encounters with Shakespeare; many of them are likely to have studied speeches as poetry and characters as people – with a 'unified network of psychological and social traits; that is as a distinct personality rather than as a functive of dramatic structure' (Elam 1980: 131). These methods, which tend to divorce study of language from its dramatic context, tend to render Jonson's ludic use of language of itself baffling, bemusing and confusing (which is, of course, quite unashamedly part of its dramatic function). In my own experience, students almost always seem to find that reading the texts aloud begins to reveal relationships between the character's voice and the function of the language (a central factor in the theatrical coding of any dramatic text).

Jonson was very much aware of the difference between a performing text and a reading text. Stephen Orgel has shown (1981) the extent to which Jonson revised his plays for publication; but, in spite of Jonson's addition of his own stage directions, there remain theatrical issues in many of the plays that are difficult to identify except through practical work or rehearsal; problems not solved by the simple expedient of reading aloud. As Sam Mendes says:

'We had to sort of decode it as a series of moves, as a series of journeys, as a series of stage shapes. The moment they were up on their feet and playing with each other they realised how alive the language was and how many options it gave them. I think it is very difficult to judge straight off the page.'[2]

The key differences, then, between reading from the page and reading from the stage include the visualisation of character, space and situations; the possibility of keeping more strands of the multiple narrative in view. There is, however, another crucial difference: in a theatrical production the silence of characters can be as significant as their speech.

Restraint and silence are not often thought of as characteristics commonly associated with Jonson's theatre. As Colin Ellwood noted when reflecting on the workshop on *The New Inn*:

'It's easy to see Jonson's work as existing entirely in the written text. But what's not said, and what's understated, is at least as powerful as what is said. Sometimes this is very comical, sometimes very moving.'[3]

In the theatre, when staged sympathetically, his plays demonstrate a remarkably diverse understanding of silence as a theatrical signifier. Close examination of the significance and theatrical power of silence in his plays is crucial to interpreting them – as audiences and as practitioners. Consider, for example, the following extracts from Sam Mendes' account of his rehearsal process for *The Alchemist*:

'There are moments that . . . are for me pure Jonson – like when Face is being the Captain, and he's got the Roaring Boy, Kastril, and he's trying to teach him how to quarrel, and there's a lot of thigh-slapping and shoulder-punching and this sort of stuff; and Kastril is thinking "God this guy's *it*, you know . . ." and Drugger's just watching the scene. He watches them doing their RSC kneel with their legs up on the table . . . and he thinks "I'll try that" – Kastril and Face are talking all the while – and Albie Woodington (who was fantastic as Abel Drugger) gradually, very slowly, put his leg up on the table but he was a little too far away . . . It really is the essence of character acting. I think it pushes you into finding those moments and exploring a character way beyond what appears on the page . . . Every time you see something hinted at in the text it's worth making it graphic.'[4]

Mendes' point that character acting demands visual, graphic stage-images disguises the intuitive decision on the part of the director and the actor to allow a silent character to become the focus of the audience's attention. In the scene referred to here (3.4), Drugger introduces Kastril to Face, but otherwise he seems redundant; and reading the scene from the page would give the sense that it 'belongs' to Face and

Kastril. In the hands of a director less in tune with Jonson, the actor playing Drugger would perhaps be asked simply not to upstage the main event. In Jonson, however (as Mendes recognised), the 'main event' theatrically is frequently not where the reader from the page thinks it is; and this apparently simple shift of emphasis can animate a scene in rehearsal and breathe life into interpretations of the plays.

In a paper given at the Reading conference entitled 'Teaching Jonson in University College, Dublin', Christopher Murray discussed how he refers to the Marx Brothers and to John Cleese when he is introducing students to Jonson. Trying to imagine the Marx Brothers without Harpo, or *Fawlty Towers* without Manuel, gives an indication of the importance of the silent character in comic traditions. Jonson's best-known 'double acts' (Face and Subtle, Volpone and Mosca, Meercraft and Engine) may appear to be masters of quick-thinking repartee, but they all use silence as an essential part of their repertoire, and that should alert us to the dramatic possibilities of silence elsewhere in the plays.

Epicoene

The play in which Jonson most forcefully foregrounds silence as theatrically significant is *Epicoene*, in which the eponymous silent woman is revealed to be neither a woman, nor silent. Morose's desire for silence is presented initially as a symptom of his melancholic humour, or (to use post-Freudian vocabulary) the anally retentive desire to control what we have come to think of, rather possessively, as our very own late twentieth-century problem: the invasion of personal space by noise. I propose here to focus on the play's use of silence as a signifier and to sketch out the dramatic functions of Epicoene's silence in the play.

The form of the play would have seemed initially familiar to a contemporary audience (who might have anticipated that the twist at the end of the play would be that the 'silent woman' would become a virago as soon as she married Morose). As Richard Cave has argued, however, the twist at the end, when Epicoene is revealed to be not a woman, but a cleverly trained boy-actor, subverts the stereotypical and conventional by asking whether the monster who 'finds release after the wedding is any more typical of the quintessentially feminine than the dutiful mouse?' (Cave 1991: 66). *Epicoene* is remarkable for the way in which Jonson subverts the conventional and questions the audience's own assumptions about the much-vaunted Jacobean 'virtue' of silence in a woman. Morose's obsession with silence is presented in fierce contrast with his own garrulousness: 'All discourses, but mine own, afflict me' (2.4.4). His desire to shut out noise is highly selective: an ill-tempered rejection of anything originating outside himself. In this context, his search for a silent wife is clearly presented as symptomatic of a deviant personality, especially given that he only wants marriage in order to disinherit Dauphine. His desire for a silent wife is presented as a manifestation of misogyny; and his misogyny unequivocally linked to cantankerous misanthropy.

Epicoene's silence is of crucial structural importance in the play. As a narrative device it keeps an audience guessing: how long will 'she' remain silent? Who is 'she'? It also implicates other characters (and an audience) through their, and our, attitudes to 'the silent woman'. Just as Epicoene's silence allows Morose to indulge his fantasy of female perfection, so it also seems to provoke Daw and La Foole to sexual boasting (5.1) and encourages members of an audience to indulge our own fantasies (for we are nothing if not voyeurs in a theatre). If the twist of plot at the end of the play forces us to question gender stereotypes and convention, it also makes us think about our own voyeuristic participation in the action of the play, and perhaps leads us to reconsider the very notion of 'the perfect partner' as a fantastical imposition on another.

The Devil is an Ass

Trickery is at the heart of many Jonson plays. We are encouraged to enjoy the tricksters' deceptions – not least because they reveal to us the craft in their craftiness; they show us the art in the artful. But audiences' relationships with the tricksters are complex. They are attractive because they emanate so much theatrical energy. Denied the comfort of passing judgement on the tricksters, audiences are encouraged to examine their own complicity in the action: even in *Volpone*, where the old fox is sentenced to imprisonment, the judgement of the court is itself subverted by the sudden elision of the distinction between actor and role in Volpone's final direct address. Manly's lines (which refer directly to passing judgement on Meercraft and Engine) at the end of *The Devil is an Ass* epitomise Jonson's challenge to us at the end of many of the plays:

> Let them repent them, and be not detected.
> It is not manly to take joy, or pride
> In human errors (we do all ill things . . .)
>   The few that have the seeds
> Of goodness left, will sooner make their way
> To a true life, by shame, than punishment.
>   (5.8.168–74)

I cannot, however, unreservedly agree with Genista McIntosh's assertion that Jonson is 'not a moraliser': if there is a moral drive to the plays it is that the characteristics of the gulls are held up to degrees of mockery, scorn and contempt. Although he defies us to judge his tricksters, there is little room for sympathy for the gulls; the ridicule we feel for them is perhaps the most damning of judgements.

Whereas in *The Alchemist*, Subtle and Face take on all comers, Meercraft and Engine, the tricksters in *The Devil is an Ass*, specifically target Fitzdottrel, who shares with Morose (and John Cleese's Basil Fawlty) an obsession with control which verges on a kind of madness. His behaviour reveals a mismatch between interior and exterior models of reality that is both richly comic and profoundly disturbing. Fitzdottrel's perception that his wife and his clothes are goods for barter is but one strand of a complicated plot; but in each strand his own desire for self-aggrandisement is his undoing. His extraordinary capacity for vanity convinces him that his obsession with conjuring up the Devil will get him a better deal than Faustus. He is a prime target for Meercraft and Engine (and Wittipol) because they all understand what he does not: namely that his real genius is for self-deception, and his blindness lies in his inability to distinguish between his own bizarre perceptions of the world and any rational model of it. His determination to silence his wife, to deny her a voice, to lock her up, to have her schooled in manners by 'the Spanish lady' (Wittipol in disguise) are all symptoms of this 'madness'. It is a madness in which all things and all people are commodities to be bought, borrowed and sold in his own interests. This 'madness' is perhaps most evident in the smug self-satisfaction Fitzdottrel expresses when he thinks he has struck a deal with Wittipol: in exchange for Wittipol's plush cloak, the young gallant is to be allowed fifteen minutes with Fitzdottrel's wife, Frances (of whom Fitzdottrel is obsessively possessive and jealous), on the condition that he always keeps

> The measured distance of your yard, or more,
> From my said Spouse: and in my sight and hearing.
> (1.6.68–9)

Fitzdottrel thinks he has outsmarted Wittipol by insisting:

> What'er his arts be, wife, I will have thee
> Delude him with a trick, thy obstinate silence.
> (1.6.53–4)

When Wittipol 'tastes a trick' in Frances's silence, he 'makes answer' for her, conducting a dialogue between himself and Frances, using Frances's voice to ridicule Fitzdottrel's 'asinine nature'. Frances is actively silenced by her husband; the denial and appropriation of a woman's own voice could not be made more visible. As in *Epicoene*, where the most profoundly misogynist character is a misanthropic and melancholic fool driven by the desire to deny others what he most fears and dislikes, so too in *The Devil is an Ass*, Fitzdottrel's treatment of Frances is held up to ridicule and contempt. His humiliation in this episode results directly from his attempts to manipulate his wife and to deny her a voice of her own. To a modern audience, however, Wittipol's readiness to step in and speak not just *for* her, but *as* her, is a moment that has the potential to be profoundly unsettling. Fitzdottrel's silencing of Frances is an attempt to exploit her as part of a commodity exchange; and although we may laugh at Wittipol's ability to see through the trick, he is effectively colluding in Frances's oppression. As with those moments referred to above in *The Alchemist*, the weighting of the silence is crucial, and the scene has the potential to be far more of an 'open text' than many of Jonson's conservative critics commonly allow. Frances's reaction to Wittipol's appropriation of her voice (which can range from delight through mild-mannered approval to horror) is a key not just to a reading of the scene, but also to modern interpretations of the play.

The Magnetic Lady

> 'Stay, and see his last *Act*, his *Catastrophe*, how he will perplex that, or spring some fresh cheat, to entertain the *Spectators*, with a convenient delight, till some unexpected, and new encounter break out to rectify all, and make good the Conclusion.'

> (The Boy of the House, *The Magnetic Lady*. 4. Chorus. 27–31)

The Magnetic Lady is Jonson's last completed play to be performed in his lifetime. Peter Barnes refers to it as a personal favourite:

> '. . . a blending of satire and fairy tale, realism and fantasy. The framing device of this play is . . . uniquely Jonsonian. Two would-be theatre enthusiasts, Probee and Damplay, go into a shop that sells plays. They want a new play by Ben Jonson and the shop stages his latest, *The Magnetic Lady*, for them.'[5]

As the Boy of the House says, when he offers it to Probee and Damplay, 'An attractive title the author has given it' (Induction 76). But for all the attractions of its title, the play has not had a good press over the years. There are records of three performances of the play in 1632. Apparently the actors took considerable liberties with the text, swearing profusely on occasions, and Inigo Jones ridiculed the play.[6] Jonson himself did not attend any of these performances (the stroke he had suffered in 1628 had left him more or less permanently confined to bed) and the play was scorned and mocked. The text was not published in his lifetime. In 1640 it appeared in the third volume of a new *Folio of the Collected Works of Ben Jonson*. The few published texts of the play are based on this 1640 Folio. In 1987, to mark the 350th anniversary of the death of Ben Jonson, the BBC mounted a radio production of the play, using a text adapted for radio by Peter Barnes with a superb cast, including Dinsdale Landen (Compass), Elizabeth Spriggs (Nurse Keep) and John Moffatt (Sir Diaphanous Silkworm). Barnes recalls that the radio production was a joy; and that every actor who was contacted immediately accepted the invitation to play the offered role. Apart from the radio production, there had been no theatrical revival of the play since 1632.

It had been written off as a 'dotage' by Dryden,[7] and most critics have either concurred with that judgement or damned it with faint praise. Although C.G. Thayer proposes that 'The art that conceals art is . . . so strongly present in *The Magnetic Lady* that one is likely to overlook it entirely' (Thayer 1963: 233), and suggests that this play has 'the neatest of all Jonson's plots', he claims that *The Magnetic Lady* represents a far more 'tolerant' Jonson; a Jonson who is 'resigned and rather amused' (236). The implication is that the play does not have the cutting edge of the earlier plays; and, perhaps more relevantly here, that its tolerance and amusement make it less theatrically vibrant than the great 'middle-period' comedies. Anne Barton refers to it as 'both a self-conscious and an oddly guarded play' (Barton 1984: 295) in which 'Jonson is contemplating the imminence of his own death' (290). She notes its 'cool precision' (299) but she tends to praise Jonson's late plays for their Shakespearean qualities (thereby reinforcing the Shakespeare/Jonson binary). Perhaps the critic who has been warmest in his praise for the play is Larry S. Champion, who considers *The New Inn* and *The Magnetic Lady* to be 'the ageing dramatist's final attacks upon what he considered the decadence of romantic comedy' (Champion 1967: 6). Even here, however, there's a sting in the tail – for he does 'not attempt to defend these works as effective stage plays', contending that they are 'too complex for success on the public stage' (Champion 1967: 7). I note this critical history to focus on the extent to which it is not only possible but necessary to use rehearsal and production as a means of researching Jonson's theatre. Fuelled by Peter Barnes's enthusiasm for *The Magnetic Lady*, I recently directed undergraduates in a production of the play. My interest in it arose partly from its very lack of stage history and partly from a fascination with its highly theatrical and metatheatrical qualities. What follows is an account of the discoveries that were made by myself and the company of undergraduates who worked on the production (performed at the University of Reading in December 1996), which provided an opportunity to clarify and experiment with many of the approaches to rehearsing and exploring Jonson through practice that have been outlined in this section. None of the cast had ever before acted in a Jonson play; none of them had heard of *The Magnetic Lady*. We approached rehearsals as a collaborative exploration. Perhaps one of the most gratifying aspects of the production was the extent to which relatively inexperienced actors became confident with Jonson's language, and grew to enjoy it. Audiences, too, were very positive about the play and the production (even young children seemed perfectly capable of following the plot). This does, perhaps, shed an interesting light on Sam Mendes' assertion that for Jonson 'You need wonderful acting from top to bottom and it's very difficult in a company outside the RSC or The National.' The wonderful acting, is, of course, desirable; but student productions can clearly be immensely pleasurable and rewarding both for actors and audiences. What is needed is time to explore the text thoroughly and playfully, time to find the driving forces of a play. In this context, Mendes' discovery through his rehearsals of *The Alchemist* that 'the real comedy comes from the gulls, and they do a lot of the work; they motor the play . . .' was immensely stimulating, and set a continuing task, an overriding aim for many rehearsals: to find the 'comic motor' of *The Magnetic Lady*.

Compass appears to be the central character in the play. He persuades his brother, Ironside, to assist him to organise a banquet in Lady Loadstone's house. Thayer (1963: 240–1) suggests that Ironside is Compass's alter ego. Although I was not wholly convinced by the argument, I did find it useful in that it led to explorations of the notion of pairings within the play. Jonson's names may be archetypes – Face, Subtle, etc. – but they are always precise. Needle is, of course, an excellent name for a sexually active tailor; but, given the title of the play, we might assume that Needle and Compass are closely associated. By the end of the play we know that Needle is the father of the 'false' Placentia's child and has to marry her, whilst Compass will marry the 'true' Placentia and inherit the fortune. In theatrical terms, the association did not deliver much in itself; but as we explored it, it became increasingly evident that Compass functions as a trickster. He may be more apparently benign than Face or Meercraft, but he is just as much an opportunist, throwing everything into the air, turning the world upside down (with the help of his brother, Ironside) and waiting to see what gives . . .

Compass is, however, not the only trickster operating in the play: Polish (the housekeeper who substitutes her own child for the heiress) also tries to turn the world upside down. Her attempts to subvert the aristocratic inheritance of priv-ilege and wealth may ultimately be foiled, but in attempting what she does, she demonstrates an acute awareness of her social class and status. She may proclaim that she knows 'To yield to my Superiors,' (1.5.44), but she is driven by her determination to get her own daughter, the 'false' Placentia out of the poverty trap:

> . . . a Lady
> Of the first head I'd have her; and in Court . . .
> And be a viscountess to carry all
> Before her . . .
>
> (2.3.57–60)

At the end of the play she is forced to admit:

> I plotted the deceit, and I will own it.
> Love to my child . . .
> Provoked me . . .
>
> (5.10.85–7)

Crucially, in terms of the judgement of characters, she is not gulled. Polish may not achieve what she wants, but it is Sir Moth Interest, Politic Bias, Sir

Diaphanous Silkworm, Doctor Rut, Parson Palate and Master Practice who are ridiculed.

The words 'business' and 'commodity' appear no less than thirty-five times in *The Magnetic Lady*. It is a play whose central concern is the commodification of women: Placentia, at the age of fourteen, is 'ripe for a man, and marriageable'. The plot hinges on the legal catch which makes it impossible for her to gain access to her personal fortune unless she accepts one of the dreadful suitors. That much is clear from a first reading of the play. Early on in rehearsal it became clear that Polish is the 'comic motor' of the play; and that the theatrical energy of the play lies to a remarkable extent with the women and with the 'below-stairs' class.[8] In *The New Inn* (in many ways a companion piece to *The Magnetic Lady*), the nurse (Lady Frampul's mother in disguise) makes a telling indictment of Stuart society. When she asks Lord Beaufort 'Is poverty a vice?', he replies unhesitatingly, 'The age counts it so.' She retorts: 'God help your Lordship, and your peers that think so . . .' (5.5.56–7). Bearing this in mind, and given the effervescence of the scenes in which the women appear without men, we were prompted to ask, 'Just who is the "Magnetic Lady" . . .?'

The title is itself enigmatic. In the Induction, the Boy of the House tells Probee and Damplay:

> The author . . . hath fancied to himself, in idea, this Magnetic Mistress. A Lady, a brave bountiful housekeeper, and a virtuous widow: who having a young Niece, ripe for a man, and marriageable, he makes that his Centre attractive, to draw thither a diversity of guests . . .
>
> (Induction.99–109)

From this some critics have read Lady Loadstone as the 'Magnetic Lady', but the syntax is not clear. Is the 'centre attractive' the Lady or the young niece? 'The essential accompaniment to the magnetic needle was a lodestone with which to magnetise it and with which to keep it magnetised, for iron loses its magnetism unless specially treated' (Waters 1958: 22). Lady Loadstone effectively 'magnetises' her niece. Thayer has noted that Lady Loadstone's house functions, like Lovewit's, as a comic theatre (1963: 243); but the similarity with Lovewit's house does not end there. As in *The Alchemist*, the gulls come swarming to the house in the hope that they will be transformed – in this instance not by alchemy, but by marriage and the prospect of wealth inherited by proxy.

If Placentia is the eponymous Magnetic Lady, the 'centre attractive', then her silence throughout most of the play becomes theatrically highly significant. In the whole play she speaks only *five* lines, all of them in the second act, yet she appears in no fewer than ten scenes. Placentia apart, the women in *The Magnetic Lady* are not silent; far from it. The structure of the play itself draws attention to her silence. And when her voice is heard she is a cynical commentator on her own situation. 'And will you make me a viscountess too?' (2.5.76) she asks Sir Diaphanous Silkworm, then wryly adding before he has a chance to reply:

> How do they make a countess; in a chair,
> Or on a bed?
>
> (2.5.77–8)

Placentia's silence becomes increasingly uncomfortable. Her silence and Frances Fitzdottrel's are demonstrably imposed upon them by specific social situations. Their silence may be passive, in that neither character is seen to be someone who *chooses* silence for herself, but the dramatic function of the silence is theatrically active in that theatrical realisations of *The Magnetic Lady* and *The Devil is an Ass* can focus the attention of an audience on it. This is what we chose to do in the Reading University production. The most notable effects of this were firstly to create a sense that this was Placentia's play, and secondly to make the ending of the play profoundly uneasy and disturbing (see Plate 5, p. 137).

As the play ends, Ironside is to marry Lady Loadstone and Compass is to marry the 'true' Placentia. The brothers have landed on their feet, each of them about to achieve what all the gulls have striven for: transformation through wealth. To claim, as Thayer does, that 'The two couples are paired off as they are because nature is chaotic without morality . . . ' (Thayer 1963: 245) is to deny the moral drive of the play. Compass tricks his way into marriage with Pleasance (the 'true' Placentia) and he is able to do so for no other reason than that he has been fortunate enough to overhear the argument between Polish and Nurse Keep which exposes the swapped-baby plot. If this is Jonson's version of romantic comedy, it is deeply ironic.

The twist of plot at the end of *The Magnetic Lady* may not actively shift an audience's perception of gender roles, sexual stereotypes and conventions to the extent that the ending of *Epicoene* does, but as in *Epicoene*, a silent woman is revealed to be other than what she seems. And, as in *Epicoene*, silence itself can potentially become a focus of the play. Focusing on the silence of characters like Placentia, Frances Fitzdottrel, and even Dame Pliant may not of itself amplify their voices, but directors and actors can use it to position these characters in such a way as to foreground issues of exploitation, oppression, brutalisation and commodification.

In this brief consideration of four plays, we have seen Jonson using silence as an active signifier in very different ways. Any rehearsal process that does a Jonson play justice needs to explore these silences; and I would suggest the strategy would be equally productive in a workshop situation. The work might begin, for example, with a simple exercise in which workshop participants are asked to consider any given scene from the point of view of each of the non-speaking characters. This can provide useful insights, especially if the participants are encouraged to shift away from a psychological approach – 'What do you feel about what's going on?' – and towards something more visual, 'What does Drugger/Placentia/Frances/Dame Pliant *see* here?'

Sam Mendes spoke of 'the gift of the actor' in Jonson's theatre. Silence in Jonson's plays is a gift for the actor, the teacher and the director. To ignore it, to leave the silence of those characters who do not speak in a scene unweighted and unfocused, is to deny a key theatrical signifier and to pass up golden opportunities for exploring the meanings of these plays for modern audiences. To honour the silences and to seek to explore their potential meanings for modern audiences through workshop and rehearsals begins to address those critics who would themselves restrict the available meanings within the plays by insistently linking their readings to but one of Jonson's many voices.

Notes

1 Christopher Murray gave a paper at the Reading conference entitled 'Teaching Jonson in University College, Dublin', in which he noted references to Jonson in the work of James Joyce:

> When Stephen Dedalus has the discussion with the Rector of the university (to become University College, Dublin, in 1909) he sees the Rector as a countryman of Ben Jonson. Stephen does not think of the Rector as a countryman of Shakespeare but of Jonson . . . In *Dubliners* we are given a cross-section of pretenders, double dealers, self-seekers and hypocrites, for whom language is never neutral but always charged with moral meaning. For Joyce as for Jonson, character is defined and discriminated by the choice of words employed, whether voiced publicly or internalised. The opening of *Ulysses*, where Buck Mulligan parodies the opening of the Mass as he bids good morrow to the day with his shaving bowl on the roof of the Martello Tower at Sandycove invites direct comparison with the opening scene of *Volpone*, where Volpone blasphemously elevates a piece of gold as the world's soul. More broadly, the way in which Ulysses traverses the whole of Dublin, high and low, in the course of a single day, and lets us hear speech and dialogue in countless settings unified by the sense of Dublin as the world, is Jonsonian if we take *Bartholomew Fair* as representative.

2 Interview with Brian Woolland (p. 80 of this volume).
3 Colin Ellwood in his workshop on *The New Inn* at the Reading conference.
4 Interview with Brian Woolland (pp. 81–2 of this volume).
5 Extract from Peter Barnes's lecture, given at the Ben Jonson and the Theatre conference, 10 January 1996.
6 Herford and the Simpsons' brief account of the early stage history of the play includes the following 'scurrilous lines' by Alexander Gill the younger:

> And Inigo with laughter grew fat
> That there was Nothing worth the laughing at.'
> (Herford and the Simpsons, vol. 9: 253)

7 Herford and the Simpsons, vol. 2: 204.
8 In their *Introduction to The Magnetic Lady*, Herford and the Simpsons note that 'Women figure in unusual numbers among the characters and play an even more than

correspondingly important part in the action . . . In *The Magnetic Lady* the dramatic capacities of feminine intrigue are explored with a security rarely exhibited elsewhere than in this play . . . The below-stairs women have all touches of vivacity, and the "gossip and she-parasite" and arch intriguer, Polish, is perhaps the best woman Jonson ever drew' (Herford and the Simpsons, vol. 2: 208–9).

Plate 5   'The silent Placentia' in the 1996 University of Reading production of *The Magnetic Lady*, showing from left to right: Polish (Rosemary Hughes), Placentia (Nicola Disney) and Silkworm (Edwin Wills).
(By kind permission of the photographer, Lib Taylor.)

Plate 6 Pug (John Dougall) being subjected to the *gaze* and predatory hands of Lady
Tailbush (Sheila Steafel), while Fitzdotterel (David Troughton) feigns lack of interest, in
Matthew Warchus's 1995 production of *The Devil is an Ass*. Note the details of the design by
Bunny Christie: the central placing of Pug on the circular table and, above, the gilded
model of Jacobean London.
(By kind permission of the photographer, Ivan Kyncl.)

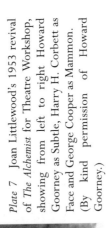

Plate 7 Joan Littlewood's 1953 revival of *The Alchemist* for Theatre Workshop, showing from left to right Howard Goorney as Subtle, Harry H. Corbett as Face and George Cooper as Mammon. (By kind permission of Howard Goorney.)

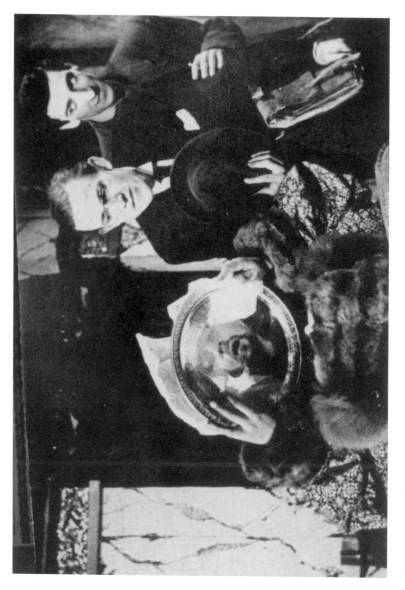

Plate 8 Joan Littlewood's 1955 staging of *Volpone* in modern dress for Theatre Workshop, showing from left to right George Cooper as Volpone, John Moffat as Voltore and Max Shaw as Mosca.

Plate 9 Geoffrey Rush as Subtle and Hugo Weaving as Face in Neil Armfield's 1996 staging of *The Alchemist* at the Belvoir Street Theatre in Sydney. (By kind permission of the photographer, Heidrun Löhr.)

Interlude II

Genista McIntosh: Casting and marketing Jonson[1]

I studied *Volpone* for A-level. That was my first major confrontation with Jonson. I remember not feeling as drawn to him as I was to Shakespeare – which I was doing at the same time – and some of what I felt at the time I probably still carry forward which is a sense that Jonson sometimes gives you a hard time as an audience or as a reader – he makes you work very hard, and it is more difficult to dig into it and make connections with it. But I have got fonder of Jonson as the years have gone by. That's always to do with performance. Things that are written to be performed in the end don't really take life until you see them performed.

Although I studied Jonson at school, my children didn't; they studied Shakespeare and I don't think either of them – both of whom did A-level English – will ever have read a Jonson play. They've seen them; but they will not have come at them as a separate bit of study.

When the Swan opened at Stratford and lesser-known plays started to get done there – there was a significant broadening of our understanding of who Jonson was. When you're being glib and cynical you say if a play hasn't been done for three hundred years there's probably a very good reason, but the Swan was set up partly to challenge that and to say there is this enormous body of work, most of which is not performed because nineteenth-century theatre conventions don't suit it. The Swan gave us the opportunity to look at certain plays again and some of them did emerge well and did seem to have a kind of newness and sparkiness which nobody had quite understood up to that point.

The New Inn at the Swan was a play I didn't know at all, and actually, of all the Jonson plays that I've been in and around, it was the one that was least successful as an audience-pleaser. They liked it, but they didn't really get it. And the actors never felt entirely comfortable with it. It struck me as less vibrant, less vivid and alive than some of Jonson's other plays. The RSC did *The New Inn* because John Caird was the director and he at that time was very keen on digging around in the lesser-known Jonson plays; and *The New Inn* had a very good part for Fiona Shaw. You start with a director and a play.

Trying to cast *The New Inn* was considerably less easy in my experience than casting *The Alchemist* or *Volpone* and there are three reasons for this: firstly, people are familiar with *The Alchemist* and *Volpone*; secondly, the characters are much more achieved; thirdly, even the better-known Jonson pieces are still quite a challenge for actors. Actors like John Nettles and Simon Russell-Beale are highly intelligent, literate men and probably have a way into Jonson which includes some kind of intellectual response to the pieces as well as their instincts and skills as actors but somebody without that background can get a bit phased by some of it. The language is tricky.

Bartholomew Fair is interestingly a play which is difficult to cast. The risk is undercasting. With Jonson's plays you have to get the mechanisms very well oiled; the style and the speed and the accuracy of the playing are quite critical in how the comedy works. You can't linger or hang about with it and think about it very deeply. If you have people that aren't up to speed, it can go very soggy.

Something similar applies to *The Alchemist*. You can have people working away very hard at the top – but you can't get the thing going – and if you have too much energy going in at the top and not enough going underneath it falls flat. Sam Mendes' RSC production of *The Alchemist* worked because of the sheer brilliance (and I use the word advisedly) of the playing. It was so quick, and the actors were so tuned to one another, it was like watching a tennis match or a very, very smart bit of team sport, they were playing it with a kind of deftness that you just don't very often see. Some people didn't like that production because they thought that that was all there was to it, that it was a bit slick, but it's the best production of *The Alchemist* that I've ever seen *because* of that. Jonson demands a kind of bravura, a kind of daring from actors that actually Shakespeare doesn't. It's a much gentler kind of energy that you need to make something like *Twelfth Night* or even *The Comedy of Errors* (which is pretty helter-skelter) work and you don't need that driving, linear energy in the same way as you do in a lot of Jonson. That's why Jonson's plays are rather wonderful because, once they get going, they carry you along in a way that takes your breath away when they're going at speed.

You do need really good actors all the way down with Jonson, an ensemble, because they do have to inhabit, to have a world and a life for those characters. It's also a problem if you don't have *time* or resources to think about what you're doing. On the surface Jonson's are plays that you can throw on fairly quickly – get the plot going and all's well – but then you start to ask yourself who these people are. Who are Subtle and Face? What have they been doing before the play started? Why are they engaged in this extraordinary con racket? You have to ask some of those questions so that what the actor brings on is a history that the audience can get very quickly.

There is a problem with casting Renaissance plays now: when you come to cast in depth with those plays, there is a lack of skill in certain areas because actors don't get to practise certain ways of actually *being* on the stage, which means that you sometimes get a rather uncomfortable bumping of a modern sensibility with a very much more classical text. The traditions of classical acting are being handed on less well than perhaps they should be. The problem is not as bad with Jonson as with some playwrights, because Jonson rolls along being 'of now' pretty much all of the time; you also need modernity to play Jonson. The RSC has fairly consistently – not every year, but most of the time – kept alive a tradition of playing Jonson. But whether in fact there are different skills and a different sensibility from this, which you need to play Shakespeare or Webster or Marlowe, I'm not sure.

Marketing Jonson? These days what you really need to market is not just Jonson but an awful lot of other things as well. Particularly with a Jonson you need an actor or actors that people will recognise, because audiences are much less prepared to take risks with that sort of work now than they were twenty or thirty years ago. Who you'd market to is an audience that is fundamentally the core audience for Shakespeare who will venture out into the Jonsons which they feel they are familiar with, but who are a little bit worried that they might not have a very good time at the lesser-known Jonsons.

You're also trying nowadays to sell those plays as being in the same territory as work with which a younger audience might be more familiar and that's pretty difficult. You can try to tap the plays into another kind of audience by hooking in a modern sensibility through a writer. That is what Trevor Nunn did with *The Alchemist* when he got Peter Barnes involved in it, because Barnes is a Jonsonian spirit, but also, at that time, he had had these great big successes with his own plays in the preceding decade.[2]

What we did with *Volpone* was to cast Michael Gambon who had been out of the theatre for quite a long time and had been saying that he wanted to come back but we couldn't hit on the thing that he wanted to do. We felt Volpone was a very good part for him and it was a happy accident that the play and the director and the actor were sympathetically linked. The previous time that the National did *Volpone* it had Paul Scofield and Ben Kingsley and John Gielgud as Sir Politic; you don't get much more classy than that. I don't know how well the RSC did with *The Devil is an Ass*, but they did have John Nettles in it and he's known for television and that would have brought in a certain audience that perhaps wouldn't have bothered to come to see *The Devil is an Ass* with Joe Bloggs. I suspect that for John Nettles Jonson is close to his own sensibility, close to where he *is* as an actor and so he is much more relaxed in that sort of world. There is a demotic quality in Jonson's writing, which, if you can catch an actor, like John, who combines an ability to understand the complexities, the mechanisms both intellectually and as an actor, but also is of now, is modern, you do get a very extraordinary kind of spark. Actually Gambon has the same thing; he has tremendous presence but he's also a very modern, rather urban character.

If you were going to market *Sejanus*, you would probably have to do it either in an environment like the Edinburgh Festival, where you've got very young actors and nobody is being paid, or in a very, very protected environment such as one of the big subsidised companies where it would spin off from other things. What you could not do is stage it in a context where it would have to bear very much weight in terms of how many people you're going to get to go and see it. Ian McDiarmid is an actor who should have played much more Jonson than he has but I fear that unless you had the likes of him, Ian McKellen *and* Paul Scofield in *Sejanus* people wouldn't come. I don't know how you crack that.

With marketing you have to acknowledge that people have this vision of Shakespeare as the Great Master against which everything else is measured; and it is really difficult to create a different view not just of Jonson but also of the other Jacobean writers who are also seen as being somehow connected to Shakespeare even though their sensibilities are entirely different. That problem is likely to get worse rather than better; and when you come to market them you're stuck with this difficulty of, on the one hand, not wanting to say, 'Come to this because it's quite like Shakespeare' (because it isn't) and, on the other hand, wanting to say to people you know would come if they thought it were like Shakespeare, 'Do come to this'. It's quite complex and when people who come think that they are going to get something that's pretty much like Shakespeare and are unfamiliar with Jonson and are then confronted with Jonson, they do go a bit glassy-eyed; because it's absolutely not at all what they expected. They *can* have a very good time, but sometimes they are just confounded by it.

You can make a comparison with opera: the known repertoire is *very* small. There are composers who are very good but have suffered by living in the shadow of somebody who is thought to be better – in exactly the same way that Jonson suffers. And even the composers who are the 'big hitters' – Verdi, Puccini – suffer. Audiences will come for *Otello* and *La Traviata* but there is this 'top soil' that everybody knows and it's very, very difficult to get an audience to respond enthusiastically outside quite a narrow band of repertoire; and they're not very good at tackling new work.

Jonson additionally suffers from not being thought to have literary merit in the way that Shakespeare does, or even that Webster does, or Marlowe. This means that the dependency on performance is even greater. There's a sort of literary snobbery. You can't point to specific passages in Jonson and say 'This is Great Literature' in the same way you can with Shakespeare. It seems entirely paradoxical that because Jonson's a great theatre dramatist he should therefore suffer from not being performed in the theatre.

Both the RSC and the National try to incorporate all their classical work into their educational programmes; but to an extent you are dependent on the market, what people want. And both organisations these days tend to be led slightly more than they used to be by what they're asked for. That comes from a variety of different sources. It comes sometimes from teachers. It'll come from the A-level syllabus and GCSE and further down. But when you're dealing with Jonson plays, then you tend to be dealing with sixth formers and above.

At the RSC the Jonson plays have tended to come late in the season for several reasons: the company would by then have had some experience of getting a real company *feel* before actually tackling Jonson; but also Jonson is still relatively quite hard to sell so we tended to keep a Jonson until we had several other things in the repertoire to support it, so it wouldn't be too exposed, which it would be at the front end of a season where there might be only one other show in the rep.

What *can* market Jonson is the fact that the revival of interest in Jonson is absolutely not accidental and absolutely not just to do with the Swan or smaller playing spaces becoming popular; and it *is* to do with the way that our social organisation is nowadays and how Jonson maps onto that. And yet at the same time, despite the number of productions that there have been of a variety of his plays over the last twenty, thirty years, Jonson is still hard to market.

Part of the problem is that comedies are hard to market. Modern audiences are not good at sitting through very long comedies. They don't mind sitting there for four hours if they think it's doing them good and it's *King Lear* and they can come away thinking that they've had a very serious experience but they're less keen on something that's supposed to be funny going on for three and a half hours – which *Volpone* can easily do.

Comedies, and particularly comedies that are of another age, are also risky enterprises. They survive less well. With comedy it's pretty unambiguous if you fail and there are too many elephant traps in them into which you can disappear very suddenly and comprehensively. You can do an indifferent production of *'Tis Pity She's a Whore*, for example, but in some ways the grandeur of the themes and the terrible dénouement with the blood on the carpet will transcend it; whereas if you've had an unfunny evening with *Every Man in his Humour* you've had an unfunny evening and that's it. Jonson suffers from the fact that his great tragic or epic work is even less well known than his comedies.

With Shakespeare's comedies – people think they're being done good to by Shakespeare no matter what he's doing – whether it's *King Lear* or *Twelfth Night* or *Comedy of Errors* – and I find that extremely annoying because I don't think you should go into any theatre expecting to be 'improved'. But in Shakespeare's comedies he manages to be more clearly attempting to give them some kind of moral weight than Jonson is. Jonson comes at you much less obviously in attempting to give you a message. Jonson isn't entirely distanced from the moral questions that he raises but he is in some way leaving you to come to the conclusions rather more for yourself than Shakespeare often is. With Shakespeare it's ambiguous what he's trying to tell you – but it's perfectly clear that there are messages; but in Jonson there's a less superior tone about what he's doing. He actually respects an audience's intelligence. Because when you get into a good production of a Jonson, you come away thinking about human behaviour very actively. He's not judgmental. When Volpone and Mosca get their come-uppance, you feel that it's right and proper that they should because they've been ripping people off. On the other hand there is a bit of you wants them to get away with it because Jonson's given them such extraordinary intelligence and ingenuity; and you admire their human ability to make something of their lives albeit criminally. I don't think Jonson is a moraliser at all.

One of the things that liberated Jonson again for our generation of theatre-goers was the advent of small spaces because when you get Jonson's plays in a little room, where the actors aren't having to push it out and when you can dwell on the almost surreal complexities of character and situation that he gives you (but you're looking in on it very much more intensely than you can from behind a proscenium arch), then I think that releases his quality as a dramatist.

The thing that really sets Jonson apart is the city base, the kind of profoundly urban and streetwise tone and atmosphere of the plays. They're not courtly; fundamentally, they are plays about people who are hacking life out of pretty raw material; and that makes them in some ways ideal for modern actors to tackle and, if you look at Jonson in the context of writing for television or writing for the theatre now, there's a much more obvious direct line than there is between most other contemporaries of his and modern writing. Not the very posh television drama but a lot of run-of-the-mill television drama which relies upon being familiar with certain ways of being, with people in certain situations, and a kind of character that is reliably who it is, and it doesn't very much matter what's happening because you just tune in and tune out again at different times; but there's that sense of it being a world and a set of circumstances that we recognise, that we know about. And Jonson does this, he's giving you a slice of something that people can recognise and feel familiar with immediately, even though bizarre and ridiculous things then happen.

There is still this gap in the way that our language has mutated and that's more true because of the immediacy and demotic quality of Jonson's language; just as some of what Mark Ravenhill, for example, is writing now will be lost in fifty or a hundred years time, and people will be saying, 'What on earth was that joke about? What was that contemporary reference that seems to motor this whole section?'

Cutting is virtually unavoidable because Jonson's plays are so long. The RNT *Volpone* was certainly three hours and yet Matthew Warchus did cut that. I don't have any particular axe to grind about editing either in itself or in relation to particular texts or authors but Jonson writes in a way which gives the appearance of being less sacrosanct; there's a sort of roughness – he has occasional flights of such absolute brilliance that he's as good as anybody ever – but at other times you don't get the feeling that he was writing very reverentially; he didn't regard his own work with any great reverence. Perhaps he did, but you don't *feel* that he did.

Cutting is an issue for modern audiences, although there's a slightly vogueish thing about playing a full text now. There are directors who make it an article of faith that they play a Full Text but I don't think you could do that with Jonson.

There was a time when what we got of Jonson in the theatre was in versions like Peter Barnes's version of *The Alchemist*. There were various writers at various times who took a hacksaw to a play and also added their own gloss and rethought it. That's marginally less fashionable now. There's been a tendency in more recent productions (this is just an impression) to let the plays largely stand or fall on their own merits. But you have to do *some* editing.

I very much like *The Devil is an Ass*. I think it's delightful and very funny; and a wonderfully 'off the wall' kind of play, quite a surreal invention. I would like to see *Epicoene* again; maybe now it would have a different kind of resonance. I've only ever seen that once. I do think that *The Alchemist* and *Volpone* are as good in their way as any plays that have ever been written. I mean simply that in terms of the achievement of intention and their stature as living pieces of theatre, they are as good as anything Shakespeare wrote.

Notes

1 The material for this Interlude is edited from an interview which took place on Thursday, 21 August 1997.

2 Peter Barnes's adaptation for Trevor Nunn's 1977 production chiefly involved cutting the text to streamline the action and modernising the language. Peter Barnes is a self-professed Jonsonian, a writer and director whose plays for the theatre include *The Ruling Class* (Nottingham Playhouse and Piccadilly Theatre, London), *The Bewitched*, *Red Noses* (both for the RSC) and *Laughter* (Royal Court). He has adapted and directed *The Devil is an Ass* and *The Magnetic Lady* for radio. His television work includes *Revolutionary Witness* (BBC). He was nominated for an Oscar for the screenplay of *Enchanted April*, and regularly writes for British and American television.

Part III

Marginalised Jonsons

Elizabeth Schafer

11 Introduction

Elizabeth Schafer

Genista McIntosh's discussion offers an appropriate introduction to this section. McIntosh is an immensely powerful voice in British theatre and yet because she does not work in the areas which get most high-profile attention in the media – acting and directing – her name is not well known to the general public even though she has such a major part to play at the Royal National Theatre, as formerly at the Royal Shakespeare Company, in determining what plays the public will see, who plays which roles and how the public will be targeted in terms of marketing. In a sense her professional location puts her on the margins in terms of the dominant public perception.

The margins in operation in this section are those brought into play first by gender and secondly by geography. Thus this section concentrates on theatrical responses to Jonson by women, predominantly in the UK, and then theatrical responses to Jonson in Australia. It seeks to examine the theatrical productions under consideration in some detail to compensate for the marginalisation of these responses in traditional mainstream Jonson scholarship; however, being positioned on the margins, as much recent feminist and post-colonial criticism has suggested, can simultaneously offer empowerment as well as disempowerment; margins offer a position of low status, from the perspective of the patriarchal and/or imperial centre, but much freedom, away from the policing gaze routinely operating nearer to the perceived centres of power.

12 Daughters of Ben

Elizabeth Schafer

Jonson still has something of a testosterone-ridden image. Peter Barnes claimed that Jonson needs playing 'with balls' and 'groin heat'; Simon Russell-Beale described Jonson as 'a young man's playwright' because 'there's something about those plays that is very cynical, that can take a lot of macho things thrown at them'; John Nettles agreed with Beale and went on to characterise Jonson's writing as showing 'a great flashiness, a great desire to show off – bang! wallop! look at this theatrical effect! this *coup de théâtre!*' Sam Mendes characterised Jonson as a playwright who in today's terms could be seen as a beer-drinking, non-PC lad.

Jonson's many, eloquent articulations of misogyny in his plays have undoubtedly contributed to his image of Renaissance man behaving badly, anti-feminist, boozing at the tavern, loud-mouthed and boorish. Not surprisingly, many feminist scholars of the early modern period have been less than enthusiastic about Jonson's work, which at worst is 'misogynist' and at best is baldly and uncompromisingly reminding us that Jonson inhabited a fallen, misogynist world which, unfortunately, is in some respects only too familiar.[1] Feminist discomfort with Jonson is perhaps most paradoxically on display in the work of the high-profile media feminist Rosalind Miles, who sadly records Jonson's repeated acts of anti-feminism in detail in the process of producing two full-length books on him, books which help to sustain the Jonson industry, which exposes more readers and audiences to the anti-feminism she deplores.[2]

As a counterpoint to the still persisting association between Jonson and rampant masculinity, this section looks at a sample of the work of 'daughters of Ben', women who have produced, directed, adapted and acted in Jonson's plays and masques. The intention is partly to counter Jonsonian scholarship's almost exclusive focus on the sons of Ben, whether these 'sons' be male poets, theatre practitioners or literary critics. Jonson himself collected 'sons' about him in the tavern, a masculinised, public space where respectable women, as the Gossips in *The Staple of News* suggest (Intermean 2. 42–5), were less likely to venture. Yet Jonson *could* appreciate daughters as well as sons, as is demonstrated by the poignant Epigram 22, 'On my first Daughter'.

MsDirecting Jonson

Women theatre directors have responded inventively and memorably to the challenges of staging Jonson and yet their work has been almost entirely ignored by much mainstream Jonson theatre history.[3] The extraordinary ease with which these women's work has been forgotten and the inappropriateness of this forgetfulness is perhaps epitomised by the example of Joan Littlewood who, despite directing three Jonson comedies, including an internationally acclaimed *Volpone*, and despite being an eminently *un*forgettable figure in so many ways, has still received scant attention in Jonson scholarship.[4] Grouping women directors together, as I do here, simply because of their gender, and despite their diverse politics (for example, Lena Ashwell was an ardent Royalist, Joan Littlewood was the complete opposite) is clearly contentious. These women would probably not acknowledge any sisterhood amongst themselves (and Jonson himself might disown several of these daughters) and class, ethnicity and religion, for example, can be as significant as gender in relation to the politicised question of how directors work, who gets work in which theatres and who gets into the theatre history books. However, I would argue the case for considering the work of these women together not only on the grounds of compensating for sexism in theatre history and theatre practice, where the role of theatre producer/director has until recently been seen largely as a male preserve, but also on the grounds that forgetting the work of these women theatre practitioners is particularly significant in relation to Jonson because this helps to perpetuate the idea that Jonson is once and for all a bloke's bloke.[5]

A major antidote to the blokeish Jonson is offered by Lena Ashwell (1872–1957). Ashwell's Jonsons were feminine, feminised and also contributed, if indirectly, to the women's suffrage campaigns in which she was involved. Although she worked extensively as a director during her career, Ashwell didn't direct (in the modern sense of the word) her Jonsons; however, she took the decision that the Jonson texts were going to be performed and because, in all three of these productions, the performance occasions were overtly political and working for the benefit of women theatre practitioners, Ashwell radically influenced the way Jonson was to be presented.

Ashwell is largely remembered nowadays as the director who (quite rightly) sacked the young Laurence Olivier for unprofessional conduct, while her other astonishing theatrical achievements have been largely forgotten.[6] Ashwell was an acclaimed actress, a director, a producer and a risk-taking manager; she ran the Kingsway Theatre from 1907, where she promoted plays written by women (for example, Cicely Hamilton's *Diana of Dobsons*) and plays dealing with women's issues. Ashwell was an accomplished administrator – during the First World War she organised for over 600 artistes to tour, entertaining troops in France, Malta, and Egypt. She was also a suffrage activist and a high-profile member of the Actress's Franchise League.

Ashwell (1936: 167–8) describes the events surrounding her most sensational production of a Jonson text in her biography, *Myself a Player*:

> At the time of the coronation of King George and Queen Mary a Gala Performance was arranged to take place at His Majesty's Theatre. The arrangements were advertised, a programme of plays in which all the leading actors of the day could take part with just the two or three women needed to support them. I appealed to Sir Charles Wyndham that it should be a matter for discussion for the Managers' Association, out of courtesy, to include a play in which all the women might appear. Nothing was done, however, and so I composed a letter to Her Majesty the Queen expressing the regret of the actresses that we were excluded. I submitted a copy to Sir Charles with a note to say that, unless something was done, I should most certainly send the letter. Sir Charles told me that the Association had decided to do nothing. The meeting had, indeed, broken up when he said that it would be as well for them to hear the letter which I was sending, and they all hastily sat down to review the situation. I was then given twenty-four hours to get the approval of the actresses and find a suitable play in which they could appear. Both these obstacles were easy to overcome as everyone wanted to be included and I had already produced 'The Vision of Delight' by Ben Jonson for a benefit performance at the Kingsway and had had special music written for it. On that memorable night this lively little masque ended the programme.

The Vision of Delight was produced under the direction of Herbert Tree and, despite the extremely hurried rehearsal process, the reviews were enthusiastic. The *Globe* (28 June 1911) reported that 'everyone taking part looked exquisite, and moved gracefully' and that 'the Masque moved along to its last pretty conceit, when the audience was pelted with roses and carnations, and Mdme. Clara Butt and the whole of the vast company sang with overwhelming effect the National Anthem'.

Despite the chauvinistic razzmatazz inevitable at a coronation shindig attended not only by royalty but also the cabinet and 'the cream and flower of English Society' (*Star*, 28 June 1911), Jonson provided a suitable vehicle here for what amounted to Ashwell's equal opportunities protest because her main aim was to get as many women onstage as possible, looking decorative, celebratory and not having many lines to learn in twenty-four hours. *The Times* (28 June 1911), like many reports of the performance, certainly suggested that the primary appeal of the masque was to the audience's gaze:

> Our real pleasure was pleasure of the eye, the pleasure of gazing at troops of beautiful women moving rhythmically and posturing with grace. Nearly every actress of importance was there, not so much to act (Miss Lena Ashwell had the

only 'speaking part' of importance) as to be seen, and they were certainly well worth looking at.[7]

The masque also seems a particularly appropriate theatrical form for the coronation celebration of a monarch, George V, who lacked the constitutional power of James I but whose British Empire was massive. As Orgel (1975: 53) points out, in *The Vision of Delight* 'What is expressed through the unseasonable glories of nature and the scenic marvels of Vitruvian mechanics is royal power'. Consequently Fantasy's lines:

> Behold a king
> Whose presence maketh this perpetual spring,
> The glories of which spring grow in that bower,
> And are the marks and beauties of his power
>
> (201–4)

seem tailor made for coronational compliments, as do the lines identifying the monarch as 'lord of the four seas,/ King of the less and greater isles' (199–200), although the syntax of Fantasy's 'free-associative' (Orgel 1969: 486) speech may have proved challenging to the audience after the day's celebrations.

The text of *The Vision of Delight* was clearly adapted for Ashwell's production;[8] Jonson's text specifies male presence in the burratines and pantalones but Ashwell's production was all-female, something true also of her earlier production of the masque in 1908, when the masque was produced at the Kingsway Theatre as a benefit for the elderly actress Mrs John Billington. This production appeared in a matinée programme entirely dominated by women; the *Referee* (10 May 1908) reported 'As only ladies will appear on the stage at this matinée, the balance will be redressed by gentlemen being turned on to sell programmes'.[9] The masque was considered ideal for the occasion because it 'furnishes plenty of opportunity for dancing' (*Referee*, 10 May 1908).

In 1911 Ashwell also got Jonson working on behalf of professional woman performers living alone in London. Ashwell (1936: 181) was campaigning to raise funds to set up the Three Arts Club, in imitation of the club in New York, that was to provide cheap and safe accommodation for young women studying and working in the arts, to 'safeguard young girls engaged in the theatrical profession' (*Sunday Times*, 7 May 1911). Ashwell staged several pieces as part of her fundraising campaign, and one of these was Jonson's *The Hue and Cry after Cupid* or *The Haddington Masque*.[10] The stellar cast included Ashwell as an imposing looking Juno (*Daily Sketch*, 19 May 1911), something which immediately indicates the nature of the adaptation. In addition to Ashwell's unJonsonian Juno, Marion Terry played Ceres and Lilian Braithwaite played Iris, suggesting a considerable cross-fertilisation from *The Tempest*. The Jonsonian credits included Evelyn Millard as Venus and Lady Tree as Hymen; the three graces were played by Evelyn D'Alroy, Alexandra Carlisle and Eva Moore. Distinguished actors and actresses played wedding guests but it is predominantly actresses and children who are mentioned in relation to Cupid's antic train and Cupid was played by Vera Fleming. No one is credited as playing Vulcan or Pyracmon which suggests that another feminisation of a Jonson masque had taken place. The performance ran at about half an hour.

Ashwell's production was praised as a 'bonne Bouche' (*Daily Telegraph*, 20 May 1911) which 'If hardly to be described as wildly exhilarating . . . served at any rate the pleasant purpose of introducing' a host of famous actresses. *Hue and Cry* was also described as 'exquisite' and 'one of the sweetest, most haunting little fancies imaginable' (*Daily Chronicle*, 20 May 1911) by a reviewer who went on to describe the action in detail:

> As the curtain rises upon a tree-embowered glade, Cupid comes running down the stage, steps over the footlights, and loses himself among the audience. Soon enough, with statelier tread, along come the Goddesses, the Graces, and all the rest of the Olympians to find him. They plead with the ladies of the audience to give him up . . .
>
> When the truant comes back there is no doubt what he had been about, for he brings back with him from the audience his train of victims, all in gorgeous Elizabethan dress. These are headed by the Bride and Bridegroom, whom, though he be blindfolded, Cupid still leads with threads of gossamer. A pavane upon the greensward, some sanctioning verses – 'Hesperus, shine forth, thou wishéd star!' – and mortals and immortals pace out together in the quiet richness of the sunset.
>
> The masque was produced by Mr. Philip Carr, and no praise could be too high for the way in which he had perceived and preserved the beauty of the thing, avoided all cheaply theatrical effects, and made it all a most precious memory for everyone who was there. The grace that pervaded the stage, with all these wonderful women clad in flowing classic robes, set against the gilded splendour of the Elizabethan wedding party, was, it need hardly be said, quite indescribable.

The Stage (25 May 1911) also praised the choreography by 'Miss Martel, of the Empire', the music 'collected from the work of Seventeenth-Century composers' and commented 'As thus revived, *The Hue and Cry after Cupid* would well bear repetition.' The emphasis, in reviews of *Hue and Cry*, is on sweetness, prettiness and decoration; not words immediately associated with Jonson today.

Ashwell used *Hue and Cry* to make space for forty-five performers onstage. This was an advantage not only because it gave all the performers concerned an opportunity to demonstrate their support for the cause of the Three Arts Club but also because a potentially large number of fan clubs might be drawn in to swell the audience. Consequently, as with the original Jacobean performance, the emphasis was on display, dance, music but also giving a large number of people the opportunity to participate. The masque form, possibly, had more currency in the early twentieth century than now because of the revival then of interest in theatrical pageants. Related to the masque by its emphasis on visual display as well as its extreme ephemerality, the pageant form was particularly brilliantly handled by Ashwell's fellow suffrage worker, director, designer and actress Edy Craig. The suffrage pageants promoted very different politics from the Jonson masques but used related dramatic devices: they were short pieces, very decorative, partly instructive, partly dress-ups and partly heavy politics but also, significantly, partly valued for the experience of participation; Craig commented on how, with each new staging and each new cast, she always had too many unsuitable but enthusiastic pro-suffrage women who wanted the thrill of playing Joan of Arc (Hamilton 1949: 43).

Ashwell's feat of making Jonson's masques contribute to the cause of early twentieth-century feminism at such big, public events – George V's coronation, and the benefits for the elderly Mrs Billington and for the Three Arts Club – constitutes a creative, interventionist and clearly feminist appropriation of Jonson's masques; as such it is only too predictable that this feat should be almost entirely ignored by traditional criticism.[11]

Director Olga Katzin (1880-1976) ought also to be identified as a daughter of Ben because of her double success with *The Alchemist*. Katzin first directed *The Alchemist* in June 1931, a production F.H. Mares (1967) identifies as the earliest production of the play he has been able to trace in the USA.[12] The play was presented in three acts by the Fortune Players at the New School for Social Research and the *New York Times* (5 June 1931) commented approvingly 'This is research with a point in it'. The reviewer felt that the cast, which included Broadway actors, 'fell upon [the play] with sufficient spirit to keep it at a gait almost unremittingly funny' and stresses roar, rant, fast pace and 'the broad, very broad, style of such farce'.

Katzin returned to *The Alchemist* in 1935 at the Embassy Theatre, Swiss Cottage, London (11 March); this production then transferred, with several cast changes, to the West End Prince's Theatre (1 April). *The Stage* (4 April 1935) listed it as a production 'arranged' as well as directed by Katzin; the play was presented in 'three acts of six scenes' (*The Stage*, 14 March 1935) with the play 'pruned down to a certain extent, but most of the essentials . . . retained'. The three-act structure suggests Katzin was building on her New York production. Some reviewers felt that the farce became too dominant. *The Times* (2 April 1935) felt it was 'very definitely not a version for scholars' but 'a boisterous modern farce' evoking references to contemporary dupes 'still to be found flocking to the doors of any occultist charlatan or vendor of tickets in the Irish Sweep'. Although reviewers were divided over whether the production was a success – the *Spectator* (12 April 1935) thought it 'better to leave Jonson in the study rather than degrade him in this manner to the level of the circus' while the *Daily Telegraph* enthused over Katzin's 'rousing performance of a rollicking play' – certain constants emerge: the pace was fast and furious; the verse was neglected with the exception of Bruce Winston as Mammon whose verse-speaking was much praised; the audiences laughed a lot; it was a successful return for *The Alchemist* after a long time away from the London stage.

The most energetic, iconoclastic, enthusiastic and extraordinary daughter of Ben must surely be Joan Littlewood who directed *The Alchemist* (1953), *Volpone* (1955), and *Every Man in his Humour* (1960).[13] Littlewood's politics gave her enthusiasm for Jonson a very individual slant and she is still passionate, extreme and proprietary on the subject of Jonson:

> 'I think *Volpone* is the greatest comedy ever written because Jonson knew about money and monopoly and poor old Shakespeare just rants about it and then goes straight back to Stratford to spend and get himself a decent bed to die in. I did so many of those Shakespeares because we had to but I don't like his comedies compared with Ben Jonson. I did *Volpone* and *Every Man In* and *The Alchemist*; I couldn't stop.'

Littlewood admires what she constructs as Jonson's vigour, his insubordination and energy and this tells us a lot about what she was looking for in Jonson:

> 'I think Ben must have been a good fucker from what he wrote and his life was long compared with all the rest. I like Jonson because first of all he was no Christian; "But if, once, we lose this light, / 'Tis with us perpetual night" (*Volpone* 3.7.172–3). He didn't believe in any afterlife and he knew about money and monopolies. He used to hold court and he would sit and all the young poets and writers would come and he was their guru . . . incidentally Ben was 424 the other day. He's getting on a bit but his mind's still fresh.'

However, Littlewood has little time for Jonson's late plays, the plays which many women critics are now finding so rewarding. Littlewood claimed that 'A bloke like Ben Jonson only sat down to write "classics" when he was old and couldn't fuck his audiences any more' (Ansorge 1972: 19) and she's clear where the blame lies.

> 'The late plays are not much good compared to the early ones; that's the fault of the bloody Scots, the Stuarts. He did hundreds of those boring masques and it's like writing for television. I don't like *Sejanus* that much. I LOVE *The Devil is an Ass* and the copulating on Blackheath – [you can imagine] maybe this very spot for the stealing of the clothes. Such great fun. I tremble to think [the RSC] are doing it. I wonder if they've fucked it up – such a difficult play. Are they using that Shakespearean voice?
>   You can't do Jonson the way they do it now – it's so brilliant: the English, it's

like diamonds and rubies and pebbles and granite – wonderful words. His love to Celia in *Volpone* is so erotic and so is Epicure Mammon's speech about riches but it's difficult to read Jonson. They do Jonson, and they may have all these English degrees from university but they're illiterate. I'm scared in case they do a Shakespeare on him; you might as well compare Hugh McDiarmid and Rupert Brooke. It's so different that you cannot make that same noise.'

Littlewood's admiration for Jonson accounts for the fact that he gets mentioned twice in the Theatre Workshop Manifesto:

> The great theatres of all times have been popular theatres which reflected the dreams and struggles of the people. The theatre of Aeschylus and Sophocles, of Shakespeare and Ben Jonson, of the Commedia dell'Arte and Molière derived their inspiration, their language, their art from the people.
>
> We want a theatre with a living language, a theatre which is not afraid of the sound of its own voice and which will comment as fearlessly on Society as did Ben Jonson and Aristophanes.
>
> (Goorney 1981: 41–2)

In discussing the creativity of theatre (Bramwell 1997: 106), Littlewood also asserts a model of Jonson in line with Theatre Workshop practice: 'Nobody ever really wrote on their own. Aristophanes or Ben Jonson or Brecht. Theatre is collaborative.' When Littlewood wants to illustrate her ideals of theatre, she often refers to Jonson; however, she acknowledges that getting an audience for Jonson at Stratford East wasn't easy:

> 'Of course the only place we could get was that shithouse in the East End. You have to make an audience and we spoilt them for anything else in Stratford East but they didn't know really what they were coming to see, they didn't know they were coming to Jonson. We had lots of lures; we had a good bar, coffee and food; we pinched whisky to open the place.'

Given Theatre Workshop's existence – relentlessly hard up but always managing to put on an act to tempt the punters in – it seems appropriate that Littlewood's first Jonson at Stratford East was *The Alchemist* (see Plate 7, p. 139).

> 'Some of those situations in *The Alchemist* are so complex; we had some bright wits emerging in that company and we'd swop until we got the actual movement which is subtle and difficult to pin down. Do you realise how many entrances and exits, what quick cutting Jonson had? A wonderful woman, Avis Bunnage, played Doll Common.'

In *Joan's Book*, Littlewood (1994: 450) records that George Cooper 'was carried on as Sir Epicure Mammon in an open sedan chair' and that at one performance the iron safety curtain fell and nearly killed him; she also reminisces (451):

> Ben Jonson's English was our riches. Howard [Goorney] as Subtle, Harry C[orbett] as Face and the incomparable Avis as Doll Common revelled in the play and at the end when the gang split and Subtle kisses Doll with:
>
>> My fine flitter-mouse,
>> My bird o' the night; we'll tickle it at the pigeons
>> When we have all, and may unlock the trunks,
>> And say, this's mine, and thine, and thine, and mine . . . (5.4.88–91)
>
> I wondered if he meant the same Pigeons as the old pub of the same name on the [Stratford] Broadway.

Whether Jonson meant this inn or The Three Pigeons at Brentford is less significant than the indication here that, for Littlewood, Jonson's identity as a local, as a Londoner, as an urban laureate, was part of his great attraction.

The production was almost entirely ignored by reviewers, although in retrospect the *Daily Worker* (13 November 1953) called *The Alchemist* Theatre Workshop's 'biggest box-office success so far'. Fortunately the local paper, the *Stratford Express* (30 October 1953), reviewed the production, pronouncing that *The Alchemist* 'is quite unlike anything Stratford has seen before' and that on the opening night the production was 'given such a warm welcome that at the curtain call Mr. Harry Corbett was moved to exclaim with evident relief, "Thank goodness you have enjoyed it".' The *Stratford Express* reviewer described the production's initial contextualising of the comic action: 'With the cry of "Bring out your dead" ringing out we see the alchemist at his work'; commended the company effort of all the performers 'who, even taking the play at a breakneck pace, have all their resources strained to the utmost for practically three hours'; but reserved chief praise for George Cooper as Mammon 'for an immaculate performance of an ancient knight, fat, asthmatical and lecherous'. The reviewer also felt bound to suggest that 'Audiences may well be bewildered by the comings and goings, by the drollness of Jonson's humour and not a little shocked by some of the lines' and mentioned especially the goings-on 'in the upper room where a curtained four-poster occupies so prominent a place'.

Littlewood's next Jonson production, *Volpones*, was internationally acclaimed and, unusually for theatre reviewers, *all* were in agreement that this was a triumph. The play was located in contemporary Italy: 'Mosca rode a bicycle laden with pineapples and champagne, Corbaccio wheeled himself around in an invalid chair and Sir Politic Would-Be, the Englishman abroad, wore swimming trunks and carried a snorkel' (Goorney 1981: 101–2). According to R.B. Parker (1979:

150–1) 'modernisation had the effect of emphasising the play's farcical element' and the modern props included 'an accordion, a telephone, a cocktail shaker, a bath chair, and a frogman's suit (to replace Sir Pol's tortoise shell)'. This frogman's suit allowed Sir Pol to 'exit by a dive into the orchestra pit' (Parker 1979: 164). The production programme depicted Jonson in Littlewood's inimitable style, with Jonson constructed as a working-class, brilliant subversive: 'BEN JONSON: Son (sic) of a hod-carrier: self-educated: the intellectual scourge of the University wits of his day. A good actor'. Jonson was firmly placed as the sort of playwright who could wander in off the streets of Stratford East and join Theatre Workshop. The programme also includes quotations from critics whose politics were rather different from those of Theatre Workshop – T.S. Eliot, G.E. Bentley, L.C. Knights and Roy Walker – something which reflects the extensive research and critical reading all the Theatre Workshop company were expected to undertake.

Joan Littlewood recalls that reviews of *Volpone* were extremely enthusiastic:

> 'The French went mad about it. They said there's been no one since Orson Welles who could touch George Cooper who played Volpone in Paris; Max Shaw, who died young and was a beautiful actor, played Mosca.'

The French reviews particularly stressed energy, enthusiasm and spirit as keynotes of the production.[14] *Figaro* complained about modern gimmicks such as guns, martinis, electric door bells, dancing the rumba, and several reviews mentioned that a bicycle was unlikely in Venice. Two reviews thought Celia was dressed as Boulevard Sebastopol prostitute in a short, black skirt, tight-fitting white sweater and stockings embroidered with stars: *France-Soir*, which felt the production was not close to the spirit of Jonson, detailed Celia's 'Lollobrigidesque' breasts; *Le Monde*, which felt the production was extremely Jonsonian, concurred with this view of Celia. *Le Monde* was squeamish about the belly-dancing hermaphrodite and disapproved of turning Peregrine into an American tourist but, apart from that, thought the production perfect, even though the stress on the monstrosity of the characters was nightmarish: Corbaccio was a leprous, shaking, living corpse; Corvino a swollen, sweaty, grotesque baby with his tongue hanging out, spluttering, spitting and grabbing suddenly with swollen claw-like fingers; Voltore was a Uriah Heep.

British critics were absolutely unanimous in praising the production; *Plays and Players* (20 April 1955) claimed this 'was the most stimulating theatrical experience enjoyed in London this year', that Littlewood's 'brilliantly imaginative production of *Volpone* blew the accumulated dust of ages off Jonson's savagely satirical masterpiece' and that 'Greed, lust for wealth and slimy obsequiousness oozed their way across the stage in grotesque procession'.

Plays and Players particularly praised Maxwell Shaw's Mosca as 'a velvet-tongued, ever-so-common spiv', whose costume changes progressed 'ever farther along the more wayward side of Charing Cross Road'. The *Evening News* (4 March 1955) thought Shaw was 'the most plausible, cigarette-sucking spiv that ever grew from dead-end kidhood' and Parker (1979: 161) described Mosca as 'elaborately coiffed and dressed in ever flashier suiting as his fortunes rose, to end the play in an extravagantly draped white tuxedo'. The *Spectator* (11 March 1955) protested at the production's 'truncated ending' which left 'Mosca in triumph and cut Volpone's speech in which the whole intrigue is pulled down on the heads of its contrivers' and *The Times* (4 March 1955) confirms that the production 'denies [Volpone] his last desperate throw, leaving Mosca in possession of his ill-gotten gains'. Such a major rewriting of the ending seems worthy of more comment and, perhaps, protest, except for the fact that this left the class underdog Mosca in control and critics expected 'extreme class emphasis' (Parker 1979: 161) from Littlewood. In addition Bernard Levin (*Truth*, 18 March 1955) argued that Littlewood had 'rightly divined that the central character is not the Fox, but the Fly' (see Plate 8, p. 140).

Plays and Players also praised Harry Corbett 'as the almost unactable Sir Politic' who 'gave a fascinating study of an eccentric Tory back-bencher' and Littlewood's Lady Pol, 'a memorable comic fuss-pot'. The *Spectator* thought Littlewood's Lady Pol an 'exquisitely funny old Roedean girl'; she was 'a mistress of the obscene nudge' (*The Stage*, 10 March 1955) and 'all gaucherie and Girton' (*The Times*). The *Evening News* commented 'Naturally women, in a nightmare charade of this kind have only two functions; to nag men to a state of boredom and to incite them to a state quite otherwise. These functions are well exercised by Joan Littlewood and Deidre Ellis' (as Celia).

Significantly, given the controversy over whether Littlewood ever won over local support or not, the *Stratford Express* (11 March 1955) was particularly enthusiastic:

> The charge so frequently levelled against the Theatre Workshop Company is their tendency to stage productions which are – to use a cliché – over the heads of their patrons.
>
> There can be no fault in this respect over 'Volpone'.
>
> This is as funny as anything on the stage to-day, and it deserves to keep the box-office very busy throughout its run.

Such an ecstatic review must have read rather ironically to the company who were so under-funded that actors had to take the set to Paris as personal hand luggage (Goorney 1991: 150), and didn't have the fare home (Littlewood 1994: 464).

Littlewood's last Jonson, *Every Man in his Humour*, was a play she had 'always wanted to do' (Littlewood 1994: 555–6); Brian Murphy was to be a 'dashing' Bobadil; Victor Spinetti was to 'delve into his darker side for Brainworm'; Roy Kinnear played Matthew; Bob Grant played Kitely. The production was very fast paced and again Littlewood stressed commedia elements. Indeed with *Every Man In*, Littlewood (1994: 557) declares that Jonson brought 'the *commedia dell'arte* to the

London stage: his Captain was a dead ringer for the swaggering braggart he had probably seen in one of their troupes, when he was soldiering in the Low Countries'. Jonson's language again was primary: 'The more attention we paid to detail, the more interesting the play became. It was exhilarating to watch the actors responding to the challenge of the language' (Littlewood 1994: 557).

Several reviews commented on the extent of the adaptation: the *Spectator* (15 July 1960) remarked that Littlewood 'has treated Ben Jonson with no more, but also no less, respect than she would Brendan Behan'; the *New Statesman* (9 July 1960) commented 'It goes without saying that she has monkeyed a good deal with the text. Master Matthew, the poetaster, quotes Shakespeare not Kyd. There are local jokes, interjections and backchat Jonson never dreamed of' and felt that 'A great deal of the . . . production has more in common with *Guys and Dolls* than with *Every Man in his Humour*'. Goorney (1981: 120–1) confirms that 'Topical allusions had been included, and Joan's production carried it along at great speed and with a wealth of slapstick – which was not how some people felt Ben Jonson ought to be treated'.

The *Spectator* felt that one thing which was missing from the production was a clear sense of Jonson's class and social distinctions; however, the communist *Daily Worker* (5 July 1960) had a different reading:

> Brain-Worm, the 'wide-boy' servant, is contemptuous of the rich, and ever ready to use their foibles and conceits to make a quick and easy penny. Victor Spinetti with his 'what can you do with them' gestures has our complete sympathy.

Spinetti's 'admirable Soho spiv' (*Evening Standard*, 5 July 1960) was generally appreciated; however, reviews were more negative than for *Volpone*: complaints were made about a lack of unified playing style, the lack of sufficiently biting satire, but complaints were also made about the play itself. Indeed *The Times* (5 July 1960) spoke patronisingly of Littlewood's 'researches at Stratford, E., among the comedies and tragedies of the lesser Jacobeans'. This reviewer felt Littlewood was attracted to the plays' 'frequent rawness and bounding vitality, to the pawky urban knowingness of their character, not so different, perhaps . . . from those in *Fings Ain't Wot They Used T' Be* or *Make Me an Offer*'. The reviewer disliked the 'mass of funny business, endless irrelevant movement, and dialogue delivered in that monotonous gabble usually reserved for the more ritualistically predictable sections of music-hall cross-talk acts'. However, even this disdainful reviewer has to concede that the second half seemed an improvement and mentions several entertaining performances including 'Mr. Roy Kinnear's poet Matthew, like a refugee from *Hancock's Half Hour*'. This concession is significant in a reviewer who also somewhat sweepingly asks 'what pre-Restoration comedy *does* remain genuinely funny?'.

Littlewood's failure to find a secure place in the Jonson theatre histories, despite her extensive work with and her enthusiasm for Jonson, has a lot to do with the alternative to mainstream class politics propounded in her productions as well as the alternative, marginalised theatre space in which she was working; away from the centre of London theatre, Theatre Workshop were trying to build up a working-class audience base and, at the time of *The Alchemist*, were so hard up that they couldn't afford to advertise their productions. Although Littlewood herself values her Jonson productions, and her classical work in general, as among her best work, her name continues to be known primarily as the force behind the big Theatre Workshop hits and West End transfers such as *Oh, What a Lovely War!* However, in many ways, she is the most Jonsonian of the daughters of Ben.

Another important woman director who was attracted to Jonson was the feminist and communist Buzz Goodbody, whom many saw as carrying on a tradition partly inherited from Joan Littlewood in terms of theatre practice – theatre that was politicised, often starkly presentational and nearly always anathema to the traditionalists. Goodbody had begun work on a production of *Epicoene* (Chambers 1980:36), which she had worked on earlier in 1967 as an internal production in the Conference Hall at the RSC, Stratford (Chambers 1980: 27), when her career ended with her death. Genista McIntosh remembers:

> 'We did *Epicoene* at the RSC in 1989 because Buzz Goodbody had always wanted to do the play and she was very, very, very keen on Jonson. I think, had she lived, she would have been the one who would have picked up the baton and done the plays in the Swan.
>
> Buzz was exactly the same age as me and we grew up through the 60s in that generation when feminist thinking was beginning to really take hold and she was very committed to feminist politics. It's over 20 years ago and it's hard for me to remember exactly what it was that drew her to the play but I'm sure it was to do with the sexual ambiguity at the heart of it. But I think she had quite a powerful academic interest in Jonson that was nothing particularly to do with her feminism and it hadn't had much chance to assert itself on the stage before she died.'

Genista McIntosh's wide experience of working with Jonson doesn't include any women-directed Jonson productions:

> 'They've all been directed by men. Why is that I wonder? Certainly the big plays are driven by the men, and the women are quite significantly marginalised: even Doll. It's a good showy role for an actress, and actresses like to do it but in terms of contribution to the plot, although she certainly makes an impact on the outcome, she isn't the engine. Neither are Lady Pol and Celia in *Volpone* although again Lady Pol is a wonderful, an absolutely marvellous part for an actress to show off in.'

Moving away from the well-known Jonson plays, it is noteworthy that one play on the fringes of the Jonsonian canon, *Eastward Ho*, has quite a substantial percentage of its stage history made up of productions by daughters of Ben. Perhaps the most significant of these productions was Charlotte Ramsay Lennox's adaptation of *Eastward Ho*, *Old City Manners* which was first performed on 9 November 1775 at Drury Lane, and was 'received with the greatest Applause' (*The Public Advertiser*, 10 November 1775). The text was published on 28 November but on the title-page Lennox announced that she took: 'this opportunity to acknowledge her obligations to Mr. Garrick, for recommending to her, the *Alteration of Eastward Hoe*, and for his very friendly assistance throughout this Comedy.' Lennox thus ensured that most of the credit for her work would in future go to Garrick rather than to herself, the successful author of the best-selling *The Female Quixote*. The prologue to *Old City Manners*, written by George Colman, declares a rationale for Lennox's adaptation: the original had become 'by time, perhaps, impair'd too much'.

In fact, Lennox updated little: she shortened the play and, unsurprisingly, cut crude language, cut the *Hamlet* jokes and cut Slitgut. Her additions build up the sense of a longstanding romance, which is completely absent from *Eastward Ho*, between the virtuous apprentice, Golding, and his master, Touchstone's, equally virtuous daughter, Mildred; for example, on abruptly being offered Mildred as a wife by Touchstone, Golding responds 'This blessing is beyond my hopes, tho' not my wishes, for I long have lov'd your daughter' (Lennox 1775: 13) and Touchstone later comments of Golding and Mildred 'I know you were agreed long ago' (Lennox 1775: 18). Sir Petronel Flash, the suitor to Touchstone's snobbish daughter Gertrude, is modified by Lennox into a name-dropper who claims to be much at court and who is very effusive in his public statements of love for Gertrude. Unlike *Eastward Ho*, *Old City Manners* ends with Sir Petronel revealed as a bigamist (Lennox 1775: 51), so his marriage to Gertrude is void, but he also has a long history of fraud and is finally taken off to York to stand trial for robbing and assuming the title of his late master (Lennox 1775: 56). In keeping with the increased sentimentalisation of *Old City Manners*, Winifred, under siege from Sir Petronel, not only resists his gift of a diamond (Lennox 1775: 27) but is fulsomely penitent after eloping with him and being shipwrecked – this Winifred feels 'the wholsome stings of conscience' and is 'bound to bless' the storm which 'has preserved me from actual guilt' (Lennox 1775: 42–3). The *Eastward Ho* Winifred, by contrast, is simply focused on retrieving her reputation. Lennox added a character, a disappointed suitor to Gertrude, Mr. Fig, a grocer, who sees through Sir Petronel, warns Gertrude of her danger and, after being insulted by her, reappears (Lennox 1775: 47) to exult over Gertrude in her misfortune in a single speech which bizarrely appears mid-scene without Fig being given either an entrance or an exit.

The process of adaptation which produced *Old City Manners* can be contextualised by reference to Lennox's three-volume work on Shakespeare's sources, *Shakespear*

Illustrated (1753). In this Lennox took Shakespeare to task for consistently ruining the stories he took from his sources. By contrast, *Old City Manners* was a respectful adaptation of *Eastward Ho*, and a moderate success in its day. However Lennox's biographer, Miriam Small (1935: 181) dismissively comments: 'Mrs. Lennox's position as a dramatic writer is not important' and gives much credit for *Old City Manners* to 'Garrick's own supervision' (Small 1935: 182). This seems unfair; Garrick's own production of *Eastward Ho* (October 1751) had failed in the theatre and Garrick clearly felt the need for outside input from Lennox, before tackling *Eastward Ho* again.

Nearly two hundred years later Bernard Miles's Mermaid Company produced *Eastward Ho* on no fewer than three occasions and two out of three of these productions had daughters of Ben directing: Joan Swinstead and Josephine Wilson. Swinstead's 1953 production had the *Spectator* (19 June 1953) reviewer complaining that Bernard Miles was too 'much in the background, leaving Joan Swinstead to direct and himself to play a fat but very short part as Slitgut. I do not find such modesty in an actor-manager at all becoming, especially when his company is one that needs leadership'. The *Daily Telegraph* (11 June 1953) by contrast, in a slightly loaded compliment, commented that 'the invention of [the play's] plot pales beside the ingenuity of its acting and its production' and that 'the real star of the evening was Joan Swinstead, who produced with pace and wit'. *The Times* (11 June 1953) felt Swinstead completely subverted the play by her cynicism and by looking at all the characters from the point of view of the dissolute apprentice, Quicksilver, something which rendered all virtue dull and painted 'the picture of London life in poster colours where it should surely be painted in oils'. However, the reviewer also felt 'it is worth going just to hear Mr. Bernard Miles bellowing and stamping in gargantuan glee as each new rascal is fished out of the Thames'. Generally reviewers stressed the energy and the fun of the production, how much the audiences seemed to be enjoying themselves and how well the three levels of the stage, a replica early modern stage erected at the Royal Exchange, were used.

The production was to a large extent revived when the Mermaid produced *Eastward Ho* for the second time, on this occasion directed by Josephine Wilson (Miles's wife, who played Winifred in Swinstead's production) working alongside Denys Palmer. The *New Statesman* (2 November 1962) felt this production was 'a typical Mermaid romp', disliked the play and complained 'some pleasant lightweight actors have been encouraged to rollick with village-hall abandon, and the hilarity on-stage is sadly disproportionate to the audience's enjoyment'. The *Daily Telegraph* used similar vocabulary: the headlines '17th Century Carousal' and 'Robust Humour at Mermaid' were followed by an account which stressed 'romping', 'vigour and roar' and which saw the production as a 'Christmas show' except 'for the bawdiness and an occasionally daring décolletage'. The reviewer also attacked the play as 'nearly incomprehensible' and commented in relation to the three authors and two directors 'many hands do not always make light work'. By contrast the *Observer* (21 October 1962) considered that 'The production, incredibly at this address, is a model of organised exuberance'. *The Times* (18 October 1962), like the *Observer*, was highly critical of the Mermaid's house style but felt with *Eastward Ho* 'for once, the result is satisfying' and although the cast 'assist in draining away whatever Jonsonian savagery might linger in the text' overall 'it is a buoyant and warm-hearted encounter with the past, much helped out by the playing of contemporary dance tunes on a variety of old instruments'. *Theatre World* (December 1962) included three photographs of the production and remembered the previous Mermaid *Eastward Ho* in the Coronation Year as 'an outstanding success'.

Further evidence for the existence of a hidden sorority of daughters of Ben, women directors and women adapters of Jonson, can be gleaned from that editorial venture tripartite, Herford and the Simpsons. This celebrated editorial team, of course, contains its own, often hidden daughter of Ben, Evelyn Simpson. It is only in the preface to volume 6 that Evelyn Simpson's co-workers admit that 'Mrs. Simpson, who has given valuable help in the past, has in this volume become a collaborator. The fact is recorded on the title-page'.[15]

In their Stage History of Jonson's plays, Herford and the Simpsons record three women-directed *Epicoene*s; Miss C.M. Edmonston directed an all-female cast on 11 May 1912, at Birkbeck College; Miss A.G. Caton adapted the play and performed Truewit in a production at Palmer Hall, Fairford; Mrs Abbey Sage Richardson adapted *Epicoene* for a production which played at Harvard University (30 March 1895) with an all-male cast on an Elizabethan-style stage – Richardson's main adaptation was to shorten the last act (Herford and the Simpsons, vol. 9: 221–2).[16] Herford and the Simpsons also record an all-female *Bartholomew Fair*, 30 April 1940, at Bryn Mawr College, Pennsylvania ('An eyewitness records that the performance went unexpectedly well' (250)) and an all-female *The Sad Shepherd*, 18 May 1935 and 24 May 1947 (additions by Alan Porter), at Vassar College, Poughkeepsie, performed by the Philalethean Society. In addition Margo Jones, famous for her arena stage productions, directed *Volpone* in Dallas, September 1954; June Abbott directed a national tour of *The Alchemist* in the UK in 1982; Sam Shammas directed an all-male *Epicoene* for her own theatre company at the Tristan Bates Theatre in London in July 1997; Louise Warren adapted and directed *The Alchemist* for the Rugeley Arts Theatre Society in March 1998.[17] However, perhaps one of the most tantalising records of production I've encountered in hunting down daughters of Ben is the wholesale adaptation of *The Alchemist* directed and adapted by Evelyn Rudie (Santa Monica, 1976). Rudie cut many male characters, added music and ended with a double wedding – Face married Doll by mistake. The review in *Research Opportunities in Renaissance Drama* (1977, vol. 20: 65) commented: 'Doll Common, played with tremendous zest by Miss Rudie, was Eliza Doolittle gone wrong, just waiting for Face to make an honest woman of her'.

Women who direct and/or adapt Jonson of course are in a powerful position if they wish to intervene in, modify, and sometimes even subvert Jonson's plays; however, while women performers are not in the same powerful position as far as influencing the overall impact of a production, it is also important to recognise some of the radical and challenging interventions which they have made in Jonson's plays, even in playing some of the smallest of roles.

Women act Jonson

On one level, any woman who performs in a Jonsonian play thwarts what we know was the authorial intention simply because Jonson wrote all his theatrical roles, except for certain roles in his masques, anticipating that they would be embodied by males. However, almost as soon as Jonson became available to women in the professional Restoration theatre, actresses started making radical interventions in Jonson's playtexts which went far beyond simply taking over the boy players' roles. Thus a 1669 performance of *Catiline* was transformed by the insubordinate contributions of two women. The first, Nell Gwynn, performed a prologue and epilogue 'merrily' and significantly 'in an *Amazonian* Habit' (Herford and the Simpsons, vol. 9: 242). Gwynn's epilogue speech was particularly insubordinate towards the play's author and attacked Jonson for his already established reputation for being anti-women:

> No *Dance*, no *Song*, no *Farce?* His lofty Pen,
> How e'er we like it, doubtless Wrote to Men.
> Height may be his, as it was *Babel's* fall;
> There *Bricklayers* turn'd to Linguists, ruin'd all.
> I'de ne're spoke this, had I not heard by many,
> He lik't one silent Woman, above any:
> And against us had such strange prejudice;
> For our applause, he scorn'd to write amiss.
> For all this, he did us, like Wonders, prize;
> Not for our Sex, but when he found us Wise.
>   (Herford and the Simpsons, vol. 9: 243)

The second insubordinate woman in this production was Catherine Corey, whose playing of Doll Common in *The Alchemist* was memorable enough for Pepys to use that role name as Corey's nickname. Corey appropriated the role of Sempronia in *Catiline* and made it an easily recognisable parody of Lady Harvey and so Jonson's play became embroiled in a high-level quarrel between Harvey and Lady Castlemaine. Harvey complained about the insult and Corey was imprisoned; however, when she was released Corey repeated her performance, and for her pains she was hissed at and had oranges thrown at her (Pepys 1913, vol. 8: 188).[18]

The various women who played Epicoene also annoyed and irritated many commentators. Mrs Knepp, who was probably the first female Epicoene, appeared in that role in 1663, and Noyes (1935: 177) comments that this malpractice 'was corrected only by popular disapproval in 1776, just as the play was to leave the stage'. It is suggestive that Noyes here juxtaposes the disappearance of *Epicoene* from the stage with the transfer of the role of Epicoene from women to men after Sarah Siddons's performance, as part of her disastrous London debut in the winter of 1775–6. After three performances Siddons was replaced by Philip Lamash but, despite *The Public Advertiser* (24 January 1776) commenting that the performance of Epicoene 'by an Actor rather than an Actress, according to the original Intention of the Author, was received with particular Marks of Approbation', only four performances later the play 'was banished from the stage' (Noyes 1935: 217).[19] Women Epicoenes may have been contrary to Jonson's theatrical vision but they made the play better long-term box office with late seventeenth- and eighteenth-century audiences than men playing the role.

The grumblings about female Epicoenes are illuminating in relation to this deeply disturbing play; for me, in complaining about a female Epicoene, the grumblings don't go far enough. Jonson wrote *Epicoene* for a company of boy-actors, who mocked grown-up behaviour in a play where no character can be seen to be admirable. In Jonson's original playhouse, the ending of the play could then be constructed as offering an abrupt, in-your-face emphasis on the male over-determination of female characters on the contemporary stage: the audience is confronted with the fact that Epicoene is a male performer directed by a male, Dauphine, speaking words a man wrote – and, given the abruptness of this revelation at the very end of the play, something which constitutes a startling *coup de théâtre* not easily accessed when reading the text on the page, this underscores the fact that *all* female characters in the professional Renaissance playhouse are similarly overly determined by maleness.[20] This, of course, disappears when a woman plays the role of Epicoene but crucially it also disappears when *all* the other women characters are not played by males. In addition as Cave (1991: 63) comments: 'The fact of . . . self-consciousness about female impersonation in the modern theatre means that the major strategy of *Epicoene* can no longer work in the way it was devised to do'; only in Jonson's original theatre could the moment of Epicoene's uncasing have its full shock value, a moment where Jonson tears 'apart the whole fabric of illusion on which the art of performance in their theatre rested' (Cave 1991: 71). For me all productions of this play which do not have all-boy-casts are missing the point.

Despite these early and clearly disruptive interventions by women in Jonsonian theatre history, the cliché that Jonson does not offer much space for the modern, feminist woman performer is still dominant. Indeed the experience of performing in *The New Inn* inspired a diatribe from Fiona Shaw:

I loathe Jonson's work and have no wish ever to do any of his plays again.
Whatever his sensibility is, it doesn't reach me at all.

(Mulryne and Shewring 1989: 133)

Such condemnation from an intelligent and articulate performer like Shaw has to be
taken seriously; however, other women performers have found more latitude than
Shaw even in some of the Jonson texts which received wisdom would have us
believe offer little scope for women. For example, Julie Peasgood played Celia in
Volpone (RSC 1983) as fiercely resistant to her husband and Volpone. Celia's
appalling victimhood was stressed, the constraints on her emphasised and made
overtly political, and her silences were played extremely forcefully. This Celia was
'lying rigid on the floor' while Corvino was 'trying forcibly to shift her' (Cave 1991:
61) while Volpone and Mosca sat watching it all, laughing, so that when the audience laughed they found themselves implicated in Celia's oppression.

Peasgood's performance was much commented on in reviews both at Stratford
and London, and several reviewers picked out this moment in the production as one
of the most telling of the entire evening. Amongst the many descriptions of Celia
being dragged 'screaming to the monster's bed' (*Daily Telegraph* in *London Theatre
Record*, 1983: 861) are comments which acknowledge the political content
Peasgood was able to inject into the role here: the *Guardian* remarks on 'John
Dicks's stubbly, haunted Corvino who drags his wife towards Volpone's bed like a
brutal cop manhandling a sit-down protester' (*LTR*, 1983: 860) and a year later,
reviewing the London revival, the *Daily Mail* claimed 'The production's best
moment comes with Corvino (John Dicks) dragging his wife (Julie Peasgood) to
Volpone's bedside like some military policeman giving short shrift to a Greenham
Common protester' (*LTR*, 1984: 300). Although both comments focus on Corvino,
Celia's not so passive resistance is forcefully registered and Peasgood's performance
to a certain extent pre-empts recent feminist readings of Jonson which stress his
clarity in depicting how appalling an institution marriage was in the early modern
period for a woman with a worthless husband.

Women performers were also a phenomenon that, unlike some canonical playwrights of the period, Jonson had to deal with. The experience of working with
women's bodies as part of the masque *mise en scène* must have impacted on a playwright as self-conscious as Jonson, although he was never one to privilege the
visual over the verbal, and indeed fought with Inigo Jones over the primacy of the
verbal text of their masques. Feminist performance theory, however, has made us
more attentive to the subversive and disturbing potential of the performed gendered
body and this can inform our reading of Jonson's creation of contexts in which aristocratic and privileged women performers danced, displayed, demonstrated
physical expertise, stamina, skill, precision.[21] Clare McManus (1998: 98, 99) argues
that these women were participating in 'court society' rather than performance and
'can be more fruitfully considered as dancers rather than actors'. Certainly the

women's aristocratic status is as important as their gender in dictating their performative role – silent as the working, professional performers were not. However, the still unconventional (in England) bodily presence of the women in the context of performance, even if it is the rarefied, special space of the court, was signalled particularly unambiguously when, as is suggested by designs drawn by Inigo Jones, costumes exposed women performers' breasts or when, as with Queen Anne for *The Masque of Blackness*, a dancer was heavily pregnant. McManus (1998: 98) argues that the women masquers 'occupy an ambiguous, liminal position, transforming apparent tools of constraint into the means for near-autonomous self-fashioning'.[22] However, my focus here is not on the possible meanings of the masquing women – although I am tantalised by the notion of the frank display of aristocratic women's bodies, performing in masques primarily conceived of as playing to the privileged gaze of a homosexual king;[23] instead I would like to relate the presence of female bodies in the *mise en scène* of Jonson's masques (where boy players with speaking female roles would be juxtaposed with the silent aristocratic women's bodies dancing and displaying) to a period of Jonsonian self-consciousness about the use of boy players to represent women in his plays.

Kate D. Levin argues, from the experience of directing *Epicoene*, that there is 'cross-pollination between [Jonson's] work in different forms' (Levin 1997: 128). Levin concentrates on 'cross-pollination' between the masques – particularly *Queens* – and *Epicoene* and identifies features of masque writing – writing star turns, leaving traffic management to a choreographer or scenographer, and expecting an audience to be extremely capable – which are problematic when they occur in play writing.[24] Another possible cross-pollination between Jonson's masques and his plays is the foregrounding of the staginess of his theatrical women. The major period of Jonson's writing women's masques is 1605–11. Riggs (1989: 182) suggests economics were important in the decline of women's masques because 'gentleman dancers' did not 'need to be so expensively decked out as the Prince and the Queen, or the earls and their ladies, whose opulent display graced Jonson's earlier entertainments'. Possibly equally significant would be Queen Anne's increasing ill health and indeed her increasing age – masque dancing is something of a preserve of the young and beautiful. The fact that masques and entertainments were commissioned meant that Jonson would have limited power in terms of subject matter and casting; however, in his plays he had more freedom, and a cluster of plays, *Epicoene*, *Bartholomew Fair* and *The Devil is an Ass*, suggest that performing femaleness was a subject Jonson was thinking about in the period during and following the writing of the Jacobean women's masques.[25]

In *Epicoene*, as noted above, the audience retrospectively have to confront the masculinity of all the female characters, and a homosexual marriage takes place. In *Bartholomew Fair* a puppet memorably demonstrates that the Puritans' 'old stale argument against the players . . . will not hold against the puppets; for we have neither male nor female amongst us' (5.5.88–90). In *The Devil is an Ass*, a play which contains what Anne Barton (1984: 224) describes as 'the first woman in a Jonson comedy who can fairly be described as a heroine', the hero Wittipol disguises himself as a Spanish Lady.[26] Helen Ostovich (1998: 172) suggests a background text here is Sir Philip Sidney's *The New Arcadia* and its narrative of the cross-dressed man who 'gains strength from the feminine principle and becomes a more compassionate, sensitive male' (Ostovich 1998: 173). My reading of this episode is that it emphasises theatrical self-consciousness, specifically in relation to the representation of women onstage.

The Devil is an Ass is very upfront about the staged physicality of Frances Fitzdottrel;[27] when Wittipol caresses her breasts, or 'plays with her paps' (at 2.6.70) as the stage direction bluntly phrases it, he simultaneously catalogues details of her physical beauty, and goes on to sing a song dwelling on female physicality.[28] This stage moment, as Jonson envisioned it, had a boy player, playing Frances, presenting 'breasts' to be caressed by a fully grown male player, Dick Robinson, playing Wittipol. Robinson is mentioned in *The Devil is an Ass* as being particularly convincing when playing women (2.8.69–73) but as having become too tall now for these roles (3.4.14). In *The Devil is an Ass* Robinson/Wittipol performs two 'female' turns. Firstly, he performs 'Frances', to an onstage audience of Frances herself, Fitzdottrel and Manly, when Frances is prevented from speaking because of her vow to Fitzdottrel; this is a powerful and memorable stage moment (although it is significant that when it was reused by a woman, Susannah Centlivre, in her phenomenally successful comedy *The Busybody* (1709), it was turned around, so that the woman concerned has made the decision herself to remain silent). Secondly, Robinson/Wittipol cross-dresses as the Spanish Lady, which is when the in-jokes are made about Robinson's skill in playing women. All this produces a big stress on the constructedness of gender in performance in *The Devil is an Ass*.

Robinson/Wittipol/the Spanish Lady also becomes an object of homoerotic desire when Fitzdottrel is so enthralled by 'her' that he signs over his property at 'her' bidding, even though this 'woman' is signalled in the verbal text as appearing physically masculine because of 'her' height. Richard Cave (1991: 132) also describes the 'covert effeminacy in his temperament' that Fitzdottrel betrays as 'He enters himself with the Ladies' (4.4.153) and eagerly claims:

> I ha' my female wit,
> As well as my male. And I do know what suits
> A *Lady* of spirit, or of fashion!
>
> (4.4.154–6)

In addition Fitzdottrel is not only seduced by the opportunity of exchanging access to Frances for an extremely expensive and splendid cloak for him to show off in but is also much concerned with what Frances wears: Wittipol tells us Fitzdottrel keeps Frances

Very brave. However
Himself be sordid, he is sensual that way.
In every dressing he does study her.

                     (1.4.16–18)

When he is upbraiding Frances for betraying him by meeting with Wittipol, Fitzdottrel's primary stress is the lack of gratitude for the care with which he was planning 'to dress [Frances] at all pieces!', that is, perfectly (2.7.37). In addition Pug comments on the sheer excess of the clothing Frances wears (2.5.6–23). There is a hint of what would now be called campness here, a notion which is further enhanced by the presence of a character named Manly.

Discussions that queer Jonson (e.g. Chedgzoy, Sanders and Wiseman 1998: 16–21; DiGangi 1997; Bredbeck 1991) have concentrated on *Volpone*, *Epicoene*, *Sejanus* and the background to *Mortimer His Fall*; however, *The Devil is an Ass* deserves further consideration here, particularly since DiGangi has made us alert to the fact that ass/arse interplay can suggest arse play – and kissing the Devil's arse was something of a cliché in early modern visions of human interaction with the Devil. Another play of the same period, *Catiline*, also warrants less coy commentary on this subject. Immediately after drinking a mixture of wine and the blood of a slave whom he has killed especially for the occasion, Catiline reprimands one of his slave boys for 'coying it/ When I command you to be free and general/ To all' (1.508–10) and appearing 'Somewhat modest' (1.505) to the suggestively named Bestia. Catiline promises if the boy shows 'But any least aversion i'your look/ To him that boards you next' (1.511–12) his throat will be cut. As Richard Cave points out to me, when men 'board' 'coying' boys, what is at stake is sodomy and, indeed, Catiline has just been promising the conspirators free access to everyone's wives, boys and daughters (1.476) once they are victorious.[29] Sodomy is here demonised – it's what blood-drinking conspirators get up to, it's what Jacobean rhetoric associates with sedition and behaviour that is beyond the pale – but, as with Jonson's vicious attack on Cecilia Bulstrode in 'An Epigram on the Court Pucell' (*Underwood* XLIX), which accuses Bulstrode of a 'lesbian rape' (Chedgzoy, Sanders and Wiseman 1998: 21), Jonson's frankness here still has some shock value and such frankness encourages us to acknowledge the comic homoerotic dynamic in *The Devil is an Ass* more fully.

While I have chosen to read Spanish ladies and Frances Fitzdottrels as all, originally, men's writerly and actorly creations, a completely different approach to the subject of interactions between women and Jonson is taken by Helen Ostovich (1998). Ostovich persuasively reads *The Devil is an Ass* as reflecting on the real-life troubles of Lady Mary Wroth and suggests the play acknowledges 'a woman's right to challenge and change the inequities of her life' (157). In this approach she is very much in sympathy with Julie Sanders's reflections on how real historical women may have impacted on Jonson's late plays. Sanders focuses on high-profile aristocratic women but in relation to one late play, *The New Inn*, one historical woman who for me hovers in the background is Jonson's wife. At the end of *The New Inn* a husband and wife, the Goodstocks, are unsentimentally reunited after years of separation. This moment inspired Fiona Shaw's scorn (Mulryne and Shewring 1989: 133) but Jonson had personal knowledge of a marriage based on long-term separation.

Notes

1 For example, McLuskie (1989); Newman (1991).
2 However, Chedgzoy, Sanders and Wiseman (1998: 22) optimistically find a 'sea-change' in recent moves away from simply stressing misogyny in Jonson's texts.
3 An exception here is R.B. Parker who discusses Joan Littlewood's *Volpone* in detail in an article on the stage history of the play; however, when Parker writes the stage history of *Volpone* for his high-profile Revels edition, the Littlewood material is radically cut back.
4 Thus Jensen (1985: 98) is incorrect to claim Frank Hauser as 'the only director in this century to have superintended the production of three different Jonson comedies on the public stage'.
5 I argue the case for looking at women directors' work as a category in *MsDirecting Shakespeare* (London: The Women's Press, 1998).
6 For Ashwell's career as a director of Shakespeare see *MsDirecting Shakespeare* and Margaret Leask's PhD work (University of Sydney).
7 The cast included: Lily Brayton, Lillie Langtry, Marion Terry, Clara Butt, Agnes Nicholls, Evelyn Millard, Constance Collier, Gertrude Kingston, Lillah McCarthy, Evelyn D'Alroy, Lilian Braithwaite.
8 *The Times* (27 June 1911) prints the 'Prelude' to the performance, written by Herbert Trench and delivered by Mrs. Patrick Campbell. *The Times* of the following day describes the text as 'touched up' by Trench.
9 The *Daily Mail* (11 May 1908) attempted to undercut Ashwell's gesture in its report by listing all the male programme sellers before naming the actresses taking part in the performances.
10 *Hue and Cry* had also been revived in 1903 by the Mermaid Society, and was performed three times (alongside a *Comus* starring Nigel Playfair) in the Royal Botanic Gardens, Regent's Park, opening on 1 July. *The Review* (9 July 1903) reported '*The Hue and Cry after Cupid* is the merest trifle, but none the less charming for that'. As masques are so infrequently staged and many at the Reading conference expressed the wish to see a staged masque or entertainment, it is worth mentioning that James Knowles's production of Jonson's *The Entertainment at Britain's Burse* (1609) at the Amadeus Centre, London 30 May 1997 was videoed as well as being reviewed in the *Independent* and *Early Music Times*.
11 The Herford and the Simpsons' stage history mentions the coronation production but not Ashwell's contribution. For discussion of Jonson's masques in the context of their original performances, see below.
12 Jensen (1985: 86) mentions Katzin's London production but doesn't credit her as director of the New York production (79).
13 *The Alchemist* ran at the Theatre Royal, Stratford for two weeks from 27 October 1953; *Volpone* at the Theatre Royal, Stratford, 3 March 1955, then 22-24 May at the Théâtre

Hérbertot, Paris Festival; *Every Man in his Humour* 27–30 June 1960 at the Sarah Bernhardt Theatre, Paris Festival and then for four weeks from 2 July at the Theatre Royal Stratford. *Joan's Book* also records that there was some thought of working on *Eastward Ho* (372), *The Devil is an Ass* (138) and *Bartholomew Fair* (307). Elizabeth Schafer's interview with Joan Littlewood took place in June 1996.

14 Digest of reviews based on: *Figaro*, 24 Mai 1955: 10; *France-Soir*, 26 Mai 1955: 9; *Le Monde*, 26 Mai 1955: 12; *Théâtre Populaire*, Mai–Juin, 1955: 90. Three ideas in circulation through these reviews were: that the French could congratulate themselves on the generous funding of the Théâtre National Populaire which compared so starkly with the poverty experienced by Theatre Workshop; that what the English thought was *avant garde* was old hat to the French; that the standard against which Theatre Workshop's production of *Volpone* was measured was the pre-war production by Charles Dullin. In March of 1955, Dullin's Corbaccio, Jean-Louis Barrault, had revived *Volpone*, adapted by Stefan Zweig and Jules Romains (see e.g. *Plays and Players* March 1955) so Dullin's ideas were still current.

15 The power of the editor to construct and contest meanings from the marginalia of the textual apparatus is, of course, enormous. Since Evelyn Simpson, a few women have edited Jonson but a very significant advance appears in Helen Ostovich's edition of Jonson's middle comedies; Ostovich has a track record of feminist interrogation of Jonson.

16 Noyes (1935: 220) offers a slightly different information: the revival took place on 7 February 1895, performed by students of the American Academy of Dramatic Art, and was revived at Harvard on 20 March 1895.

17 For the work of Australian women directors and adaptors of Jonson, see the listings in 'Jonson down under'. I make no claims to a comprehensive listing of directorial daughters of Ben here.

18 *Catiline* was again associated with insubordinate women in the anonymous anti-women play *The Female Wits* (c.1697). Marsilia, a caricature of Mary Delarivier Manly, is presented as a ridiculous, vain and meddlesome woman who has 'laid a design to alter *Catiline's Conspiracy*' (1.1.) although she intends 'to make use only of the first speech'. The audience is treated to a taste of her adaptation:

> MARSILIA: Thy head! Thy head! Proud city!' I'll say no more of his, I don't love to repeat other people's works. Now my own: 'Thy solid stones, and thy cemented walls, this arm shall scatter into atoms, then on thy ruins will I mount! Mount, my aspiring spirit, mount! Hit yon azure roof, and justle gods.'

One of Marsilia's major changes is to 'make Fulvia a woman of the nicest honour'.

19 Herford and the Simpsons (vol. 9: 219) record a single performance in 1784 with a woman playing Epicoene.

20 Orgel (1996) summarises the evidence in favour of modifying this position and acknowledging that some women did perform professionally in early modern England.

21 Some spectators clearly did respond to the physicality of the women performers; see Carleton's complaints about the blacking-up of the court ladies and their courtesan-like apparel in *Masque of Blackness* (Herford and the Simpsons, vol. 10: 448).

22 Feminist critics have generally seized on Jonson's masques as offering opportunities for reading female autonomy, authorship, and power. The most enthusiastic claims here are made by Lewalski, who posits Anne of Denmark as co-author with Jonson of the masques she commissioned.

23 This was a king who also complained vigorously when masques did not engage him; see Orazio Busino's account of *Pleasure Reconciled to Virtue*, when James felt the masquers

should get on with the dancing (Orgel and Strong 1973: 283). David Lindley (1993: 7–10) rightly cautions us against reading the exposure of women's breasts in entirely modern terms; however, exposed breasts were one performative element that women onstage could definitely do better than boys.

24 Levin's discussion of her production of *Epicoene* unfortunately doesn't address cross-casting issues.

25 Jonson's earlier encounters with the problematics of representing women onstage would include the attempt to represent Queen Elizabeth onstage at the end of *Every Man out of his Humour*. He returned to women's masques with *Chloridia*, 1631, which featured Henrietta Maria and her ladies; Henrietta Maria also appeared in *Love's Triumph Through Callipolis* in 1631.

26 Just before *The Devil is an Ass* was staged in 1616, Jonson was also consulting Selden about biblical pronouncements on cross-dressing (Riggs 1989: 198; Kay 1995: 77, 149).

27 The anecdote told by Wittipol as Spanish Lady (4.4.80–5) may also focus on women's physicality more than is usually stressed. In a period when women did not wear underclothes, falling over and disarraying their skirts exposed their genitals to view and so the line about guard-duennas being the only men 'allowed to touch/ A lady there: and he but by his finger' (84–5) is more sexualised than is usually acknowledged.

28 The RSC production avoided the physicality asked for here by the stage direction. Ostovich reads this positively (1998: 181) but it could equally be argued that this let Wittipol off the hook by not stressing his construction here of Frances as a physical object, an objectification which will be complemented by Fitzdottrel's brutal use of Frances when he strikes her, using her as a means to get at Wittipol. The play shows Wittipol moving away from this emphasis on Frances' physicality, and the onstage fondling of her breasts stresses the extent of this journey.

29 Editors are not explicit here: Bolton and Gardner (1972: xxii) comment that Catiline is offering 'a range of sexual experience to the conspirators': Herford and the Simpsons (vol. 10: 130) simply state firmly 'As Coleridge pointed out, the episode here is both undramatic and repulsive'.

13 'Twill fit the players yet'

Women and theatre in Jonson's late plays

Julie Sanders

In a letter to her intimate family friend Gilbert Talbot, Earl of Shrewsbury, written on 18 December 1603, Lady Arbella Stuart recounts that:

> The Polonian Imbassador shall have audience on Thursday next. The Queene intendeth to make a mask this Christmas to which end my Lady of Suffolk and my Lady Walsingham have warrants to take of the late Queenes best apparell out of the Tower at theyr discretion.
>
> (Steen, 1994: 197, Letter 36)

This statement registers in a very real way the transition in 1603 from one monarch to another, from the rule of Elizabeth I to that of King James VI and I. However, another queen features equally strongly here – James's spouse, Anne of Denmark. This letter suggests that Anne was planning her now famous court theatricals as early as the year of accession and helps to confirm at least some of Barbara Lewalski's sense of the strength and assertion, not least theatrical, of the new queen (Lewalski 1994: 15–44).

Arbella Stuart's description of being given warrant to raid the late queen's wardrobe for bejewelled dresses to wear in masque performances gives tangible reality to the scenes which take place between Lady Frances Frampul and Prudence, her chambermaid, at the beginning of Jonson's 1629 play, *The New Inn*. In the course of that play Prudence assumes the guise of Carnival Queen or Mistress of the Revels for the day, eliciting numerous jokes and metatheatrical references – the Host revels in the onstage kissing of a 'queen' and when Prudence first enters in her regal attire, the Host remarks: 'First minute of her reign! what will she do/ Forty year hence? God bless her!' (2.6.10–11). This recalls Elizabeth I who ruled for forty-seven years and so it seems clear that Prudence's costume is intended to be a suggestive signifier of those worn by Elizabeth and recorded in the complex iconography of the portraiture stemming from the latter years of her reign. Recall and echoes of the Elizabethan era have been persuasively traced in the playtext of *The New Inn* by Anne Barton (1984) and Michael Hattaway (1984), but it is fair to say that this now developed understanding of Elizabethan nostalgia in Jonson's Caroline texts has distracted critics from excavating other resonances of his recent history, national and personal, within the drama. Arbella Stuart wrote elsewhere in her letters of Queen Anne as 'Mistress of the Revels' and it may be that Prudence's performance is a multivalent one: connotative of a number of queens, and perhaps also of the *Masque of Queens* which Jonson had composed in 1609 and in which Anne had performed the role of Bel-Anna, Queen of the Ocean, her court ladies taking the roles of other female monarchs, characters derived from history and mythology.[1] That *The New Inn* should be seen in the light of contemporary female theatrical performance at court seems an unavoidable critical conclusion, but it leads on to wider questions about the female network of patrons, and writers, and 'real-life' examples, that feeds and shapes Jonsonian late drama and which I will address here.[2]

The Lady Walsingham mentioned in Arbella Stuart's 1603 letter was Keeper of Queen Anne's Wardrobe and thus her relationship to the play-commissioning queen seems remarkably close to that which exists onstage in *The New Inn* between Lady Frances and the level-headed Prudence. The Countess of Bedford, Lucy Russell's direct involvement in the commission and design of her masque costumes has been discussed recently by Stephen Orgel and this genuine sense of female intervention at the level of costuming would seem to lend weight to my argument that the Frances–Prudence scenes are less fanciful romance than a surprisingly accurate recording of contemporary court activities.[3]

When Prudence first arrives onstage, the dress Lady Frances has commissioned for the 'day's sports devised i'the inn' (1.6.44) has failed to arrive. Lady Frances's solution is to lend Pru a dress of her own but Pru is troubled by the social implications of dressing in her mistress's clothes for such frivolous purposes. In this, she is not so far removed from Jonson's 'anti-theatrical' contemporaries who queried theatre's use of cross-dressed boys and commoners attired as monarchs and nobles.[4] As if the dress will be somehow soiled by this use and therefore must be handed on (the *missing* dress actually has a far more debased use and is employed in the erotic and social fantasies of the tailor, Nick Stuff, and his wife, Pinnacia), Lady Frances suggests that it be sold to a company of players:

LADY FRANCES:　Twill fit the *Players* yet,
　　　　　　　When thou hast done with it, and yield thee somewhat.
PRUDENCE:　That were illiberal, madam, and mere sordid
　　　　　　　In me, to let a suit of yours come there.
LADY FRANCES:　Tut, all are *Players* and but serve the *Scene*.

　　　　　　　　　　　　　　　　　　　　　　(2.1.35–9)

Throughout the play Prudence clearly experiences discomfort with the elisions and evasions of rank and gender that theatre enables; theatre is not necessarily liberating for women performers and, in making that response, Pru is very much a product of her class and social position, and not simply a spokesperson for her sex. It has become quasi-axiomatic to state that women were silenced by the early modern theatre, ventriloquised for by boy-actors, but *The New Inn* indicates more subtle shifts and transitions in terms of reactions and responses to women and theatre in the early seventeenth century that need to be acknowledged.

The professional women actors of the Restoration did not come out of nowhere (Howe 1992: 19–26); they had distinct precedents in the private theatricals of Queen Henrietta Maria and her court ladies. The Queen Consort's French, Catholic, European theatrical inheritance was one which viewed professional women actors as entirely normative and must be regarded as highly influential by 1629, the time of *The New Inn*'s composition. Despite Kevin Sharpe's claims that the extent of Henrietta Maria's influence was 'limited to intrigues played behind the scenes', her theatrical patronage and sponsorships altered English understandings of the form and prompted virulent debate on the subject.[5] From 1626 onwards Henrietta Maria was commissioning court pastorals, performing and, most significantly, speaking in these productions. Walter Montagu's *The Shepherd's Paradise* was written with just such a court occasion in mind.

A theatrical voice, then, was claimed for women in the Caroline period not by the potentially more subversive sectors of society such as the theatres in the Liberties but by the conservative enclave of the aristocracy and the court and this may help to explicate Jonsonian interest and investment in the topic.[6] Prudence's anxieties mark out the social divisions inherent in attitudes towards theatre. The aristocratic Lady Frances feels wholly comfortable with the idea of theatre and the related philosophical concept of *theatrum mundi*: 'Tut, all are *Players* and but serve the Scene . . .' (2.1.39). The Host, himself of aristocratic 'good-stock', has also expounded on this (1.3.126–37). There is nevertheless a strong case for *The New Inn* to be regarded as an agitation for female performance, rather than a parody of it (as is often all too easily suggested by critics blinded by the 'misogynist' reputation of Ben Jonson).[7]

Jonson was not alone in enacting such agitations at this time: James Shirley's *The Bird in a Cage* within the context of its response to William Prynne's diatribe against women actors as 'notorious whores' in his one-thousand page pamphlet, *Histriomastix*, can be seen in this light. *Histriomastix* was prompted by rumours circulating about Henrietta Maria's court theatricals and Shirley responds in turn with a play that contains a central 'play-within-a-play' scene where the incarcerated Princess Eugenia and her ladies-in-waiting perform the story of Jupiter and Danae – a myth which has obvious resonances for their own situation, and which was utilised as an intervention in the ongoing Caroline debate about female agency (theatrical and otherwise).

It is also possible to employ Arbella Stuart's remarkable body of epistolary texts in a sub-new historicist reflex action to talk about how the agency of her life (as evidenced by those recently collated letters) feeds into the agency of the women characters in Jonson's Caroline plays. *The New Inn* is, as is well known, located in a Barnet drinking establishment entitled 'The Light Heart'. Arbella Stuart had lived a notorious and fluctuating life in relationship to the court, moving in and out of favour with both Elizabeth and James, largely due to the dangers inherent in her very existence and her potential, valid claim to the throne: she was James's cousin and as a relative of that other absent queen, Mary, Queen of Scots, posed constant anxiety for her reigning relatives, particularly concerning her possible marital alliances. That Stuart's claim to the throne was regarded as such a threat lends added poignancy to her suggestion that the female inhabitants of the Jacobean court consciously parodied the gestures of the late queen; although she is quick to disassociate herself from such activities, nostalgia nevertheless converts into something more politicised within Jacobean discourse as a result.

In 1611 Stuart clandestinely married William Seymour, son of Lord Beauchamps. King James had forbidden the match (which strengthened Arbella's claim to power) and once he received news of the betrothal placed Seymour in the Tower of London. Arbella Stuart was banished to the North but fell ill before she could make the journey and was forced to take lodgings in an inn in East Barnet. In an amazing turn of events, Seymour was smuggled out of the Tower and down the River Thames in disguise to be reunited with Arbella, herself disguised as a young gentleman, at Barnet. The incredible plot was ultimately thwarted when Stuart tried to disembark at Calais; her subsequent demise in the Tower of London has been the subject of much romantic writing.[8]

I would suggest that Jonson had this story from his own historical and political past in mind when he was writing his 1629 romance. *The New Inn*, Barnet-based as it is, and with its inn-house locale, has within its plot trajectory a clandestine marriage in the shape of the partnership of Lord Beaufort and Laetitia. That Laetitia has been disguised at the commencement of the play as the Host's adopted orphan son, the boy Frank, only to be 'dressed up' as a young woman by Prudence and Lady Frances (and conveniently called 'Laetitia') in order to play the Carnival Queen's lady-in-waiting, evidences the complex and layered role that cross-dressing plays in *The New Inn*. This aspect of the drama has often been seen as a textual marker of Jonson's new and belated associations with the motifs and tropes of Shakespearean romance in his latter compositional years. Cross-dressing is not a major plotline in his other works to this date, excepting the remarkable boys' company play, *Epicoene* in 1609, the complex gender resonances of which have also been associated with Arbella Stuart's biography by Karen Newman.[9] Unlike Newman, who employs the anecdotal historical relationship between Stuart and that play to confirm Jonson's attack on garrulous or assertive women in public life, I would suggest that Jonson's motivation and inspiration for *The New Inn* derives from distinctly female sources and that this can be interpreted as having a positive rather than negative influence on his female representations. That is not to argue that Jonson is in any overt way writing a play about Arbella Stuart some fifteen years after her death (although, as

Martin Butler [1991: 166–88] has indicated, this is a play concerned with political petitions; the Petition of Right was presented at Parliament in 1628, just a year before *The New Inn* was performed; and Arbella Stuart was a dedicated petitioner of the monarch during her various periods of disfavour), but it is to suggest that, like the other renowned women of his day – Lady Frances Howard, Lady Mary Wroth, Lady Anne Clifford, and Lucy Russell, Countess of Bedford amongst them (and it is interesting that all of these women had at one time or another danced in his court masques for Queen Anne). Arbella Stuart forms part of a complex matrix of feminine influence that has significant bearing upon Jonson's work and upon his attitudes towards theatre.

Another instance of female resistance and cross-dressing was available to Jonson in the life-story of Frances Coke, daughter of Sir Edward Coke, the lawyer-politician with whom Jonson was to have various encounters, textual and legal, throughout his career. The fourteen-year-old Frances had been married to Sir John Villiers, the future Viscount Purbeck, in 1617 at her father's insistence (Coke recognizing the obvious advantages of a familial alliance with the powerful Buckingham–Villiers court faction through this marriage), and against the wishes of both her mother, Elizabeth, Lady Hatton, and herself. Lady Hatton actually assisted in abducting Frances from her father's control, only to see her forcibly taken back into his sphere of jurisdiction. Once her mother was out of reach, placed as she was under house arrest by her husband, Frances was subjected to physical beatings until she consented to the match. That was not, however, the end of the story. Despite the elaborate show of the wedding ceremonies for the couple, attended by King James himself, Frances subsequently became involved in a liaison with Sir Robert Howard with whom she conceived a child. She claimed the child was nevertheless her husband's and therefore heir to the considerable Purbeck family fortune. Various courtroom trials ensued and one of James's last acts as King was to place Frances and her child under house arrest in London in 1625. She was also sentenced in 1627 to walk barefoot through the city as penance for her crime. As it was, Frances never performed her sentence; she escaped, dressed as a page-boy, and with the assistance of the Ambassador of Savoy to Howard's Shropshire estates. Her complicated personal history continued with her immediate arrest in the 1630s on returning to the capital, but suffice to say here that her agency in her own affairs and the trope of cross-dressing that emerges in her story as well as Arbella Stuart's provides a notional framework for Jonsonian considerations of female agency and performance in the late 1620s and early 1630s.[10]

Newman (1991: 143) has posited the notion that 'stories are fields of struggle' and Stuart and Coke become, in my admittedly subjective reading of *The New Inn*, and Jonson's Caroline drama as a whole, less archetypal unruly women against whom Jonson takes issue than figures of (belated) empathy and concern. If, as Rowland Wymer (1995: 65) has persuasively indicated, 1614 audiences of John Webster's *The Duchess of Malfi* 'might well have been reminded of the actual plight

of Lady Arbella Stuart' within the context of the oppressive familial control and tor-
turous incarceration endured by the Duchess in that play (Stuart herself died in the
Tower of London in 1615 amidst rumours of madness and hysteria), and if as he suggests 'it is easy to exaggerate the distance between poetic art and life' then for
Jonson's imagination to be spurred in 1629 by his recall of this significant Jacobean
woman seems less unlikely, less unique, but rather more a contribution to a general
framework of imaginings and stories about famous aristocratic women.[11]

Cross-dressing certainly had important contemporary and political resonances at
the time that Jonson was composing and staging his late drama. That Henrietta
Maria's court theatricals seem to have provoked scandal and polemic partly due to
her ladies-in-waiting dressing up for the context of the performances as male characters as well as female consolidates my sense that Jonson is employing the
cross-gender motif in 1629 to provoke discussion and debate about exactly these
issues and not merely as some nostalgic or backward-looking gesture. Jonson's
empathy towards female performance appears to have been a product of his exper-
imentations within the masque form, many of those initial masques being female
commissions. These began as early as 1605 and the now much-discussed *Masque of
Blackness*.[12] Richard Cave (1991: 136–43) has suggested that Jonson's masque work
is indeed the motivation and source for the generic and thematic variety and variations of his later Caroline drama. It could be added that Jonson's Caroline drama,
such as *A Tale of a Tub* and *The Magnetic Lady*, has a particular interest in questions of
community and that a re-evaluation of the role of women within society was con-
cordant with that concern.[13]

Unmistakeable shifts in register and tone occur within Jonsonian representations
of women, and indeed of the wider community, in his plays from 1605 onwards,
moving away from the homosocial circumstances of his earlier citizen comedy or
humours plays. The gender-blurrings of *Epicoene* have to be re-viewed in the light of
this concern with the restriction of women's voices on the English public and private theatre stages during the Jacobean period.

Perhaps the most remarkable of the Jacobean plays written by Jonson, in respect
of its treatment of the female condition and the fate of the female 'actor', is *The
Devil is an Ass*, first staged in 1616. Frances Fitzdottrel in that play marks a transition
towards the more rounded and empathetic female representations that were to
characterise Jonson's Caroline playtexts. By the time of *The New Inn*, for example,
there are no fewer than five major female roles recorded in the dramatis personae:
contrast this with the predominantly androcentric texts of the late Elizabethan and
early Jacobean period where if there were larger numbers of female roles they
were still restrained and suppressed within the action of the play. Frances Fitzdottrel
is restrained within the performances of *The Devil is an Ass* but that may indeed be
the point. *The Devil is an Ass* is a playtext that makes some remarkable and unexpected decisions – Frances, the put-upon wife, wooed by the eloquent if somewhat
ambivalent gallant-figure of the play, Wittipol, asks not for a lover but for a friend –

a friend who will assist her in the retrieval of control of her lands and wealth signed over in her marriage agreement to her irresponsible husband. In this aspect of the plot, Jonson may well have been influenced by the contemporaneous land-rights case being pursued in the courts by Lady Anne Clifford (the effects of which on her life are recorded in her own diaries). In other respects, in particular the charge of witchcraft levelled against her in the fifth act of this play, Frances Fitzdottrel's fate has been likened to that of Lady Frances Howard, who was under house arrest in the Blackfriars area of London and charged with murder at the time of the Blackfriars-located *The Devil is an Ass*'s composition.[14]

During her first encounter with Wittipol, Frances is silenced by her husband's edict and his controlling presence. In a troubling evocation of the Jacobean stage's own voicing of women by male dramatists and male actors, Wittipol ventriloquises for her in their one-sided discourse. That Wittipol in original performances is believed to have been played by the former boy-actor Richard Robinson (the text plays on this in the scenes of the 'Spanish Lady' disguise) adds weight to my under-standing that Jonson is inviting contemporary seventeenth-century audiences to consider the plight of the silenced woman – women silenced by patriarchal society and disenfranchised by Jacobean stage tradition. Like *Epicoene*, *Devil* explores the pressures of social expectations of virility and masculinity as much as femininity, and in the process becomes self-reflexive about theatre's own contribution to these social frameworks and stereotypes.

The argument over women and theatricality needs to be extended and complicated with reference to other Caroline plays such as *A Tale of a Tub*, *The Magnetic Lady* and *The Sad Shepherd* with its remarkable exposition of socially created and induced witchcraft and witch-hunts. That text contains further sophisticated and considered ruminations on the social constructions of gender roles. However, *The Staple of News* engages most openly with the polemical notion of female theatrical spectators. The onstage audience of the four Gossips – Mirth, Tattle, Expectation, and Censure – does on the surface seem to play in to more traditional concepts of Jonsonian anti-feminist satire.[15] Helen Ostovich (1994: 427) declares that the 'chorus of ignorant she-critics' in *The Staple of News* invites male audiences to respond to them as a female confederacy to be feared, much as the Ladies' Collegiate in *Epicoene* or the conspiring midwives of *The Magnetic Lady*.

Gossiping in the seventeenth century was certainly regarded as an ostensibly female (and potentially threatening) activity; the etymological root of the word is in godsibs or godparents but the attachment was overwhelmingly feminine in practice. The nomenclature attached to the four women, with its inherent implications of idle chatter and castigation, exacerbates a sense of parody and pastiche. I wish here, how-ever, to challenge a purely anti-feminist reading of the *Staple* gossips' characterisations and to review such characterisations in the light of my overall refashioning of critical understandings of Jonsonian negotiations with questions of gender and performance.

In terms of a knowledge of the theatre repertoire (and some of its political resonances and applications) these women are astute theatregoers. They are under no illusions about the double-edged role of spectatorship – that it is both to see and be seen. Tattle is often remarked upon for her regretting of the fool's absence as this is felt to be indicative of her old-fashioned theatrical tastes but she offers a cogent account of the role of the fool in much Shakespearean drama (and significantly she employs the term 'fool' not 'clown': the latter might have been more archaic or anachronistic in its applications in 1626). It is worth recalling that at this stage in Stuart history fools were not mere anachronisms and that King James's Scottish jester, Archibald Armstrong, was still a significant figure at the Caroline court; he had accompanied Charles and Buckingham in 1623 on the ill-fated trip to Madrid to secure the hand in marriage of the Spanish Infanta and he gains special mention as the 'divine *Proteus*' (1.138) and the 'Sea-Monster *Archy*' (1.172) in Jonson's masque written, although never actually performed, in the wake of their return: *Neptune's Triumph for the Return of Albion*. Tattle and company may be more politically topical than editors and critics have previously been willing to allow.

> I would fain see the Fool, gossip, the Fool is the finest man i'the company, they say, and has all the wit: He is the very Justice o'Peace o'the Play, and can commit whom he will, and what he will, error, absurdity, as the toy takes him, and no man say black is his eye, but laugh at him.
>
> (*The Staple of News*: Intermean 1.23–8)

The Gossips speak and converse in the Intermeans following each act – they are a Grex or Chorus in the Ancient Greek tradition. The Chorus is a notoriously unpredictable entity in Greek drama – it can perform the role of critical commentator upon events in the play proper; participate in the action; or be marginalised from and miscomprehending of that action. All of these possibilities must be kept in play with the *Staple* Gossips.

The Gossips are well versed in Jonsonian drama as well as the Shakespearean variety. Tattle's husband saw *The Devil is an Ass*. The editorial notes to the Revels edition of *The Staple of News* suggest that again this is evidence of this audience's taste for popular and unsophisticated drama, but in view of the earlier comments I made on the potential empathy for the female condition to be found in *The Devil is an Ass* perhaps for some astute Jonsonian theatregoers in the 'real' audience this would have had a subtler connotation.

The Gossips do prove empathetic towards the representation of women, real and fictive, throughout the play. They are concerned by the potential allusion to and parody of the Spanish Infanta in the play through the character of the Princess Pecunia: 'Ay, therein they abuse an honourable *Princess*, it is thought' (Intermean 2. 21–2). Since Pecunia is also representative of money in the play our attention is drawn to the commodification of women in contemporary Caroline society; that

Pecunia's emblematic role is also suggestive of the roles of court ladies in the masques Jonson had co-created with Inigo Jones adds to the complexity of the characterisation. Pecunia, although overtly allegorical and subject to a whole host of male-enforced interpretations and constraints and fetishisations within the play (of which Pennyboy Senior's maintaining of her under virtual house arrest at the beginning is only the most obvious), is far from silent, unlike her Jacobean female masque counterparts.[16] There is a genuine possibility here that Jonson is register-ing the shifts in female participation in masques and perhaps in the monarchy by ensuring that Pecunia is a Caroline masque performer – like Queen Henrietta Maria, determined to have her say.

In the Intermean following Act 2 the gossips also express sympathy for another real Princess who they feel has been tarnished by allusions made in the context of the play proper. There has been a dispute during the preceding scene as to whether a tavern is a fit location to take a princess such as Pecunia (noticeably she is never asked her opinion on the subject – once again men persist in speaking for women); precedent is invoked in that Pocahontas, the Amerindian princess who had visited the Jacobean court in the Christmas season 1616/17, was taken to such a place. The Gossips are appalled:

> I would hearken, and hearken, and censure, if I saw cause, for th'other *Princess'* sake, Pocahontas, surnamed the blessed, whom he has abused indeed (and I do censure him, and will censure him) to say she came forth of a Tavern, was said like a paltry *Poet*.
>
> (Intermean 2.40–5)

Pocahontas had been introduced to Jonson when she saw one of his masques per-formed at court – *The Vision of Delight* and possibly also *Christmas his Masque* – and, as with the Arbella Stuart incidences and *The New Inn*, this particular masque con-text and this other over-interpreted and exploited female figure seems to have been in the forefront of his creative imagination when composing *The Staple of News*.[17]

There is much more to be said on this theme. I am only beginning to establish a working scholarly framework for my initial hunch about Jonson's female represen-tations. This essay was in many respects inspired by the sympathetic portrayal of Frances Fitzdottrel in the 1995 RSC production of *The Devil is an Ass*, and consoli-dated in its view by the touching interpretation of Win Littlewit in the company's 1997 *Bartholomew Fair*, and I acknowledge the greater space for empathetic versions of Jonson's stage women in contemporary performance that is undoubtedly being found. But if the moment of late 1990s performance and reception was what inspired me personally, then it is equally valid to consider the initial moment of per-formance and reception for Jacobean and Caroline audiences and to consider the possibility that, as well as constituting a welcome late twentieth-century theatrical innovation, this potential for empathy for the female condition that I was responding to was implicit in the Jonsonian text as performed then.

The Devil is an Ass, *The Staple of News*, and *The New Inn* (and, indeed, *The Magnetic Lady*) are all significantly plays written for the Blackfriars theatre, a private theatre house located just within the city walls and the focus of so much of the meta-theatrical activity of *The Alchemist* in 1610. I have argued in relation to that play that the Blackfriars (on the borderline, as it was, a significant limen or threshold of the otherwise discrete spaces of city, court, and Liberties), was a transitional and hybrid location.[18] By 1629 and the composition of *The New Inn* Blackfriars was at the forefront of the debate over women and theatricals. That year it would stage a performance by a French theatre company involving professional female actors: contemporary reports suggest that they were booed from the stage but Henrietta Maria subsequently invited them to perform at court – further evidence if it was needed of the queen's influence, and deliberate intervention, in this area.[19] This event was unlikely to have had any direct effect on Jonson's play but is exemplary of a general debate at the time which feeds into the operations and stratagems of *The New Inn*.

Masque and court theatre as a whole was a genre reliant upon the blurring of the boundary between actor and part and *The New Inn*, like *The Staple of News*'s onstage audience, makes great play of the attendant confusions. Pru, Latimer, and Lovel are all confused as to the status of Lady Frances's 'love' and her 'performance' of it:

PRUDENCE: Excellent actor! how she hits this passion!
LADY FRANCES: Where have I lived, in heresy, so long
               Out o' the Congregation of Love,
               And stood irregular, by all his Canons?
LATIMER: But do you think she plays?
                              (*The New Inn* 3.2.210–14)

The blurrings inherent in the masque form prove troubling in the context of *The New Inn*: Lovel, that ultimate conservative, rails on women as actors but the truth of the situation is wholly more subtle than that. What needs to be registered is that Jonson is neither merely propagandising on behalf of the masque, or the court, nor condemning it outright, but using the transitional space of the Blackfriars auditorium as a means of critique and re-evaluation.

There is more to be said about the significance of the notion of a threshold: unlike a boundary which seems to invest a centre and marginalise a periphery (at least in the critical use of such a term by cultural materialism over recent decades this has been so), a threshold or limen acknowledges greater interaction at the meeting-points: a form of cultural osmosis. Jonson as an author wrote neither from the centre nor the margins but rather negotiated a series of somewhat fluid social, political, cultural and theatrical thresholds.

Ironically in *The New Inn* the boy Frank is commissioned to dress up and play the role of him/herself – Laetitia. (Beaufort's Ovidian physicality gains some endorsement when he marries Laetitia and thwarts the mockery of the others who think they know 'her' true sex.) As in *Epicoene* the gender confusion draws attention to the confusion and boundary-blurring inherent in the early modern theatrical tradition of boy-actors; Pru expresses experiential sympathy for the role when Lady Frances, in a typically unknowing act, blames her for the day's proceedings, dismissing her as an 'idiot chambermaid', an epithet which misses Pru's central qualities:

PRUDENCE: I will not buy this play-boy's bravery,
            At such a price, to be upbraided for it,
            Thus, every minute.
                        (4.4.321–3)

Ben Jonson had also been an admirer of the play-boy's bravery throughout his dramatic career: his complex and spirited drama for the boys' companies is evidence enough of this. As a result he was also made aware of those figures who were silenced or disenfranchised by such a tradition – women and women actors. Here I have given the merest glimpse of what I believe to be a rich seam of empathetic roles for and considerations of women in Jonson's Jacobean and Caroline plays. The success of the recent RSC *Devil is an Ass* and the renewed, and often new access it has given to that text must surely be an indicator that contemporary performances of plays such as *The Staple of News* and *The Magnetic Lady* may open up new avenues of possibility within Jonson's writing to us and that indeed we will see that it will fit the players yet.

Notes

Sections of this chapter have previously appeared in Julie Sanders, '"The Day's Sports Devised in the Inn": Jonson's *The New Inn* and Theatrical Politics', *Modern Language Review* 91 (1996): 545–60 and are reprinted here by kind permission.

1 Steen (ed.) (1994), *Letters*, pp. 181, lines 13–14: 'Our great and gratious Ladies leave no gesture nor fault of the late Queene unremembred . . .'
2 For a more extended account of *The New Inn* and ideas of female performance, see Sanders (1996).
3 Orgel discussed Russell's wardrobe commissions in a paper at the Ben Jonson conference, University of Leeds, July 1995.
4 See, for example, Howard (1994) and for a persuasive reading of Jonson's own 'anti-anti-theatricalism', see Levine (1994), especially chs 4 and 5.
5 Sharpe (1987: 226–60). See also Tomlinson (1991: 189–207 and 1992: 134–63) and Wiseman (1992: 159–77).
6 McManus (1998: 93–113) makes a related argument about the intersection of gender

and class in the rising theatrical agency of women in this period.

7 I make a related argument for *The New Inn* and agitation for female performance in "'A Woman Write a Play": Jonsonian Strategies in the Drama of Margaret Cavendish, or Did the Duchess Feel the Anxiety of Influence?', forthcoming in S.P. Cerasano and Marion Wynne-Davies (eds) *Readings in Renaissance Drama by Women* (London: Routledge, 1998).

8 Orgel (1996: 114–15) also discusses these events.

9 Newman (1991: 131–43 (especially 140–3)). See also Newman's reading of *The Staple of News* (1996: 49–69).

10 For details of Frances Coke's turbulent life see Fraser (1995 [1984]: 13–21).

11 I am grateful to Anthea Trodd for the inspiration to complicate the question of the historical and literary reception and reputation of Arbella Stuart provided by her research paper, 'Minding the Darling Heads' given at Keele University, May 1996. For further examples of possible 'real-life' influences on the debates accruing around gender and performance, including Stuart and Elizabeth Southwell, one of Queen Anne's maids of honour, who also effected an escape disguised as a page-boy, see Orgel (1992: 12–26 and 1996).

12 See for example Hall (1991) and Siddiqui (1992).

13 See also Sanders 1997 and 1998a.

14 For a consideration of other contemporary resonances in this play, including allusions to the real-life situations of Mary Wroth and Frances Howard, see Ostovich (1998).

15 Such as those endorsed by Riggs (1989).

16 For a consideration of the play's engagement with questions of gender in relation to the emergent print culture see my 'Print, Popular Culture, Consumption, and Commodification in *The Staple of News*', in Chedgzoy, Sanders and Wiseman (1998: 183–207).

17 See Hendricks and Parker (1994) and Tilton (1995).

18 See Sanders (1998b) and Gurr's Prologue to this volume.

19 See Howe (1992) and Kim Walker (1991: 385–400).

14 Jonson down under

An Australian *Alchemist*

Elizabeth Schafer

Although post-colonial theory has only comparatively recently begun to confront the multiply signifying texts of live performances, this theatrically aware version of post-colonialism offers some useful pointers in looking at Jonson in Australia. Post-colonialism reminds us that contemporary locations of early modern drama in Australia – in teaching and in theatrical production – continue to demonstrate these plays' ongoing potential to function as agents of empire, both in the reiteration of their conservative sixteenth- and seventeenth-century race, gender and class politics and in the role they play in helping to maintain the notion of a classical canon of drama, originating from outside Australia and against which Australian theatre and drama is measured and always found wanting. However, Gilbert and Tompkins (1996: 2), having suggested that post-colonialism is 'an engagement with and contestation of colonialism's discourses, power structures, and social hierarchies', also acknowledge, if only in passing, that 'the staging of the "intact" canonical play offers one kind of counter-discourse which might, through a revisionist performance, articulate tensions between the Anglo script and its localised enunciation' (Gilbert and Tompkins 1996: 16).[1]

This chapter takes up Gilbert and Tompkins's suggestion in relation to Neil Armfield's 1996 production of *The Alchemist* at the Belvoir Street Theatre, Sydney, and looks at 'tensions' generated as the production appropriated the play; my reading is also indebted to Penny Gay's post-colonial reading of recent Australian productions of *The Taming of the Shrew*, a reading which examines how these productions 'speak from an identifiably Australian position' (Gay 1998) and in particular stresses the 'larrikin' element, the non-conformist, impudent, streetwise, irreverent, and usually male, Aussie inflection.[2]

The context of competing theatre histories also needs to be acknowledged here. Post-colonialism's heightened awareness of the colonial centre/colonised margin dynamic encourages a resistant reading of dominant theatre histories of plays of the early modern period in which productions at the imperial theatrical centres of London and Stratford are privileged and extensively discussed. As a consequence of this, few Australian productions of Jonson receive much attention outside of

Australia (despite the location there of eminent Jonson scholars such as G.A. Wilkes).[3] This blind-spot (one of many) in Anglo-centric Jonson theatre histories needs to be contested and, as a consequence, there is an attempt here to begin acknowledging the recent history of Jonson in the Australian theatre.

Simply by occupying space in an Anglo-centric book, then, this discussion of an Australian *Alchemist* constitutes a politicised, post-colonial gesture. While the focus will be on the ways in which Armfield's production generated 'tensions' in taking over ownership of the play, it also seems important initially to register the lack of knowledge generally, outside Australia, of Armfield's work, and the fact that British and American colonial prejudices will impact on the critical reception of the career of a director who, so far, has deliberately chosen to work almost entirely in Australia. In addition it seems crucial to raise the question of whether in selling Jonson so successfully to Sydney, Armfield's *Alchemist* was complying with empire, accepting the canon, or insubordinately taking over and occupying imperial territory. However, invoking a post-colonial perspective on Armfield's *Alchemist* is almost irresistible: not only does the play then become newly resonant – as the figure of the absent owner, Lovewit, reaping all the profits derived from the hard labour of others, easily becomes analogous to the imperial master – but also it is tempting to imagine the fun Subtle and Face could have with the language of high theory, whether post-colonial or otherwise.

The most obvious tension between any early modern Anglo script and its local enunciation in Australia will always be location. *The Alchemist* is a particularly confrontational text here because it is so specifically located in a definite part of Jacobean London. In Australianising the play, whilst also keeping its 'London 1610' identity clearly in perspective, Armfield was creating a double vision which, although it now seems unremarkable in Australia to see a production of a classical play played with a deliberate and self-confident local inflection, is a comparatively recent phenomenon. Such productions are, to a certain extent, heirs to the Sydney Nimrod Theatre Shakespeares, which led the way during the 1970s in strenuously rejecting Anglicised performances of early modern plays. This was signalled most clearly in the abandonment of the so-called received pronunciation/upper-class English accents used by the previous generation of Australian classical actors. The Nimrod Shakespeares significantly popularised the notion of localising classical texts, as well as performing them in a brash, iconoclastic way, a tradition still carried on now in a much milder form by the Bell Shakespeare Company, headed by John Bell, one of the leading lights of Nimrod. The 1970s has been much acknowledged as the decade in which a new, energised Australian theatre and film burst upon the scene. What is less frequently discussed is the fact that this period revolutionised Australian productions of the classics as well. Theatre practitioners who valued the classics, and wanted to work on them, brought a similar sensibility to them – often as Gay (1998) claims 'larrikin' – as they did to working on new Australian scripts.

In relation to this question of locality Geoffrey Rush, who played Subtle in the Armfield *Alchemist*, comments:[4]

> 'There's always that Australian dilemma of "Are we going to localise it into England?" Neil Armfield's got a great concern for the classics having a natural voice onstage for Australia, without making it a corked hat vocal attachment. He didn't want anyone to block their own energies and instincts and comic abilities by being trapped into a whole series of regional or class accents in order to be English. The audience are watching a play in the 1990s, which they know in their heads is London in 1610, but it's really in the theatre that they're sitting in that it's set.'

Stephen Curtis, the set designer for the production, helped further this double vision – Sydney/London, 1996/1610 – by playing with local reference points. The setting suggested an expensive, 1950s, Tudorbethan house which had been converted into a cross between a King's Cross brothel/strip show theatre and a travellers' hiding hole – an hallucinogenic, inside out space made for fast fixes and nightmare awakenings, a squat cluttered with trash and fast-food cartons and a house where chamber-pots were still used.

> 'Stephen Curtis is *so* good at defining some sense of contemporary life but never strait jacketing the production into a setting. He was able to create by inference, it was never stated, some reasonably smart, upper-middle-class, north-shore Sydney home that had been taken over by these crims. He's very detailed and it was very important to him to get the right sort of panelling down the side of the door to evoke bourgeois Sydney *and* to pay homage to a Jacobean notion but also make the space an interesting playpen for this particular piece.'

The audience responded strongly to the sense of invasion and desecration:

> 'We had a strange, very bourgeois, fluffy carpet on the floor. I'd read about Tyrone Guthrie's production with Leo McKern and that, instead of having an alchemical flask or phial in his hand, Subtle had a chamber-pot. I liked that idea. When you look at the prehistory of the play, of what's happened just before "the curtain goes up", three crims in a household are basically getting up and getting ready for the day and there's a lot of tension between them. So I threw the contents of the chamber-pot over Face. Of course it had turds in there and there was just something about seeing a turd in that carpet with piss going everywhere . . . The audience would just go "yuk!" but they really registered that this is how those crims treat this house; they've just ruined the place.'

The production's localisation was hailed by *The Australian* (29 August 1996) in its opening sentence: 'Dirt, disease, poverty; vice, obscenity, blasphemy; trickery, stupidity, corruption and greed – welcome to Sydney'. This localisation extended to characters as well as setting. One contemporised reference here which worked extremely successfully for Sydney audiences was the use of New Zealand accents for Kastril and Pliant, something which reduced the audience to helpless laughter. Not only did this fit the text to a large extent – 'suster' being a good approximation of how Australians hear New Zealanders saying the word 'sister' – but it also fitted the rustic stereotype which Sydneysiders in particular would apply to New Zealanders whom they see as coming from a quiet, tranquil, slow-moving country. However, Rebecca Massey created a vigorous Dame Pliant, increasingly infuriated by Kastril's cavalier treatment of her, a woman who, once she found herself married to an elderly but clearly indulgent husband, exited after her brother, baseball bat in her hand, clearly determined that, at long last, she was going to have her say. Arky Michael's Drugger also became part of the Sydney scene as a Greek corner-shop man, earnest, eager, bespectacled. Dapper was recognisable, in Rush's words, as 'an idiot young lawyer, some yuppy, trendy lawyer'.

For Rush the main contemporary Australian reference was New Age and commercialism:

> 'Jonson's syntax of alchemy produces something so vivid and rich and it's New Age gobbledegook of the era. I'd read that when Jonson wrote *The Alchemist* there were an enormous number of books on alchemy published and it was hot on the reading list, it was a big thing. We brought into rehearsal a whole lot of New Age magazines, which were just absolutely outrageous but very comparable in terms of the scams and beliefs. It's exactly the metaphor: "we will give you 'gold'".
>
>   It's my belief that a lot of people who get involved in New Age want to change, and if you want to change you're actually really open and available to very quick, easy cures. It's so commercial and so mainstream that you can have a getaway aromatherapy weekend at the Hyatt, give yourself two or three days with seaweed baths and some crystals and come back to your business life a "new person".'

Rush combined the New Age scheme of reference with an evocation of Australian comic phenomenon Barry Humphries in speaking in detail of how the first Drugger scene functioned:

> 'This is only about six or seven minutes of stage-time, but it goes into completely preposterous stuff because he's so gullible – all this Feng shui gobbledegook of 'Show me the plans of your shop . . .' I think a trap with a lot of the classic comedy repertoire is that people think it's very musty and muted

and they lose sight of how *outrageous* some of the writing can be. Here, with Face feeding in, the whole thing escalates and by the end of the scene they're getting Drugger to hand over his life savings. But they're also making a point of coming back and going 'oh his breath's off' and being really overt and cheeky with the audience. It's like when Barry Humphries used to do a show where he'd "read" people's shoes. He had a fish net on a pole and he'd send it out into the auditorium and he'd bring up this wonderful, delicate, fawn, low heeled thing which had obviously come from this frail little pensioner down on the front row and he'd just go "ugggh!" as if at the smell. It was in that kind of spirit that we could go "Yeah, it can be that preposterous".'

Although clear connections between *The Alchemist* and contemporary culture seemed to Armfield 'so patently clear you don't need to have it hammered home' (*The Australian*, 23 August 1996), nevertheless, in the same article, he invoked Mamet's *Glengarry Glen Ross*, Tarantino's *Reservoir Dogs* and commented that *The Alchemist* was written when: 'Science and economics were forming themselves without a sense of how that gets regulated in terms of human behaviour.' So you have a crisis of social management which Armfield compared with today's situation when the law is outstripped by developments such as the Internet and genetic engineering. In another interview Armfield also connected *The Alchemist* with the scene in *Trainspotting* where the protagonists are trying to sell their heroin to the heavies; 'Everything is won or lost in that room, depending on the image you project of yourself . . . It's pure Jonson' (*Elle*, September 1996).

Despite the production's localisation of *The Alchemist* in terms of Sydney, Rush felt the play still needed opening up more to the audience, especially at the beginning:

'I liked the fact that the play had such an extraordinary opening, that the play started with a row, a fight, but the audience only really came in on the production with Abel Drugger's entrance. We were absolutely on home turf there. We suddenly just romped. But the fight, with all that information and all that Jacobean slang and the audience trying to find out who's who! After we'd opened we put the acrostic Argument in. The lights came up with Subtle and Face and Doll onstage, ready to go, in a freeze and Lovewit spoke it as a prologue. Even that was quite dense; it's very lean and pithy writing, but it does give you an inkling of story. That helped enormously; it gave the audience a chance to look at the room, look at who we were and theatrically it suited the play because it opened the play out instantly; somebody came up and spoke to the audience – whereas the fight is so inward.'

Another moment when the production sought to open up the play to the audience was 3.2., the scene with Ananias and Tribulation.

'When Subtle says to them "Have I ever told you how alchemy actually works?" and he goes through this big spiel and through that really digs into them to go for more money, then the feeling for me was that it was like he sits them down to have a cup of tea and I had this image of Michael Caine or Bob Hoskins in *The Long Good Friday* – the very nice, Cockney, gentle gangster who is very menacing. I was also thinking of the Kray twins – or Al Capone with a baseball bat walking round the table going "Everything's fine".

We got that tea-party image going, and then there's this wonderful litany of stuff and Subtle's saying "You'll see some old woman whose face is painted and you'll give her the elixir – bang! – you'll double your money". And the Puritans are going "Oh that sounds good". Neil said "We'll play that off the audience; make the people around your subjects". And it used to work fantastically. For the gag about the woman with the painted face I'd always try and find somebody in their sixties and be really nice to them – "A lady, that is past the feat of body, / Though not of mind" before the sting in Jonson's line "and hath her face decayed / Beyond all cure of paintings"(3.2.33–5).

Then I used to drag some poor chump up to join in the tea party. Nothing would happen; it was just one of those Barry Humphries sorts of moments, that terrible situation of one of the throng being made a victim. We used to just riff that for as long as the audience held it. Once we'd got too many laughs, the line was "You've had your fun, now get off" and I'd throw them an Iced Vo Vo biscuit. The prepared *ad lib* was "Did you know Ben Jonson invented the name Iced Vo Vo"? Depending on how the house was going, the situation was often "I can say anything at this point".

We also had some stuff about lighting incense in preparation for Epicure Mammon – I used to do the ABC logo.[5] I'd get someone on the front row, give them an incense stick and I just went 'Hold that!' Then I had a thing with them later when I went off after 3.2. with the tea trolley; they became a sort of stooge in the audience – I'd go "Are you keeping up with the plot?"

I thought that was very much in the spirit of the openness of the play, an openness that you need to bring out because *The Alchemist* feels like a domestic play, it's set in a house, and there's a risk that you can close the world in and then the audience don't go with it as much. So that's why all those opening up bits came in for us.'

Another contemporising idea in circulation around the production was one invented by Hugo Weaving who played Face: 'poetic grunge'. Grunge in the sense of feral filth and finery, plus an inventive use of found objects was certainly present in the costumes designed by Kym Barrett: Face appeared as Lungs in filthy overalls plus cricket pads; Subtle as guru to Mammon appeared in a makeshift turban and loin cloth; Gillian Jones as Doll became a platform-shoe wearing Queen of the

Fairies, dressed in charity-shop couture and accompanied by tinny fairy music emitted from an ancient tape recorder. Geoffrey Rush recalls:

> 'I'd been reading about alchemists and the books said that people like Subtle did come from the rag heaps; he wouldn't have to dress up much because people expected the alchemist to be slightly divine or crazed and to be quite grubby from the nature of the work.'

The grunge basis of the character helped Rush to effect a major transformation for his first performance to a client, Drugger:

> 'At the beginning I was this flea, with scabby arms and filthy old longjohns. When Drugger came in, I really changed the rhythm of the character for the first time, by putting on some glasses that made me look quite amusing, an academic's gown and this little black hat, and I suddenly became *terribly* gracious. I also used this really cheap gag; I just picked up an iron and used it as if it was a telephone for "good wives, I pray you forbear me, now. / Troth I can do you no good, till afternoon" (1.3.1–2). Then with Drugger it's as if I'm going "I'm *so* busy but you are *so* welcome I'm giving you my time" and I'm terribly open to everything that simple chump Drugger is offering.'

'Poetic grunge' was also there in the acting; the tricksters were living on the edge, they were manic, hyperactive, driven, repellent but also exuding seedy charm. *The Australian* described Rush's Subtle as 'magnificent: scabrous, vile, grotty, energetic, febrile – an exultantly life-affirming cockroach'; the *Sun-Herald* (1 September 1996) saw Rush's Subtle as 'like some antic praying mantis', one minute 'leadenly brooding', the next 'obscene, childish, dissolute and disorderly'; the *Sydney Morning Herald* hailed Rush's 'decaying, syphilitic Subtle' as a '*tour de force*'. In his own words:

> '*The Alchemist* is scurrilous and ratbaggy and I always looked at Subtle as being like someone from the sixties who'd fried their brains on acid. He may have once been a great thinker but he'd lost it, although he still had enough imagery spitting around so that he could go into raves – and stuff would come back to him, so that he was actually quite a good con-artist because there was a knowledge there. Subtle has got great spiels in his head and, like a great salesman, he knows exactly what buttons to press.
> We used the analogy that Face was the stage-manager and that Subtle was the complete prima donna within the household; at the beginning Face was there ironing his shirt, preparing to be groomed and ready and Subtle was getting up and taking his time. In the course of the fight, Face says "You're a nothing, a nobody, you're just a sham" and Subtle's going "I don't care what you think; I'm

brilliant and you can't do it without me". And it *is* a complicit thing; they actually can't survive as criminals without each other.'

Rush's Subtle was ably complemented by Hugo Weaving's suave, sleazy, sometimes even swashbuckling Face, who adopted a series of comically outrageous accents
for his different disguises (see Plate 9, p. 141). Although Weaving is best known
internationally for his starring role in *The Adventures of Priscilla, Queen of the Desert*, he
has powerful stage charisma, something which was still apparent even in the seedi-
est of his disguises. Alongside the brilliant comedy skills of Rush and Weaving's
dangerous, seductive Face, Rush recalls Gillian Jones' Doll as much less flamboyant:

'What's very hard is that Doll has to quell that opening fight. We played it for
a while in rehearsal that she had a gun, because she needs something to pull this
argument to a halt. And she talks about the possibility of them being hung,
which is a very real threat, but some of that was hard to capture, so that the
audience would understand that this is what's at stake.

Gillian played up the drug side of Doll. She was very determined that there
was something desperate about Doll, that these three people are all misfits.
There was one scene where she and Face imbibed something – Laudanum or
something that belonged to that world. After all the action is all very heightened and drugs provide the sort of energy that drives that kind of behaviour.
Gillian also played the notion that Doll wasn't really in with Face or Subtle, that
the relationships were very much close to breaking up and that she wanted out
but just needed to find an opportunity.'

Despite such contemporising and localising devices as the drugs and 'poetic
grunge' references, this *Alchemist* never descended to simplistic universalising. Even
in the costuming, with the gulls wearing a witty and eclectic mixture of codpieces,
leggings and modern suit jackets, the audience were constantly reminded that *The
Alchemist* playtext is a product of a distant historical period, whilst the production
text was a mixture of early modern text and late twentieth-century Sydney cultural
locations. These characters, no matter how modern they seemed to be, were always
also creatures of the distant past.

The box office demonstrated that this production clearly succeeded in making
The Alchemist accessible. Geoffrey Rush concludes:

'The audiences were fantastic. That was the greatest joy because we played to
something like 104 per cent capacity. Every performance we had people
crammed down aisle ways, queues outside the theatre. It was right for that
company and that city at that point in time. It wasn't just a cerebral notion of
people coming because we were treating the classics differently; they were
having a great time and really getting the play.'

At the same time the production did enhance Armfield's reputation for challenging, slightly off-beat direction, which sheds new light on difficult, literary plays, particularly the classics and the plays of Patrick White.

In distancing the production from the 'cerebral', Rush also stressed the great theatricality of the play. Rush was trained at Lecoq, training he characterises as 'very much through the actor-based traditions of theatre', focusing on 'an approach to acting through movement and a stylistic study of commedia, traditional white-face pantomime, buffoon, clowning and a lot of improvisational techniques'. Rush's vision of *The Alchemist* reflects this background:

> 'With *The Alchemist*, because of the smell of the theatre that's just in the play – that's not literature and it's not psychologically constructed – it's finally down to how you can make great preposterous leaps within scenes that are very freewheeling. It's something that Neil and I really worked with in a big way with *Diary of a Madman*; it's not a reverence for the poetry of the voiced word but how that imagery can become meaningful as a theatrical experience with an audience coming in on it.'

Rush sees this as contrasting in approach with a lot of English theatre:

> 'From what I see here in the English theatre, there's still a great reverence for the pure poetry of the text that's a little bit bloodless for my taste; it's never sexy enough, it's never funny enough, it's never dangerous enough, it's never surprising enough. It feels as though you have to make an appreciation of it as well formed; I think in Australia we're quite good at tapping the ratbaggery notion of it although not denying the text, because that's always the starting point.'

Rush's sense of an Australian 'ratbaggy' style of doing the classics resonates with Penny Gay's (1998) analysis of Australian 'larrikin' style. However, I would like to pick up on Rush's emphasis that *The Alchemist* is 'not literature' and link this to Armfield's forceful contestation of English Literature's, as opposed to theatre's, ownership of *The Alchemist* in his production programme.

Armfield's programme contained a list of reasons why he loves Jonson, a list which is both elucidating and strategic:

- I love the way that in writing *The Alchemist* Jonson was basically opening the door of the theatre onto the street outside and inviting in the passing parade of human beings trying to make their way in the jungle called the modern city. I love the way that when they arrive onstage they know they're onstage, with an audience out there wanting a show.
- I love the way Jonson starts his play with a fart.

- I love the fact that Jonson and Shakespeare were writing for the same company of actors, and that most of the original cast of *Hamlet* were, nine years later, the original cast of *The Alchemist* . . .
- I love the way these plays are so confident in their love of theatre, in the love and hunger of their audience – the sense of the security of performance just radiates from the stage.
- I love the way the play hates puritanism and all those who impede the pleasure of play and of people laughing at themselves.
- I love the way the play makes you feel that human affairs are still being trans-acted in the school playground . . .
- I love the fact that Jonson went walking from London to Scotland, to look at life . . .

Armfield concludes with a comparison with Shakespeare, constructing Jonson as equal but different:

- I love the fact that while Shakespeare could write with such awe and wonder of the human mind, 'What a piece of work is man! How noble in reason! how infinite in faculties! . . .', Jonson looked inside the brain and saw: 'Cockle shells, pebbles, fine wheat-strawes, and here and there a chicken's feather and a cob-web'.

The concluding quotation here significantly comes from *Bartholomew Fair*, the play Armfield was directing in 1978, when, as he explains in the *Alchemist* pro-gramme, he was in the second year of a post-graduate research scholarship at Sydney University.

> My professor, Dame Leonie Kramer, called me to her office to say that the time for me to submit written evidence of my research had passed, and we agreed, quite amicably, to conclude our student/professor relationship.

The fact that Armfield had that year mounted an ambitious and full production of *Bartholomew Fair* was not seen as acceptable evidence of research, and it seems appropriate that in the *Alchemist* programme letter Armfield spelled out the dangers of stifling Jonson by the forces of English Lit.:

> The subject of my post-graduate research had been 'The Theatre of Ben Jonson.' Now, as then, I have very little to say about it – it has to be *done*.

The fact that Armfield's programme letter is addressed to his English professor, Dame Leonie Kramer, is also significant. The reiteration of the title 'Dame', the construction of Jonson as falsely claimed by English studies, as opposed to theatre practice, and the fact, evident to a Belvoir Street audience, that Kramer had thrown out a student who was to become one of the major theatre directors of his generation, make this 'Letter to Leonie' extremely loaded: by politely situating the forces of English academia as foolish, anti-theatrical and stiflingly regulatory, the letter contests ownership of Jonson and claims him for theatre. The letter thus functions as part of the still flourishing territorial dispute between Eng. Lit. and theatre. The *Sydney Morning Herald* review certainly took up Armfield's hints here: the reviewer claimed Armfield had managed to breathe new life into *The Alchemist*, a play which had 'spent years in the artistic sin bin' for being 'too literary', a play 'read now only in English Lit. courses as an example of supposed classical . . . comic form'.

Armfield's profession of love for Jonson in the production programme also confronts the audience with being positioned as anti-theatrical wowsers if they resist the production; this was a tactical move, given that for many in the audience this would probably be their first encounter with Jonson in the theatre – as Jonson is so rarely performed in Australia.

Armfield himself had directed both *Volpone* (1980) and *Bartholomew Fair* (1978) before *The Alchemist*. His *Bartholomew Fair* was described as 'larrikin' by Penny Gay and aimed at democratising the text.[6] In the production programme Armfield commented that 'a post-Brecht audience in the 1970s is surely very well equipped to appreciate' the play and stated:

> We make no apologies . . . for playing our play straight to the audience, nor for having designed the production to look quite artificial. Our costumes have all been cut from a single fabric, and then very obviously 'painted' to reinforce the play's sense of its own artifice. Our aim has been to give the audience the sense of witnessing a huge puppet play.

Armfield stressed 'the patent self-consciousness of [Jonson's] art' and the Jonsonian brand of realism where 'the reality of his play as a "play", the reality of his actors as "actors" is always insisted upon'. The programme also stressed the play's historicity, included a glossary and reprinted a facsimile of the 1631 title page.

Despite this historicising gesture, Armfield used his large cast of student actors to create colourful crowd scenes which generated a feeling specifically reminiscent of the Side-show Alley at the Sydney Easter Show. The fair was staged extravagantly around three sides of the theatre space, as well as on catwalks within a semi-promenade performance layout. Accents were Australian and the one professional actress in the company, who was clearly older than the student actors around her, played a powerful Ursula, who was the centre of the action.

Two years later in 1980 Armfield co-directed *Volpone* with John Bell for the Nimrod Theatre, Sydney. Bell, a leading figure in Australian classical theatre as well as in new Australian drama, also played a foxy, red-haired Volpone, a virtuoso role which would suit his forceful and histrionic stage presence. At this time,

Armfield was a comparative newcomer to professional theatre and Bell was a long-established, star actor and director. Bell publicly (*Sydney Morning Herald*, 2 October 1980) claimed the experience of co-directing was 'very fruitful' and commented: 'as long as the directors basically agree, the more input you get, criticism and advice, the better for production'. Bell felt the production had 'touches of Fellini about its decrepitude and its grotesqueries'; that it stressed the play's materialism and emphasised the fact that every character is playing a role.

Reviewers seemed puzzled by the mixture of music hall, vaudeville, cartoons, cabaret, and theatrical excess. Kim Carpenter's set combined a Victorian theatre and funeral parlour, adorned with cupids and wreaths. *The Sydney Morning Herald* (3 October 1980) described it as 'faded art-deco magnificence, all burgundy brocade and marble statuary and candelabra'. An organ played chords at moments of high tension as well as accompanying the Kurt Weill-meets-*Cabaret* songs of Nano, Castrone and Androgyno.

Theatre Australia (November 1980: 31) described this Volpone as a 'restless, even tortured character' who also exhibited a sense of inertia. Voltore had a Dracula-style black and red cape and flaunted his incisors. Corvino was Captain Hook with shades of Long John Silver, and came equipped with a waxed moustache, high heels, frilled shirt and a metal-hook hand. The *Sydney Morning Herald* found it all overstated and disapprovingly characterised the production in terms of 'romping melodrama', 'gusto', 'theatricality' and 'caricature grotesquerie' although the reviewer approved of Peter Collingwood's Sir Pol, 'a marvellously comic, sempiternal type of English club bore and know-all, instructing lesser breeds and sniffing conspiracy everywhere'. *Theatre Australia* particularly enjoyed Colin Friel's Bonario, 'a schoolboy with Clark Kent glasses, a plastic cover on his boater and a jaw habitually dropped like Jerry Lewis's' but was less impressed by Friels' Peregrine.

Something of the scarcity of professional productions of Jonson in Australia can be gauged from the fact that the *Australian and New Zealand Theatre Record*, which ran from 1987 to 1996, records only four Jonson productions in that period, one of which was a 1995 rehearsed reading of *The Devil is an Ass*. Raymond Omodei directed *The Alchemist* in 1987, at the Hole in the Wall theatre in Perth, a production linked by several reviewers to Perth's notoriety for get-rich-quick schemes, 'conspicuous consumption' (*Financial Review*, 1 May 1987) and volatile financial fortunes, epitomised in the career of former millionaire Alan Bond. Apart from Armfield's *Alchemist*, the only other Jonson recorded in this period was a modern-dress, 'greed is good' *Volpone*, directed by Robert Draffin in Melbourne in 1988, using a script adapted by Mark Williams. Draffin wanted audiences to see *Volpone* in terms of contemporary Australian economics and the 'titanic take-over battles waged by our Elliotts, Holmes a Courts and Packers. The characters in the play, just like the high-flying entrepreneurial barons of Australian business, make their victories through quick wits' (*The Age Entertainment Guide*, 22 April 1988). In the same interview Draffin also suggested

'*Volpone* deals with the sort of people who really start to get going at 4 o'clock in the morning when everyone else is bombed out: the really conniving, greedy people. Life at 4 a.m. is the feel of the play'.

What it is crucial to acknowledge here is that not only are these productions years apart, they are also thousands of kilometres from each other. Apart from a select band of people who can fly interstate or internationally to see theatre, very few Australian theatregoers could have built much familiarity with Jonson in the theatre in this period in Australia.

The history of Jonson production in Australia previous to the publication of *ANZTR* is also sparse. I've tracked down six productions of *The Alchemist*;[7] six *Volpones*;[8] and three *Bartholomew Fairs*, mostly non-professional.[9] This comparative scarcity of Australian productions of Jonson is an important part of the context for Armfield's *Alchemist*. His audiences would be far more likely to know the play from reading it, than seeing it. The advantage, of course, is that he wouldn't be confronted with reviewers who'd seen the play too many times before.

Jonson's position as an early modern English canonical writer makes his work ambivalent in the contemporary Australian theatre, associated, as it must be, with British cultural imperialism.[10] The tendency with recent productions, and reviews of those productions, to situate Jonson productions in terms of Australia-specific scams is understandable as a theatrical strategy, given the need to connect with an audience in order to ensure good box office; tenured academic writers might designate this universalism, theatre workers would call it survival. However, there is a risk that, in hard-selling Jonson, productions perpetuate the imperial canon, unless the appropriation of the text is sufficient to pose a challenge to British imperial ownership. Armfield's *Alchemist*, in its contestation of territory via localisation – and via the territorial dispute with English Literature – seemed to me to realise a subversive potential – but then my reading is inflected by my own institutional location, the old colonial centre of London University.

Notes

1 Brian Crow and Chris Banfield (1997) although claiming to discuss post-colonial theatre, actually only focus on playtexts written by male indigenous playwrights; however, they do briefly evoke performances of canonical texts and 'the absurdity of an audience sweating its way through a stilted performance of *A Midsummer Night's Dream* or *An Inspector Calls* in an ill-equipped colonial hall on a hot tropical night in Africa or India' (11–12). Post-colonial discussions of Canadian Shakespeares exist (for example, Salter, Hodgdon) and Ania Loomba's work continues to open up this field. There's also a forthcoming edition of *Australasian Drama Studies* dedicated to early modern plays in Australasia.

2 The clichéd white maleness of 'Larrikinism' has rendered the term more problematic in recent years. I also follow Gay in acknowledging the 'conflicted nature' of the term 'post-colonial' and an obvious feature of the following discussion is its focus on the dominant white Australian culture.

3 Although the census productions in *Research Opportunities in Renaissance Drama* occasionally list Australian and New Zealand productions, these lists are not comprehensive.

4 Geoffrey Rush was interviewed by Elizabeth Schafer, Brian Woolland and Richard Cave in London, November 1997.

5 The Australian Broadcasting Corporation had a long-running campaign of advertisements where their logo was written in the air by members of the public. Complaints were made about how often these advertisements were run.

6 Penny Gay privately. Thanks also to Kate Newey for her memories of this production.

7 *The Alchemist* (adapted by Patricia Bullen Flower), New Theatre, Sydney, November 1948, revived April 1982; production at the Adelaide Festival, March 1972 (directed by George Ogilvie); production by the Sydney Old Tote Theatre (directed by John Clark), April 1977; one of the most enthusiastic of Jonson directors, Frank Hauser, directed a Jacobean-costumed *Alchemist* in Melbourne in 1979 (the imperial dynamic and Hauser's status as someone who had acquired his expertise, especially in Jonson, in England and who then bestows the fruits of that experience on Australian theatre could be detected here); production by the University of Western Australia Drama Society (directed by Chris Wortham), 1979.

8 Production by the Adelaide University Theatre Guild, August 1946; production at the Arrow Theatre, Melbourne, 1953 (directed by Robin Lovejoy and starring the flamboyant star Frank Thring); Doris Fitton directed a translation of a Stefan Zweig adaptation at the Independent Theatre, Sydney in 1947, revived July 1959; production by the University of Queensland drama society, 1973 (directed by Richard Fotheringham); production at the University of Tasmania, 1977, directed by Lisa Warrington.

9 Production by the Adelaide University Guild, August 1989, not noted in *ANZTR*; Richard Fotheringham remembers a very good *Bartholomew Fair* produced for the Intervarsity Drama Festival at the University of Queensland in the late 1960s and a Twelfth Night Theatre Co (Brisbane) production in the mid-1980s.

10 A related post-colonial dilemma pertains in Ireland. At the Reading conference Chris Murray spoke of the challenges of teaching Jonson in Ireland, where Jonson is very rarely performed. Murray spoke eloquently of using Irish authors as a way into Jonson for his students: Joyce's flamboyant use of language and the city (Dublin) milieu; the rich language of O'Casey. However, as the author of *The Irish Masque*, Jonson is always also going to be a problematic author in Ireland.

Epilogue to this 'venture tripartite'

Post-colonial appropriation of Jonson in Australia was matched the same year within the metropolis by a daring appropriation of *Volpone* as *Flesh Fly* by Graeae Theatre Company for the Disabled (Oval House, 1996). The programme actually defined their objective as a conscious 'abduction' of a classic in the wake of their success in staging Jarry's *Ubu*. The marginalised were given creative voice in a complete rethinking of the comedy; and this point was quickly established by the director's decision to present the whole play from the perspective of Volpone's servants, Nano, Androgyno and Castrone (the sexually and physically marginalised). Rarely has the imagery of disease and degeneration in the text carried such weight, which only made the counter-theme of the increasingly manic cerebral inventions of the characters seem that much more desperate and absurd. The wheelchair-bound Nabil Shaban playing Volpone opined that, as a disabled actor impersonating an able-bodied man pretending to be disabled and afflicted, he could push his comic invention to levels of the grotesque and surreal that no able-bodied performer in the role would dare to do. Consequently, the sheer physicality of the action in depicting a mass rush for wealth was marked. There were other gains, particularly in the playing of the two main female roles by a deaf actor (Neil Fox). It is a tradition with Graeae that the performance is accompanied by a Sign Language Interpreter who is integrated into the action and not marginalised, as in conventional theatre, to the side of the stage. It was therefore a considerable surprise when this hitherto mute figure suddenly spoke aloud Celia's words even as she signed them, while Fox mimed exquisitely Celia's plight. Fox transformed himself deftly into Lady Politic Would-be with a minor adjustment to his costume; his miming in this role became grosser, caricatured and more rapid, while the voice was now provided by the other female member of the cast, Mandy Colleran, who adopted a thick Mancunian accent and an unstoppable volubility. This casting decision incisively problematised the whole issue of male constructions of the feminine both in the play and in Renaissance theatre practice: women as the silenced presences whose voices are disturbingly ventriloquised. Equally disturbing was the performance of Jamie Beddard, whose speech and movement are affected by cerebral palsy, as Corbaccio. The text makes fun of the ways Corbaccio's age and near-senility affect his speech, sight and movement, which Mosca and Volpone satirise with cruel glee. Here it was less easy for the able-bodied members of the audience to laugh (the cruelty was more apparent than the fun), though the disabled members of the audience found his performance uproarious, as if they had earned the right to laugh. Here that factionalising of the audience which Jonson frequently promotes came forcefully alive to one's awareness, causing one to question the grounds on which one might laugh. A theatre for the marginalised had here appropriated Jonson, had creatively interrogated the text and had found from a distinct and unusual perspective the means to reinstate elements of danger within the performance, particularly for able-bodied spectators.[1]

Margins appear to have meant a great deal to Jonson. A cursory glance at the layout of the printed page in the 1616 Folio proves this point: a central column of text is balanced in an aesthetically pleasing manner by an exceptionally wide outer margin.[2] It is here that Jonson, deploying a different typeface, sets out those comments on the action of his drama which allow a performance text to stimulate a reader's imagination to the point where it sets up a dialogue with the literary text. The books that survive from Jonson's personal library, we are told, abound with his marginalia: texts were not for wholesale absorption but sites for opposition, intellectual debate, challenges to the authority of the printed argument, and certain proof that nothing was in his view to be taken on trust. The monovocal published text was rapidly transformed into multivocal dialogue: an insistent focus was decentred by shifting the perspective, thus widening the potential for meaning, insight and interpretation. The plays too give a voice to the marginal in society, who continually destabilise magisterial pretensions to authority. An abiding fascination throughout the range of Jonson's plays is with the art of acting, that licensed but often disturbing assumption of shifting roles and cleverly assumed voices, that transformation of an individual identity into a multivocal shape-changer which unsettles all conventional attitudes to characterisation in drama. It has been the agenda of this volume to address the margins, the better to attack the marginalised status of Jonson within our theatre today. This study has been conceived as a multivocal text resisting authoritarian closure, where perspectives are constantly changing, even as in Jonson's plays, to open up debate and excite new ways of perceiving where his excellences as a dramatist are to be sited in performance.

Postmodernism judges closure as anathema; it values plurality (especially that which occurs when what is culturally and socially marginalised as objectified 'other' is redefined as the centred subject); it respects an ability to parody or mock conventions and traditional attitudes in the search for, or recovery of, authenticity (even while problematising authenticity as an unreachable goal, given the complexities of twentieth-century cultural exchange); it welcomes *acting* as either game (masquerade) or social process (performativity); and views theatricality as either a potent means to social analysis or an expression of political dissent. It is our belief that Jonson's drama continually works within these same parameters and should be valued on precisely these grounds. This is not to argue that Jonson is in some bizarre way a postmodernist before time or even an honoured forerunner; but that postmodernism opens up critical approaches to performance which allow the complexities of Jonson's artistry to be fully registered in ways that allow his drama to *speak* to us in its myriad voices. The challenges his plays pose are remarkably akin to the challenges on which postmodernist art thrives. Accessibility should, therefore, be less of an issue now than previously. It is certainly less of an issue for all the individuals who *speak* in this book where the approach takes its directional cue from what Jonson has to *say* about acting and performance.

Given our agenda, it would seem appropriate to end with a voice from the margins. William Butler Yeats, seeking to shape a distinctly Irish theatre at the turn of this century within a colonial cultural situation that gave imperial privilege to Shakespeare, was increasingly drawn to Jonson. *The Sad Shepherd* influenced the composition of his Arcadian Faery Tale, 'The Island of Statues', published in 1885; Jonson's epigrams became a model for his own pithy cultural pronouncements and denunciations; the masques preoccupied him as his own plays moved towards a greater abstraction that nonetheless has its roots in social, psychological and emotional insight; and Jonson's relations with aristocratic women intrigued him: he wrote to the scholar-publisher, A.H. Bullen, asking where he might find information about 'the various ladies one lights upon in Ben Jonson's Masques'[3] (Wade 1954: 479). Required to defend in public the Abbey's decision to stage Synge's *The Playboy of the Western World*, Yeats turned repeatedly to Jonson for support: raging against this attempt to censor dramatist and actors in the interests of what he considered to be a bogus nationalism, he called Jonson to mind as exemplary of creative liberties now lost to playwrights:

> In the great days of English dramatic art the greatest English writer of comedy was free to create *The Alchemist* and *Volpone* but a demand born of Puritan conviction and of bourgeois timidity and insincerity, for what many second-rate intellects thought to be noble and elevating events and characters had already at the outset of the eighteenth century ended the English drama as a complete and serious art. Sheridan and Goldsmith, when they restored comedy after an epoch of sentimentalities, had to apologise for their satiric genius by scenes of conventional love-making and sentimental domesticity . . .[4]
>
> (Frayne and Johnson 1975, vol. II: 349)

His is an accurate cultural insight. Situating the work of the Abbey Theatre as oppositional to current trends in stage realism, he later wrote forcefully of the company's respect for 'a fine speaking of fine things' and claimed a precise ancestry for this in 'the fine feeling for fine oratory that made possible the rogues and clowns of Ben Jonson' (1975, vol. II: 354–5).[5]

Yeats's knowledge of Jonson's comedies in performance grew through his support for the productions of firstly Philip Carr and later Allen Wade, who severally endeavoured to find a professional stage for unperformed Renaissance plays. He was a member of the Honorary Committee of Carr's Mermaid Repertory Theatre and wrote to Lady Gregory appreciatively of their 1905 production of *The Silent Woman*: 'the details were full of invention and vitality, and the language was like a torrent' (Wade 1954: 450).[6] It was a lasting regret that he missed seeing Wade's production of *Bartholomew Fair* (1921), particularly since, as he informed Wade, the play 'was one of the things that influenced Synge' (Wade 1954: 671).[7] But he did attend Wade's production of *Volpone* with The Phoenix Theatre Company earlier that same year. The experience affected him deeply. Marginalised within the cultural hegemony in being Irish, he found a rare sympathy for the marginalised characters within the dramatic action and through that sympathy an insight into the processes whereby that condition was constructed:

> *Volpone* was even finer than I expected. I could think of nothing else for hours after I left the theatre. The great surprise to me was the pathos of the two young people [Celia and Bonario], united not in love but in innocence, and going in the end their separate way. The pathos was so much greater because their suffering was an accident, neither sought nor noticed by the impersonal greed that caused it.
>
> (Wade 1954: 665)8

A voice from the cultural margins opens up in three sentences a whole new approach to characters generally dismissed as lifeless because wanting in dramatic interest. Margins are worth exploring when they so eloquently invite us to refocus our perceptions.

Notes

1 Much of the material in this paragraph was the subject of a discussion with Colette Conroy, assistant director on the production for Graeae Theatre Company.
2 The outer margins tend to vary slightly between 6.7 and 7 cm, whereas the text in the volumes of the Folio consulted measured 12 cm for passages of prose dialogue and between 7 cm and 9.5 cm for lines of verse. This affords a ratio of roughly 11:19 for prose passages and a ratio varying between 11:11 and 11:15 for verse.
3 The letter is dated 21 September 1906.
4 The passage is quoted from an article Yeats contributed to *The Arrow* for 23 February 1907.
5 The quotation is from 'Notes' published in *The Arrow* for 1 June 1907.
6 The letter is dated 30 May 1905.
7 The letter is dated 10 July 1921.
8 The letter is dated 8 February 1921.

Appendix

The conference 'Ben Jonson and the Theatre', University of Reading, January 1996

Organisers

Richard Cave
Brian Woolland

Conference participants

Nicholas Bayley	University of Reading (student)
Mark Bland	St John's College, Oxford
Gary Bowman	University of Bristol (research student)
Tony Bromham	Brunel University College
Michael Casey	Bretton Hall College
Richard Cave	Royal Holloway College, University of London
Claire Cochrane	University College, Worcester
Rocco Coronato	University of Bologna
Gabriel Egan	The Shakespeare Institute (research student)
Andrew Gurr	University of Reading, Renaissance Texts Research Centre
Michelle Haslem	Chester College
Xenia Horne	
Doriel Hulse	Tonbridge School
Mick Jardine	King Alfred's University College
Trish Knight-Webb	
Cheri Logan	Cumbria College of Art and Design
Claudia Manera	University of Reading (research student)
Lesley Mickel	University of Northumbria
Mervyn Millar	University of East Anglia
Valerie Moon	
Christopher Murray	University College, Dublin
John O'Connor	University of Reading (student)
Amanda Penlington	University of Warwick
Victoria Redfern	Royal Holloway, University of London (research student)
Julie Sanders	Keele University

Elizabeth Schafer	Royal Holloway, University of London
Robert Shaughnessy	University of the West of England
C. Sullivan	University of Wales
Suzi Turner	Royal Holloway College, University of London (research student)
Martin White	University of Bristol
Andrew Wilson	Charterhouse School
Brian Woolland	University of Reading

Actors

Timothy Bateson
Peter Bayliss
Jasper Britton
Diana Fairfax
Martin Head
Ben Livingstone
Tina Marian
Kevin Moore
John Nettles
Vivien Rochester
Simon Russell-Beale
Andrew Wincott

Directors

Peter Barnes
Colin Ellwood
Michael Walling

Others who have contributed to the book

Joan Littlewood
Genista McIntosh
Sam Mendes
Geoffrey Rush

Bibliography

Anonymous (1981) 'The Female Wits', in F. Morgan (ed.) *The Female Wits: Women Playwrights on the London Stage 1600–1720*, London: Virago.

Ansorge, P. (1972) 'Lots of Lovely Human Contact', *Plays and Players*, July: 18–21.

Arnold, J. (1969) 'Lovewit's Triumph and Jonsonian Morality', *Criticism* 11: 151–66. Revised in *A Grace Peculiar: Jonson's Cavalier Heroes* (1972), Penn.: University Park.

Ashwell, L. (1936) *Myself a Player*, London: Michael Joseph.

Aubrey, J. (1949) *Brief Lives*, ed. O.L. Dick, London: Secker and Warburg.

Bamborough, J. (1970) *Ben Jonson*, London: Hutchinson.

Barry, P. (1995) *Beginning Theory*, Manchester: Manchester University Press.

Barthes, R. (1982), 'Inaugural Lecture, Collège de France', in S. Sontag (ed.), *A Barthes Reader*, London: Jonathan Cape: 459–69.

Barton, A. (1984) *Ben Jonson, Dramatist*, Cambridge: Cambridge University Press.

—— (1994) 'Shakespeare and Jonson', in *Essays Mainly Shakespearean*, Cambridge: Cambridge University Press: 282–301.

Bloom, H. (1975) *The Anxiety of Influence*, Oxford: Oxford University Press.

Bolton, W.F. and Gardner, J.F. (1973) Introduction to *Catiline*, London: Edward Arnold.

Brady, J. and Herendeen, W.H. (1991) *Ben Jonson's 1616 Folio*, London and Toronto: Associated University Presses.

Bramwell, M. (1997) 'A Cup of Tea with Joan Littlewood', in J. Tompkins and J. Holledge (eds), *Performing Women / Performing Feminisms: Interviews with International Women Playwrights*, Australasian Drama Studies Association Academic Publications 2: 103–9.

Braunmuller, A. R. and Hattaway, M. (eds) (1990) *The Cambridge Companion to English Renaissance Drama*, Cambridge: Cambridge University Press.

Brecht, B. (1964) *Brecht on Theatre*, trans. J. Willet, London: Methuen.

—— (1965) *The Messingkauf Dialogues*, trans. J. Willet, London: Methuen.

—— (1974) *Short Organum for the Theatre*, trans. and ed. J. Willet, London: Methuen.

Bredbeck, G.W. (1991) *Sodomy and Interpretation: Marlowe to Milton*, Ithaca and London: Cornell University Press.

Brock, S. and Pringle, M. J. (1984) *The Shakespeare Memorial Theatre: 1919–1945* (Theatre in Focus series), Cambridge: Chadwyck-Healey.

Burt, R. (1993) *Licensed By Authority: Ben Jonson and the Discourses of Censorship*, Ithaca: Cornell University Press.

Butler, M. (1991) 'Late Jonson', in G. McMullan and J. Hope (eds), *The Politics of Tragicomedy*, London: Routledge: 166–88.

Cave, R.A. (1991) *Ben Jonson*, Basingstoke and London: Macmillan.

Chambers, C. (1980) *Other Spaces: New Theatre and the RSC*, London: Methuen.

Champion, L.S. (1967) *Ben Jonson's Dotages: A Reconsideration of the Late Plays*, Lexington: University of Kentucky Press.

Charnes, L. (1996) '"What's Love Got To Do With It?" Reading the Liberal Humanist Romance in *Antony and Cleopatra*', in S.N. Garner and N. Sprengnether (eds), *Shakespearean Tragedy and Gender*, Bloomington and Indianapolis: Indiana University Press: 268–86.

Chedgzoy, K., Sanders, J. and Wiseman, S. (eds) (1998) *Refashioning Ben Jonson: Gender, Politics and the Jonsonian Canon*, Basingstoke and London: Macmillan.

Cixous, H. (1980), 'Sorties', in E. Marks and I. de Courtrivon (eds) *New French Feminisms*, Brighton: Harvester: 245–64.

Craig, D.H. (ed.) (1990) *Ben Jonson: The Critical Heritage 1599–1798*, London: Routledge.

Crow, B. with Banfield, C. (1996) *An Introduction to Post-colonial Theatre*, Cambridge: Cambridge University Press.

Derrida, J. (1976) 'Genesis and Structure of the *Essay on the Origin of Languages*', in *Of Grammatology*, trans. G. Spivack, Baltimore and London: The Johns Hopkins University Press.

DiGangi, Mario (1997) *The Homoerotics of Early Modern Drama*, Cambridge: Cambridge University Press.

Dutton, R. (1996) *Ben Jonson: Authority: Criticism*, Basingstoke and London: Macmillan.

Elam, K. (1980) *The Semiotics of Theatre and Drama*, London: Methuen.

Fraser, A. (1995 [1984]) *The Weaker Vessel: Woman's Lot in Seventeenth-Century England*, London: Mandarin.

Frayne, J.P. and Johnson, C. (eds) (1975) *Uncollected Prose of W.B. Yeats*, Basingstoke and London: Macmillan.

Gay, P. (1998 forthcoming) 'Recent Australian *Shrews*: The "Larrikin" Element', in J. Levenson and J. Bate (eds), *Proceedings of the 1996 ISA Conference*,. University of Delaware / Associated University Presses.

Gilbert, H. and Tompkins, J. (1996) *Post-colonial Drama*, London: Routledge.

Goorney, H. (1981) *The Theatre Workshop Story*, London: Eyre Methuen.

Gossett, S. (1988) '"Man-maid, begone!": Women in Masques', *English Literary Renaissance* 18: 96–113.

Gras, H. (1989) '*Twelfth Night, Every Man out of his Humour*, and the Middle Temple Revels of 1597–98', *Modern Language Review* 84: 545–64.

Greenblatt, S. (1985) '*Invisible bullets*', in J. Dollimore and A. Sinfield (eds), *Political Shakespeare: Essays in Cultural Materialism*, Manchester: Manchester University Press.

Gurr, A. (1982) 'Shakespeare's Many-headed Audience', *Essays in Theatre* 1: 52–62.

—— (1988) '*The Tempest*'s Tempest at Blackfriars', *Shakespeare Survey* 41: 91–102.

—— (1996) *The Shakespearian Playing Companies*, Oxford: Clarendon Press.

Guthrie, Sir Tyrone (1959) *A Life in the theatre*, New York, Toronto and London: McGraw-Hill.

Hall, K.F. (1991) 'Sexual Politics and Cultural Identity in *The Masque of Blackness*', in S. Case and J. Reinelt (eds), *The Performance of Power: Theatrical Discourse and Politics*, Iowa City: University of Iowa Press: 3–18.

Hamilton, C. (1949) 'Triumphant Women', in E. Adlard (ed.), *Edy: Recollections of Edy Craig*, London: Frederick Muller: 38–44.

Hattaway, M. (ed.) (1984) *The New Inn*, by Ben Jonson, Manchester: Revels, Manchester University Press.

Hayes, T. (1992) *The Birth of Popular Culture: Ben Jonson, Maid Marian and Robin Hood*, Pittsburgh, PA: Duquesne University Press.

Haynes, J. (1992) *The Social Relations of Jonson's Theater*, Cambridge: Cambridge University Press.

Heinemann, M. (1985) 'How Brecht Read Shakespeare', in J. Dollimore and A. Sinfield (eds), *Political Shakespeare: Essays in Cultural Materialism*, Manchester: Manchester University Press.

Hendricks, M. and Parker, P. (eds) (1994) *Women, 'Race', and Writing in the Early Modern Period*, London: Routledge.

Herford, C.H., Simpson, Percy and Simpson, Evelyn (eds) (1925–52) *Ben Jonson*, 11 vols, Oxford: Clarendon Press.

Hibbard, G.R. (ed.) (1977) *Bartholomew Fair*, Ben Jonson, London: New Mermaids, Ernest Benn.

Hill, C. (1996) *Liberty Against the Law*, Harmondsworth: Allen Lane Press.

Hodgdon, B. (1996) 'Looking for Mr. Shakespeare after "the revolution": Robert Lepage's intercultural *Dream* machine', in J. Bulman (ed.) *Shakespeare, Theory and Performance*, London: Routledge.

Howard, J.E. (1988) 'Crossdressing, the Theatre, and Gender Struggle in Early Modern England', *Shakespeare Quarterly* 39: 418–40.

—— (1994) *The Stage and Social Struggle in Early Modern England*, London and New York: Routledge.

Howe, E. (1992) *The First English Actresses: Women and Drama 1660–1700*, Cambridge: Cambridge University Press.

Jameson, M. (1966) *Ben Jonson: Three Comedies*, Harmondsworth: Penguin.

Jensen, E.J. (1985) *Ben Jonson's Comedies on the Modern Stage*, UMI Research Press, Theater and Dramatic Studies.

Kay, W. D. (1995) *Ben Jonson: A Literary Life*, Basingstoke and London: Macmillan.

Kernan, A. B. (1959) *The Cankered Muse: Satire of the English Renaissance*, New Haven and London: Yale University Press.

Kiernan, T. (1981) *Olivier: The Life of Laurence Olivier*, London: Sidgwick and Jackson.

Lacan, J. (1977) *Écrits*, trans. A. Sheridan, London: Tavistock.

Lacey, S. and Pye, D. (1994) 'Getting Started: An Approach to Relating Practical and Critical Work', *Studies in Theatre Production* 10: 20–30.

Lennox, Charlotte (1775) *Old City Manners*, London: T. Becket.

Lentricchia, F. (1983) *Criticism and Social Change*, Chicago: University of Chicago Press.

Levin, H. (1971), 'Two Magian Comedies, *The Tempest* and *The Alchemist*', *Shakespeare Survey* 22: 47–58.

Levin, K.D. (1997) 'Unmasquing *Epicoene*: Jonson's Dramaturgy for the Commercial Theater and Court' in J. Hersh (ed.) *New Perspectives on Ben Jonson*, London: Associated University Presses: 128–53.

Levine, L. (1994) *Men in Women's Clothing: Anti-theatricality and Effeminization, 1579–1642*, Cambridge: Cambridge University Press.

Lewalski, B.K. (1994) 'Enacting Opposition: Queen Anne and the Subversions of

Masquing', in *Writing Women in Jacobean England*, Cambridge, MA: Harvard University Press: 15–44.

Lindley, D. (1993) *The Trials of Frances Howard: Fact and Fiction at the Court of King James*, London: Routledge.

Littlewood, J. (1994) *Joan's Book: Joan Littlewood's Peculiar History As She Tells It,* London: Methuen.

Maclure, M. (ed.) (1979) *Christopher Marlowe: The Critical Heritage*, London: Routledge.

McLuskie, K. (1989) *Renaissance Dramatists*. Hemel Hempstead: Harvester Wheatsheaf.

McManus, C. (1998) 'Defacing the Carcass: Anne of Denmark and Jonson's *The Masque of Blackness*' in Chedgzoy, Sanders and Wiseman (eds): 93–113.

Mares, F.H. (ed.) (1967) Introduction to *The Alchemist*, London: Revels, Methuen.

Marshall, N. (1962) *The Producer and the Play*, Macdonald, London, second, revised and enlarged edition, 1962.

Mazer, C.M. (1981) *Shakespeare Refashioned: Elizabethan Plays on Edwardian Stages*, Michigan: UMI Research Press.

Miles, R. (1986) *Ben Jonson: His Life and Work*, London: Routledge.

—— (1990) *Ben Jonson: His Craft and Art*, London: Routledge.

Moi, T. (1985) *Sexual/Textual Politics*, London: Routledge.

Mulryne, Ronnie and Margaret Shewring (1989) *This Golden Round: The Royal Shakespeare Company at the Swan*, Stratford-on-Avon: Mulryne and Shewring.

Newman, K. (1991) *Fashioning Femininity and English Renaissance Drama*, Chicago and London: University of Chicago Press.

—— (1996) 'Engendering the News', in A.L. Magnusson and C.E. McGee (eds), *The Elizabethan Theater XIV*, Toronto: Meany: 49–69.

Noyes, R.G. (1935) *Ben Jonson on the English Stage 1660–1776*, Cambridge, MA: Harvard University Press.

O'Connor, M. (1987) *William Poel and the Elizabethan Stage Society*, Theatre in Focus Series Cambridge: Chadwyck-Healey.

Orgel, S. (ed.) (1969) *Ben Jonson: The Complete Masques*, New Haven and London: Yale University Press.

—— (1975) *The Illusion of Power: Political Theatre in the English Renaissance*, Berkeley: University of California Press,

—— (1981) 'What Is a Text?', *Research Opportunities in Renaissance Drama* 26: 3–6.

—— (1992) 'The Subtexts of *The Roaring Girl*', in S. Zimmerman (ed.), *Erotic Politics: Desire on the Renaissance Stage*, London: Routledge: 12–26.

—— (1996) *Impersonations: The Performance of Gender in Shakespeare's England*, Cambridge: Cambridge University Press.

Orgel, S. and Strong, R. (1973) *Inigo Jones: The Theatre of the Stuart Court*, volume I. London: Sotheby Parke Bernet.

Ostovich, H. (1994) 'The Appropriation of Pleasure in *The Magnetic Lady*', *Studies in English Literature* 34: 425–42.

—— (ed.) (1997) *Jonson Four Comedies*, London: Longman.

—— (1998) 'Hell for Lovers: Shades of Adultery in *The Devil is an Ass*', in Chedgzoy, Sanders and Wiseman (eds): 155–82.

Parker, R.B. (1979) '*Volpone* in Performance 1921–1972', *Renaissance Drama* n.s. 9: 147–73.

Parker, R.B. (ed.) (1983) *Volpone*, Manchester: Revels, Manchester University Press.

Parr, A. (ed.) (1988) Ben Jonson, *The Staple of News*, Manchester: Revels, Manchester University Press.

Paster, G.K. (1993) *The Body Embarrassed*, Ithaca: Cornell University Press.

Pepys, S. (1913) *The Diary of Samuel Pepys*, ed. with additions by H.B. Wheatly. London: G. Bell and Sons.

Pritchard, A. (1994) 'Puritans and the Blackfriars Theater: The Cases of Mistresses Duck and Drake', *Shakespeare Quarterly* 45: 92–5.

Rebhorn, W.A. (1980) 'Jonson's "Jovy Boy": Lovewit and the Dupes in *The Alchemist*', *Journal of English and Germanic Philology* 79: 355–75.

Riggs, D. (1989) *Ben Jonson A Life*. Cambridge, MA: Harvard University Press.

Sanders, J. (1996) '"The Day's Sports Devised in the Inn": Jonson's *The New Inn* and Theatrical Politics', *Modern Language Review* 91: 545–60.

—— (1997) '"The Collective Contract Is a Fragile Structure": Local Government and Personal Rule in Jonson's *A Tale of a Tub*', *English Literary Renaissance* 27: 443–67.

—— (1998a) 'Midwifery and the New Science in the Seventeenth Century: Language, Print, and the Theatre', in E. Fudge, R. Gilbert, and S. Wiseman (eds) *At the Borders of the Beasts, Bodies and National Philosophy in the Early Modern Period*, Basingstoke and London: Macmillan.

—— (1998b) *Ben Jonson's Theatrical Republics*, Basingstoke and London: Macmillan.

Salter, D. (1996) 'Acting Shakespeare in Postcolonial Space', in J. Bulman (ed.) *Shakespeare, Theory, and Performance*, London: Routledge.

Schafer, E. (1998) *MsDirecting Skakespeare*, London: Women's Press.

Schoenbaum, S. (1975) *William Shakespeare: A Documentary Life*, Oxford: Oxford University Press.

Sharpe, K. (1987) 'The Image of Virtue: The Court and Household of Charles I, 1625–1642', in D. Starkey *et al.* (eds), *The English Court from the Wars of the Roses to the Civil War*, London and New York: Routledge: 226–60.

Siddiqui, Y. (1992) 'Dark Incontinents: The Discourse of Race and Gender in Three Renaissance Masques', *Renaissance Drama* 23: 139–63.

Small, M. (1935) *Charlotte Ramsay Lennox: An Eighteenth Century Lady of Letters*, New Haven: Yale University Press.

Stallybrass, P. and White, A. (1987) *The Politics and Poetics of Transgression*, London: Methuen.

Steen, S.J. (ed.) (1994) *The Letters of Lady Arbella Stuart*, Oxford: Oxford University Press.

Thayer, C.G. (1963) *Ben Jonson: Studies in the Plays*, Norman, Oklahoma: University of Oklahoma Press.

Tilton, R. (1995) *Pocahontas: The Evolution of an American Narrative*, Cambridge: Cambridge University Press.

Tomlinson, S. (1991) 'She That Plays the King: Henrietta Maria and the Threat of the Actress in Caroline Culture,' in G. McMullan and J. Hope (eds), *The Politics of Tragicomedy*, London: Routledge: 189–207.

—— (1992) 'My Brain the Stage: Margaret Cavendish and the Fantasy of Female Performance', in C. Brant and D. Purkiss (eds) *Women, Texts, and Histories, 1575–1760*, London: Routledge: 134–63.

Wade, A. (1954) *The Letters of W.B. Yeats*, London: Rupert Hart-Davis.

Waith, E.M. (ed.) (1963) *Bartholomew Fair*, New Haven and London: Yale University Press.

Walker, K. (1991) 'New Prison: Representing the Female Actor in Shirley's *The Bird in a Cage* (1633)', *English Literary Renaissance* 21: 385–400.

Waters, D.W. (1958) *The Art of Navigation in England in Elizabethan and Early Stuart Times*, London: Hollis and Carter.

Watson, R.N. (1986) '*The Alchemist* and Jonson's Conversion of Comedy', in B.K. Lewalski (ed.) *Renaissance Genres*, Harvard English Studies 14, Cambridge, MA: Harvard University Press: 332–65.

Wilson, E. (1963) 'Morose Ben Jonson', in J.A. Barish (ed.) *Ben Jonson: A Collection of Critical Essays*, Englewood Cliffs, NJ: Prentice Hall: 60–74.

Wilson, R. and Dutton, R. (eds) (1992) *New Historicism and Renaissance Drama*, Harlow: Longman.

Windsor, C. (ed.) (1995) *The Prince's Choice: A Personal Selection from Shakespeare*, London: Hodder and Stoughton.

Wiseman, S. (1992) 'Gender and Status in Dramatic Discourse: Margaret Cavendish, Duchess of Newcastle', in I. Grundy and S. Wiseman (eds) *Women, Writing, History, 1640–1740*, London: Batsford: 159–77.

Womack, P. (1986) *Ben Jonson*, Oxford: Blackwell.

Wymer, R. (1995) *Webster and Ford*, Basingstoke and London: Macmillan.

Index